BARRON'S

AP*

MICROECONOMICS/ MACROECONOMICS

4TH EDITION

Frank Musgrave, Ph.D.
Professor
Department of Economics
Ithaca College

Elia Kacapyr, Ph.D.
Chair and Professor
Department of Economics
Ithaca College

BARRON'S

*AP is a registered trademark of the College Board, which was not involved in the production of, and does not endorse, this product.

ACKNOWLEDGMENT

We thank Tina Bennett, Department Assistant, for her many hours of superb services on behalf of the production of the original manuscript. She worked diligently and was able to offer suggestions that were always helpful. Her patience, understanding, and skillful assistance were more than sufficient as stress reducers and aids to the completion of the task.

DEDICATION

To Eva Mae Gifford Musgrave

All inquiries should be addressed to:
Barron's Educational Series, Inc.
250 Wireless Boulevard
Hauppauge, NY 11788
www.barronseduc.com

ISBN: 978-0-7641-4700-5

ISSN 1944-8295

PRINTED IN THE UNITED STATES OF AMERICA
9 8 7 6 5 4 3 2 1

10%
POST-CONSUMER WASTE
Paper contains a minimum of 10% post-consumer waste (PCW). Paper used in this book was derived from certified, sustainable forestlands.

Contents

MICROECONOMICS

8 Costs, Production, Supply 97

9 Product Markets: Types, Characteristics, Pricing Strategies 111

10 Perfect Competition 119

MACROECONOMICS

INTRODUCTION

The AP Exams in Microeconomics and Macroeconomics

- The exam set-up
- Multiple-choice questions
- Answering strategies
- Free-response questions

THE EXAMS

Advanced Placement (AP) exams are given each May to qualified secondary school students who wish to complete coursework equivalent to a one-semester college introductory class. There are two separate exams in economics: one in microeconomics and one in macroeconomics. Basically, the AP exam determines whether a student understands enough of the subject matter to be given college credit.

The AP exams in economics are both set up the same way. There is a multiple-choice section of 60 questions with a time limit of 70 minutes, and an essay section of 3 questions with a time limit of 50 minutes. The essay section is preceded by a 10-minute reading period where the essays can be outlined. The multiple-choice questions are graded by computers and the essays are evaluated by professional graders.

The multiple-choice section counts for two-thirds of the final score, while the free-response section counts for the other one-third. Typically, the longer essay question counts for 50 percent of the free-response score (or 16.5 percent of the overall exam score) and the two shorter questions count for 25 percent (or 8.25 percent of the overall exam score). A test taker's multiple-choice and free-response scores are combined and that number is translated into a final score ranging from 1 to 5.

College policies on granting AP credit vary. Generally, a score of 4 or 5 is required to obtain college credit. Anyone preparing for an AP exam should visit the website of the College Board (*http://apcentral.collegeboard.com*).

HOW THIS BOOK CAN HELP

This book is designed to prepare you for the AP exam in microeconomics, the AP exam in macroeconomics, or both. The College Board is very specific about what material will appear on each exam and the extent to which specific topics are emphasized. For instance, 50 to 70 percent of the AP exam in microeconomics concerns "the nature and function of product markets." On the macroeconomics exam, "inflation, unemployment, and stabilization policies" are emphasized. This study guide takes into consideration the coverage and emphases of recently administered AP exams.

This chapter goes on to give general study guides and tips for doing well on either of the AP economics exams. Chapters 2 and 3 cover material that appears on both the microeconomics and the macroeconomics AP exams.

Microeconomics

Students preparing for the microeconomics exam should continue on with Chapters 4 through 13. After Chapter 13 there is a full-size sample AP exam in microeconomics for you to try.

Macroeconomics

Students preparing for the AP exam in macroeconomics should continue with this chapter and Chapters 2 and 3, then skip to Chapter 14 and continue straight through Chapter 21. After Chapter 21 there is a sample AP exam in macroeconomics.

MICRO AND MACRO AP EXAM COVERAGE

Micro	Macro
Basic Economic Concepts (8%–14%), Ch. 2	Basic Economic Concepts (8%–12%), Ch. 2–3
Supply and Demand (15%–20%), Ch. 4–5	Economic Measurement (12%–16%), Ch. 14–15
Consumer Utility (5%–10%), Ch. 6	Aggregate Supply and Demand (10%–15%), Ch. 16
Production and Costs (10%–15%), Ch. 8	Money and Banking (15%–20%), Ch. 18
Market Structure (25%–35%), Ch. 9–12	Monetary and Fiscal Policy (20%–30%), Ch. 17–19
Factor Markets (10%–18%), Ch. 13	Economic Growth (5%–10%), Ch. 20
Market Failure (12%–18%), Ch. 7	International Trade and Exchange (10%–15%), Ch. 21

MULTIPLE-CHOICE QUESTIONS

There are any number of suggestions that have been made regarding the art and/or science of answering multiple-choice questions. If the student is thinking of "multiple-guess" questions, the student is not destined for greatness on the examination. Pure guessing will likely result in 20 percent correct (one out of five odds) on the multiple-choice section.

The Advanced Placement exams no longer assign a penalty for random or haphazard guessing. Therefore, pure guessing will most likely result in a score of 12 out of 60 on the multiple-choice section of the AP exam.

TIP

It is always better to guess than to leave a multiple-choice question blank.

Strategy

A suggested strategy would be to guess when you "don't have a clue" about the question or any of the choices. However, if you have some knowledge about the question, and if two of the five choices appear to be feasible answers, then your odds have been considerably improved if you choose an answer from one of the two (instead of five) choices.

Time is a factor in all of this; therefore the questions that are the most difficult or are causing you to spend a lot of time should be skipped until you have answered those questions with the least difficulty. Remember to take a watch with you to the exam in the event that the clock is difficult to see from your seat.

A good approach to answering multiple-choice questions would be to first read the question and any related graph and decide your answer before looking at the choices. Otherwise, you will find yourself checking each of the five choices for accuracy, which will consume too much time (a relatively scarce resource)!

Some clues can be obtained by looking at the structure of the five choices for any "pairing," modifying clauses, or "far-out" (such as apparently irrelevant even if true) statements.

The "pairing" of choices can involve two or four choices. If there are two pairings, for instance, two of the five choices are paired, then the odds are that one of them is the correct answer. For example:

Which of the following is correct?

(A)   The law of diminishing returns applies to the long run.
(B)   The law of diminishing returns applies to the short run.
(C)   The law of diminishing returns explains how total output decreases as inputs are added.
(D)   The law of diminishing marginal productivity applies to consumer demand.
(E)   The law of diminishing marginal utility applies to production of output.

The correct answer is **B**, "the law of diminishing returns applies to the short run." Since choices **A** and **B** did *not* contain the word "only" after "applies" so that the law might apply to both the long run *and* the short run, the answer to the question has to be **A** or **B**. In other words, the law of diminishing returns *must* apply to either the short run or the long run; you have effectively eliminated the other three choices! Of course, you now must choose between **A** or **B**. Your study of economics and your review of this book (see Chapter 8: Costs, Production, Supply) should indicate to you that the correct answer (**B**) reflects that in the short run, supply has not fully adjusted to changes in demand. This means that the quantity of at least one input, say capital, remains fixed, while the quantity of another input, say labor, varies. The law is framed in these terms of "allowing" labor (input) to vary while holding capital (input) constant. At some level of production, the addition of labor to this fixed quantity of capital will mean each additional unit of labor has less capital with which to produce (additional labor must "share" the fixed capital with the previous units of labor). This leads to diminishing returns or smaller and smaller additions to output (marginal physical products of labor) with additional units of labor. The law of diminishing returns does *not* hold in the long run since all inputs vary in the long run. That is, the time frame for the long run is whenever supply fully adjusts for changes in demand; all inputs are variable in the long run.

Incidentally, as indicated above, choices **C**, **D**, and **E** are incorrect by process of limiting the choices to **A** or **B**. However, we have provided a basic reason for each of these choices being incorrect in their own way, as follows:

C—The law of diminishing returns explains how additions (marginal products) to total product decrease.

D—The law of diminishing returns applies to production.

E—The law of diminishing marginal utility applies to consumer demand.

Remember, we provide these reasons for rejecting **C**, **D**, and **E** only for information and instruction on diminishing returns. However, you should not have to examine these other choices too carefully for want of time.

The "pairing" may involve four of the five choices. Be careful of the structure of the choices, particularly if absolute terms such as *always* or *never,* are used. For example, which of the following is *true* about the relationship of the average product (AP) curve and the marginal product (MP) curve?

(A) AP and MP are always equal.

(B) AP and MP are never equal.

(C) The AP curve intersects the MP curve at the minimum point of the MP curve.

(D) The MP curve intersects the AP curve at the minimum point of the AP curve.

(E) The MP curve intersects the AP curve at the maximum point of the AP curve.

Absolutes

If you look at the structure and pairing of the choices, you might find some revealing differences. First, beware of absolutes, such as *always, never, every, none, forever,* etc. This is especially noteworthy, as in this question, since *two* absolute terms are used in a question about relationships. If there is any significant or defining mathematical relationship, it is rarely *always* or *never*. Knowing this, you should figure that choices **A** and **B** can be eliminated. You should *not* expect that the mathematical or conceptual "relationship" between AP and MP would be either *always equal* or *never equal.* Now, you are left with choices **C**, **D**, and **E**. You should have a clue that **C** can be eliminated since one of **D** and **E** are contrasting points— either MP intersects AP at its minimum or its maximum point. Choice **C** has no contrasting choice. Conceptually, you should know that since MP is the addition to total product (TP), when MP is greater than AP, AP must be rising. Conversely, when MP is less than AP, AP must be decreasing. Therefore, when MP = AP the average product curve is neither rising nor decreasing. In other words, the addition (MP) to total product is equal to the average product (AP). Thus, **E** is the correct answer: "The MP curve intersects the AP curve at the maximum point of the AP curve."

You may see the symmetry between this MP/AP relationship and the MC/AC relationship; however, the marginal cost curve intersects the average cost curves (average variable cost *and* the average total cost curve) at the minimum of the average cost curve (see Chapter 8: Costs, Production, Supply) for graphs depicting MP/AP and MC/AC.

Two Similar Answers

Some multiple-choice questions will offer two answers that are identical except that one contains a clause that modifies the statement. If you do not have another substantive clue, choose the response with the modified statement. For example:

> Which of the following *best* expresses the profit-maximizing condition for a firm that uses labor and capital?
>
> (A) The marginal physical product of labor equals the marginal physical product of capital.
> (B) The marginal physical product of labor is greater than the marginal physical product of capital.
> (C) The marginal physical product of labor is less than the marginal physical product of labor.
> (D) marginal revenue product of labor = marginal revenue product of capital and marginal factor cost (price) of labor = marginal factor cost (price) of capital
> (E) marginal revenue product of labor = marginal revenue product of capital = 1 marginal factor cost (price) of labor = marginal factor cost (price) of capital

You will observe that none of the first three choices relates directly to the question primarily since one cannot establish the most profitable combination of labor and capital without any revenue data. So, toss away choices **A**, **B**, and **C**.

You are left with choices **D** and **E**, which are identical except that choice **E** modifies choice **D** by adding *=1*. If you have no further clue, you might figure that choice **E** is correct. The knowledge you need to answer this correctly would start with your attempt to sketch the answer without looking at the choices. The modification, *=1*, suggests that $MRP_L = MFC_L$ and that $MRP_K = MFC_K$ where L = Labor, K = Capital, MRP = Marginal Revenue Product, and MFC = Marginal Factor Cost. If we had been considering profit maximizing for the firm separately for labor and for capital, we would need $MRP_K = MFC_K$ for profit maximizing in

TIP

To the extent that you have time, check over your responses.

the hire of capital and we would need $MRP_L = MFC_L$ in the hire of labor. Therefore, each of the ratios in the profit-maximizing condition for the hire of both inputs (labor and capital) would have to be $=1$. Then, the correct answer is **E**. If each ratio is $=1$, then we must establish that the two ratios would equal 1. Without the *equals 1* modification, you could have something such as $MRP_L = 8$, $MFC_L = 4$; $MRP_K = 20$, $MFC_K = 10$. Thus, $8/4 = 20/10$ or $2 = 2$. This would not represent the most profitable combination of the two resources.

Another step in the process of reducing the choices to a few instead of five is to see how many of the choices are on "the same page" or, better yet, which choices are on "the same *correct* page." We can use the previous example to illustrate this point. As we explained, if the question refers to profits we need to have revenue data. No revenue data exists for choices **A**, **B**, **C**. Only choices **D** and **E** include the word "revenue." Thus, you need to select as choices those options that are relevant or "on the same page."

Another approach is to sketch a graph, if one applies to the question and is not provided on the test. This would be particularly useful when seeing if your answer matches one of the choices. For example, a shift in aggregate demand may produce an effect on the price level and real GDP that is much more easily identified on your graph than trying to visualize the answer in your head. Similarly, on the micro side, shifts in demand and supply are much better identified in their effects on equilibrium price and quantity if you sketch a graph.

Before taking the AP exam, students would be advised to test themselves by recreating the major graphs, given only the titles of these graphs. The students should check their work with the text graphs. They would then know their strengths and weaknesses and the major concepts could be identified and related to the graphs.

FREE-RESPONSE QUESTIONS

It is much more difficult to give advice for the writing of answers to free-response or essay questions than to render assistance for answering multiple-choice questions. However subjective these questions may appear to be, there are very specific objective factors that the readers (graders) look for in the answers. The student should be advised to take three steps before answering the free-response questions:

1. Quickly review the questions. Often, there is a suggested allocation of time, such as, "use one-half of the time to do question number one and divide the balance of the time for the other two questions." (Usually there are 50 minutes to do three questions.) Make a time schedule for yourself and remember to have a watch with you. *No buzzers or alarms are allowed!*

2. Make short "sketch" notes on the questions about points that you may well forget later in the rush to complete your answers on time. You can do this during the 10-minute "reading period" that precedes the free-response section of the exam. Think of evidence you can provide that demonstrates the correctness of your answer. A graph often fills this requirement.

3. Draw graphs when required. Be sure to label the axes, curves, and any other requested points. If you are unsure of a graph label, search the question for clues. Do not leave an axis unlabeled. As a last-ditch effort, guess at the appropriate label. ("Quantity" is often a good guess for the horizontal axis.)

4. Number your responses. The free-response questions typically have several parts. You should clearly demarcate your responses. For example, you should write "2 (c) ii," to preface your response to question 2, part c, section ii.

5. Be definite in your response. Even if you are unsure of your analysis, give a definite answer. Partial credit may be awarded for asserting the correct conclusion.

6. Be consistent. If your graph indicates one thing, make sure your written analysis points in the same direction.

7. Embellish and improve your response if you have time. There is no penalty for adding extraneous information to your response. Consider your response and look for additional points and perspectives. However, remember to be definite and consistent.

The Night Before the Exam

The night before the exam should be reserved for a brisk review that builds confidence. If you require more than a brisk review, then any confidence you have of doing well on the exam is misplaced. You should read the chapters in this book relevant to the exam you are taking, do the end-of-chapter questions, and take the practice exam well before the exam date. This will allow time to brush up on the areas that are problematic for you.

The practice exams provided in this guide are critical. They will give you the experience of having already taken the exam. In addition, the areas you need to work on will be revealed. Review the explanations for the correct answers on the questions you missed and re-read the relevant sections of the chapter.

Then, just before the exam, you should review the major topics by flipping through the relevant chapters, reading the summaries, and making sure you understand the key terms and formulas.

Graphs are critical. There are no unimportant graphs anywhere in this guide. For the exam you should know their titles (regulated monopolist, loanable funds, etc.); their axes (price, quantity, real interest rate, etc.); their curves (marginal cost, marginal revenue, demand for loans, etc.); and their important points (profit maximization, equilibrium, etc.).

If you give yourself a couple of weeks and do a chapter a day, then you will need only a brief review the night before the exam. You will be well-rested and confident on the exam day. You won't need it, but . . . best of luck!

TABLE 1.1

Supplies

Items to Bring to the Exam

- No. 2 pencils (for multiple-choice answers)
- Black or dark-blue ballpoint pens (for free-response answers)
- Your secondary school code number
- Your Social Security number (optional)
- Watch (turn off the alarm and beeper)

Items That Are Strictly Forbidden

- Calculators
- Scratch paper
- Rulers, correction fluid, compasses, dictionaries, and the like
- Pagers and cellular phones
- Food and drinks

The Discipline of Economics

CHAPTER 2

- What is economics?
- Micro vs. macroeconomics
- Positive vs. normative economics
- Opportunity cost
- Production possibilities frontier
- Comparative advantage

ECONOMICS DEFINED

Economics is a social science that studies how resources are used and is often concerned with how resources can be used to their fullest potential. Is it wise to use our resources to explore outer space or should we build low-income housing instead? Should we explore for oil fields in the United States or should we use our resources for other endeavors while we import the oil we need?

Consider the case of a student who has only 24 hours to spend each day. Some of this precious resource (time) must be spent on the necessities of life such as eating and sleeping. But of the hours remaining, how many should be devoted to studying? Socializing? Relaxing? Too much socializing and relaxing will not allow the student to live his or her life to its fullest potential. Neither will going overboard on the study time. One problem every student faces is just how much time should be allocated to each of the various activities that make for a full life. This is an economic problem, since the student must decide how the resource (time) will be used to its maximum potential.

The discipline of economics is not directly concerned with money or politics or the stock market; however, economic problems abound in each of these areas. People want to spend their money in the best way. Politicians want to make decisions to achieve the maximum benefit, and investors want the highest return from their savings. Any time someone is trying to make the most out of what he has, we are in the realm of economics.

It is only natural for families, firms, and nations to strive for the best outcomes, given their initial endowments of resources. For that reason every person and institution must grapple with economic problems every day.

Macroeconomics Versus Microeconomics

The discipline of economics is broken into two fields: macroeconomics and microeconomics. Macroeconomics involves economic problems encountered by the nation as a whole. For example, do we spend too many of our resources on national

TIP

The general distinction between macroeconomics and microeconomics is that the former deals with the overall economy whereas the latter is concerned with particular individuals, firms, industries, or regions within the economy.

defense and not enough on education of our youth? If households are required to pay fewer taxes, will national savings be affected? Will prices rise or fall because of a tax cut? Will increasing the money supply increase production levels in the economy?

Microeconomics is concerned with the economic problems faced by individual units within the overall economy. Here we will be focusing in on particular families, individuals, and firms. Some examples of microeconomic issues are: Does a particular family save enough to provide for its future needs? How will a tax break affect XYZ Corporation's output? If the Smiths win the lottery, how will their spending patterns change?

Positive Versus Normative Economics

The discipline of economics can be split in another way—positive and normative economics. Positive economics is based on the scientific method. That means hypotheses are formulated and tested. For instance, one theory holds that if a family's income increased, their spending will increase but not by as much as the increase in income. There are several ways that this theory could be tested. One way is to observe how a group of families behave when their income is increased. Another might be to survey lottery winners to see how they disposed of their winnings.

Normative economics involves value judgments. Someone may feel that resources are better spent exploring outer space than providing free breakfasts for elementary school children. If this is the person's opinion, not based on a scientific investigation of the matter, then we are in the realm of normative economics. Normative economics is economics based on the way someone believes things *ought* to be.

It may appear as if positive economics is a superior form of the discipline since it is grounded in the scientific method and normative economics is based on opinions. However, normative economics is a crucial part of the economics discipline. Any scientific study will require an experiment, and experiments can be designed to highlight a scientist's prejudices. Even if an economist can keep his biases out of a study, why did he choose this particular question to investigate? However much economists strive to be like biologists and physicists, there will always be a large normative aspect to economics. Some economists claim that the normative side of the economics discipline is the more interesting.

RESOURCES

Economists, like most professionals, have special words and phrases that are used to describe concepts and ideas that occur frequently in their work. In order to understand economics, one must master the jargon. Familiar words and expressions can take on new meaning as economic jargon. The term "resource" is a case in point. To the layperson, a resource is something that can be used or drawn upon in a particular situation or endeavor. Economists do not dispute this definition, and use the word "resource" to mean much the same thing. However, the economist gives the term a special, more particular definition. *A resource is anything that can be used to produce a good or service.* This definition is broad enough to cover such dissimilar things as farmland, crude oil, machinery, and even intellectual ability.

In macroeconomics every resource is classified into one of three categories: land, labor, or capital.

- **Land** does not only refer to the ground we walk on, but all natural resources. Therefore resources such as farmland, crude oil, timber stands, oceans, and mineral deposits are all classified under the term "land."
- **Labor**, the second classification, encompasses all human attributes that are productive. Humans have the ability to perform a multitude of tasks, so there are many forms of this type of resource. Labor can be the person pounding nails at a construction site or the neurosurgeon in the operating room. Any time anyone is performing a service, function, or task, it is the resource "labor" at work. The professor in the classroom is using his intellectual capability to provide a service, just as a professional basketball player uses her athletic ability to produce points. In both cases, humans are using their attributes to produce things society finds valuable.
- **Capital**, in the economic sense of the term, is productive equipment or machinery. Again, many disparate items can fit into this classification: factory buildings, forklifts, computers, and paper clips are a few examples.

Not all resources fit neatly into this classification scheme. Resources such as time, health, money, adventurousness, and the willingness to take risks would all be difficult to categorize. Some economists have added categories to the classification system so that hard-to-classify resources have a place of their own, but most economists stick with the jargon and maintain that the productive assets of an economy are land, labor, and capital.

OPPORTUNITY COST

Opportunity cost is what must be sacrificed to obtain something. The concept of opportunity cost is quite general and ubiquitous in everyday life. When someone decides to spend two hours studying—obtaining wisdom or better grades—something must be sacrificed. For some individuals this might be two hours of watching TV; for others the opportunity cost of two hours of study time may be two hours of lost quality time with the family.

When someone decides to attend college, costs are always a consideration. Even if the money cost of tuition and books is not an issue for the student, the opportunity costs are. The opportunity costs of attending college will be different for each student, since each student sacrifices something different to attend. For most students the opportunity cost of college is the work experience or leisure activities that must be foregone in order to be in college.

In the macroeconomic sphere, opportunity cost takes on a more specific meaning. If a nation decides to produce one more unit of product A, how many units of product B will have to be sacrificed? Producing another unit of product A will use up resources. Exactly how many units of product B could have been produced with those resources?

TABLE 2.1

Hypothetical Production Possibilities		
Point	**Guns**	**Butter**
A	0	30
B	3	25
C	6	20
D	9	15
E	12	10
F	15	5
G	18	0

Table 2.1 shows various combinations of guns and butter that an economy could produce using all of its resources fully and efficiently. Using resources efficiently means that they are not used foolishly or wasted in the production process. Efficiency implies using resources to their maximum potential.

It may seem peculiar that this society produces only guns and butter. Guns can be thought of as all types of national defense, while butter represents consumer goods. The number of products in our example could be increased, but that would complicate the analysis unnecessarily.

Notice that each time the country portrayed in Table 2.1 produces three more guns, it must give up five pounds of butter. If it were decided to produce one more gun, then 1.67 pounds of butter would have to be sacrificed. Therefore, the opportunity cost of guns is 1.67 pounds of butter for this nation.

Conversely, if one more pound of butter were produced, society would have to forego the production of 0.6 guns. The opportunity cost of butter is 0.6 guns.

To calculate the opportunity cost of guns, divide the change in butter production by the change in gun production as you move from one line of Table 2.1 to the next.

$$opportunity\ cost\ of\ guns = \frac{change\ in\ butter\ production}{change\ in\ gun\ production} = \frac{5}{3} = 1.67\ pounds\ butter$$

The opportunity cost of butter is the reciprocal of the opportunity cost of guns.

$$opportunity\ cost\ of\ butter = \frac{change\ in\ gun\ production}{change\ in\ butter\ production} = \frac{3}{5} = 0.6\ guns$$

The concept of opportunity cost illustrates the simple fact that some amount of one product must be given up when more of another product is desired.

PRODUCTION POSSIBILITIES FRONTIER

The production possibilities frontier is the graphical portrayal of the information contained in Table 2.1. It shows the combinations of two goods that can be produced if the economy uses all of its resources fully and efficiently. Figure 2.1 is the production possibilities frontier that corresponds to Table 2.1. Points A through G are plotted with gun production measured on the vertical axis and butter production along the horizontal axis.

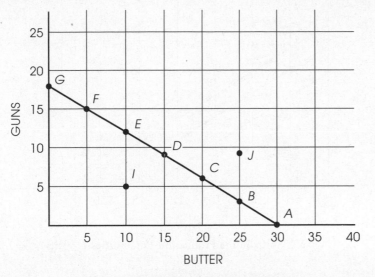

Fig. 2.1 Production Possibilities Frontier

The economy has the option of producing any combination of guns and butter along the frontier. At Point B most of the economy's resources are devoted to butter production. Only three guns are produced. At Point F gun production is predominant. Still, the economy is using its resources fully and efficiently at both points. A normative analysis is required to determine which point is preferred. On efficiency grounds all the points along the frontier are equal.

Points inside the frontier (Point I) are possible also. However, if the economy is operating at a point inside the frontier, resources are not being used fully or efficiently. Consider Point I, where 10 pounds of butter and five guns are being produced per year. By the definition of the production possibilities frontier we know that when the economy produces 10 pounds of butter, 12 guns could be produced if resources were used fully and efficiently (Point E). Point I represents a combination of guns and butter that does not require full or efficient resource utilization. The economy could do better by producing some combination of the two goods that lies on the frontier.

Points outside the production possibilities frontier (Point J) are unobtainable. Point J represents a combination of 25 pounds of butter and nine guns per year. By the definition of the production possibilities frontier we know that if 25 pounds of butter are produced, only three guns can be produced (Point B) if resources are used fully and efficiently. Therefore, points outside the frontier cannot be attained at this time.

Points outside the production possibilities frontier may be attained at some future date because the frontier may shift so that points like J lie along the new frontier. The frontier can also shift inward representing a change for the worse. Two factors cause the production possibilities frontier to shift:

1. changes in the amount of resources in the economy, and
2. changes in technology and productivity.

Fig. 2.2 Shifts in the Production Possibilities Frontier

It stands to reason that if the economy obtains more resources, larger combinations of guns and butter could be produced. This would shift the frontier to the right as in Figure 2.2. Similarly, a technological advance that made a given amount of resources more productive would also shift the frontier to the right.

The amount of resources in a country can increase for a variety of reasons. The amount of labor could increase through population growth. New territories could be acquired or existing land could be opened up for oil exploration or mining. The amount of capital could be increased by producing and putting in place more equipment and machinery.

TIP ✎

A decline in unemployment does not shift the production possibilities frontier. If unemployment exists, then the economy is operating inside the frontier. A decline in unemployment would move the economy to a point closer to or onto the frontier.

The production possibilities frontier would shift to the left if the amount of resources were decreased or technology took a step backward. It is easy to imagine the amount of resources in an economy decreasing due to devastating weather, war, or a decline in population. But why take a technological step backward? However, economies sometimes do use less efficient production techniques because of government regulation or tradition.

Government regulations to ensure worker safety or protect the environment often force firms to use less efficient production techniques. Hopefully, the benefits of increased worker safety and a less polluted environment are worth the cost of lower output. By tradition, Amish farmers still use horses to plow their fields. When less efficient production techniques are adopted, the production possibilities frontier shifts to the left. Again, the costs of maintaining this tradition (less output) might be worth the benefits (a more wholesome life).

LAW OF INCREASING COSTS

The production possibilities frontier is not typically a straight line as in Figures 2.1 and 2.2. You may have noticed that each time gun production increases by three in Table 2.1, butter production decreases by five. The opportunity cost of gun production is $^5/_3 = 1.67$ pounds of butter between all points. In other words, opportunity cost is constant throughout Table 2.1. This gives rise to the straight-line production possibilities frontier.

However, there is a good reason why opportunity cost will not be constant in the real world. The law of increasing costs states that as more of a product is produced, the opportunity cost increases. Table 2.2 presents data that comply with the law of increasing costs. The opportunity cost of guns is $^2/_3 = 0.67$ pounds of butter between Points A and B, and rises to $^3/_3 = 1$ pound of butter between Points B and C. A quick check will show that the further down Table 2.2 we go, the higher the opportunity cost of guns. The more guns we are initially producing, the more expensive it will be to produce one more gun in terms of butter production lost.

TABLE 2.2

Hypothetical Production Possibilities with Increasing Costs		
Point	Guns	Butter
A	0	25
B	3	23
C	6	20
D	9	15
E	12	8
F	15	5

This holds true for butter production also. In this case we move up Table 2.2 since more butter is produced as we go toward the top of the table. Between Points D and C the opportunity cost of butter is $^3/_5 = 0.6$ guns, whereas the opportunity cost is $^2/_3 = 0.67$ between Points B and A. These numbers are in line with the law of increasing costs, which states that the more of a product that is initially being produced, the higher the opportunity cost will be to produce still more.

When the numbers in Table 2.2 are graphed to form the production possibilities frontier the result is a line that is curved concave to the origin. This is shown in Figure 2.3. Concave-to-the-origin production possibilities frontiers are due to the law of increasing costs.

Fig. 2.3 **Concave to the Origin Production Possibilities Frontier**

CAUSES

But what is the cause of the law of increasing costs? Why does it cost more (in terms of butter) to produce another gun when a lot of guns are already being produced? To see the answer to these questions you must imagine the situation in an economy that is already producing a lot of guns. Most of the resources in the economy will be devoted to gun production, while only a few resources, such as farmers, cows, milking machines, and so forth, are engaged in butter production. Now, if that society wants to produce more guns, resources will have to be taken from butter production and used to produce guns. This means some farmers and cows will be employed in gun manufacture. (The cows could be used to turn mills that polish gun bores.) But farmers and cows are good at making butter and are not used in gun production, so when the resources are shifted from butter to gun production, not many more guns are produced, but a lot of butter must be sacrificed. In short, the opportunity cost of producing guns is high when gun production is already at a high level.

When gun production is low, the opportunity cost of increasing gun production is low. That is because most of society's resources are employed making butter. Imagine gunsmiths and gunmaking equipment being used to make butter since they are not needed to make the small number of guns being produced. Now, when gun production is increased, the resources that are adept at making guns can be shifted off the farm and into gun production—not much butter will be lost, but many more guns are produced. The opportunity cost of guns is low when a low level of guns is being produced.

The law of increasing costs is due to the fact that some resources are more adept at the production of one good than another. When resources are forced to work in an industry where they are not proficient, they are less productive. Thus, the opportunity cost of producing a good becomes greater as more resources are forced into industries where they are not as productive. This causes the production possibilities frontier to be concave to the origin.

COMPARATIVE ADVANTAGE

A survey of economists undertaken in the early 1990s indicates that 93 percent of them believed that restrictions to free trade, such as tariffs and quotas, reduce economic welfare. The basis for this widespread support of free trade is the law of comparative advantage.

The law of comparative advantage was delineated convincingly by David Ricardo in the early 1800s. The law is an important element in introductory micro- and macroeconomics courses. It is also an application of the concept of opportunity cost.

The law of comparative advantage advocates specialization for increased output. The idea that specialization can improve productivity impressed Adam Smith when he visited a pin factory in the 1700s. In his famous tome *The Wealth of Nations* he wrote about his observations:

> One man draws out the wire, another straights it, a third cuts it, a fourth points it, a fifth grinds it at the top for receiving the head; to make the head requires two or three distinct operations; to put it on is a peculiar business; to whiten the pins is another; it is even a trade by itself to put them into the paper; and the important business of pin making is, in this manner, divided into about eighteen distinct operations, . . .

Smith showed how the division of labor into specialized tasks could increase productivity and output. The law of comparative advantage shows that the notion of specialization for increased productivity and output applies to nations as well.

When David Ricardo wrote about the benefits of free trade it was in opposition to the Corn Laws of England. The Corn Laws prohibited the importation of grains from outside England in order to protect domestic farmers. Ricardo, like 93 percent of today's economists, felt that the economic well-being of England suffered because of this restriction of trade.

To prove his point, Ricardo set up a scenario very similar to the one depicted in Table 2.3.

TABLE 2.3

A Hypothetical Example of Production Costs

Country	Labor Hours Needed to Produce a Unit of:	
	Wheat	Cloth
Portugal	10	20
England	20	60

The table shows how many hours of labor are required to produce one unit of wheat or cloth in England and Portugal. According to Table 2.3, Portugal can produce both products more efficiently than England. In Portugal, a unit of wheat can be produced with 10 hours of labor, while it requires 20 hours in England. One unit of cloth can be produced in Portugal with 20 hours of labor, while the corresponding number in England is 60.

Portugal is said to have the absolute advantage in the production of both wheat and cloth. Absolute advantage implies that the product can be produced more efficiently, that is, with fewer inputs. You might wonder why Portugal would want to trade with England at all, as England is an inefficient producer of both products. That was the genius of Ricardo's exposition—trade can be mutually advantageous to both countries even if one country has the absolute advantage in all products, because mutually advantageous trade is based on comparative advantage, not absolute advantage.

Comparative advantage means that a nation can produce the good with a lower opportunity cost. Consider the opportunity cost of wheat in Portugal. It takes 10 hours to produce a unit of wheat. If it was decided to produce another unit of wheat in Portugal, then half a unit of cloth would have to be given up since the labor would be pulled off cloth production and it takes 20 hours to produce a unit of cloth.

Opportunity cost, you will recall, is how much of one thing must be sacrificed in order to obtain a unit of something else. Here half a unit of cloth must be given up in order to obtain an extra unit of wheat. By similar reasoning, the opportunity cost of cloth in Portugal is two units of wheat. Table 2.4 outlines the calculations required to determine the opportunity costs of wheat and cloth in Portugal and England.

Portugal has the lower opportunity cost in cloth production (two units of wheat), and England has the lower opportunity cost in wheat production ($1/3$ unit of cloth). Portugal has the comparative advantage in cloth, and England in wheat. Ricardo showed that if each country produced only the good in which it held a comparative advantage and traded for the other product, then both countries could consume more of both goods.

TABLE 2.4

Calculations of Opportunity Costs from Table 2.3
Portugal
Opportunity cost of wheat = 10/20 = 1/2 cloth
Opportunity cost of cloth = 20/10 = 2 wheat
England
Opportunity cost of wheat = 20/60 = 1/3 cloth
Opportunity cost of cloth = 60/20 = 3 wheat

You might convince yourself of this by assuming that each nation has 120 hours of labor to divide between the production of both goods. For instance, England could use 120 hours to produce a unit of cloth and three units of wheat; Portugal could produce five units of cloth and two units of wheat. Total cloth production by both countries would be six units, and total wheat production would be five units.

TABLE 2.5

Production of Wheat and Cloth in 120 hours

In Isolation		Wheat	Cloth
	Portugal	2	5
	England	3	1
Total		5	6
Specialization		**Wheat**	**Cloth**
	Portugal	0	6
	England	6	0
Total		6	6
With Trade		**Wheat**	**Cloth**
	Portugal	2.5	5
	England	3.5	1

However, if Portugal devoted its entire 120 hours to cloth production, there would be six units produced and England could use 120 hours to make six units of wheat. This is specialization according to comparative advantage. Notice that total cloth production is six units as it was before specialization, but total wheat production is now six units, not five. The extra unit of wheat could be shared by the citizens of each country through specialization of production and trade.

In fact, we could determine what the terms of trade would have to be so that the extra unit of wheat would add to the welfare of at least one, if not both, countries. Suppose England offered to trade 2 units of wheat for 2 units of cloth. Portugal would not accept since she would be left with 4 units of cloth and the 2 units of wheat. In isolation she could have enjoyed 5 units of cloth and 2 units of wheat.

The terms of trade would have fallen somewhere between 2 units of wheat for 1 unit of cloth (which would leave Portugal no better off than in isolation) and 3 units of wheat for 1 unit of cloth (which would leave England no better off than in isolation). Let's say the two countries strike a deal to trade 2.5 units of wheat for 1 unit of cloth. Then both countries would consume 0.5 units more wheat than in isolation and the same amount of cloth. In other words, the countries would share the extra unit of wheat production that was gained by specialization according to comparative advantage and trade.

Notice that the terms of trade must fall between the opportunity costs of both countries. Portugal's opportunity cost of cloth from Table 2.4 is 2 wheat and England's is 3 wheat. So the terms of trade must lie between 2 and 3 wheat, for one unit of cloth. It amounts to the same thing to state the terms of trade as falling between $1/2$ and $1/3$ cloth for one unit of wheat.

The idea that trade is beneficial to all parties involved even when one party has an absolute advantage in everything has an analogy in microeconomics. Consider a lawyer who happens to be very fast and accurate at keying legal documents. It would still pay for the lawyer to hire a secretary to do the keying, even if the secretary is not as efficient. That is because the secretary has the comparative advantage (lower opportunity cost) in keying. If the lawyer does her own keying, the opportunity cost is the income that could have been earned writing law briefs.

SUMMARY

- Economics is about using resources wisely. When we focus on one individual or one household or one firm and analyze its use of resources, we are practicing *microeconomics*. When we study whether a nation is allocating its resources in an efficient manner, we are practicing *macroeconomics*.
- Both macro- and microeconomics will require some normative analysis. That is, value judgments will have to be made at some point to answer most economic questions, but there is a tendency to be as positive as possible. Being positive means sticking to the scientific method of reaching conclusions and avoiding personal biases and opinions.
- Even if you have never studied economics before, you are well acquainted with it because everyone strives to make the most out of what they've got. Many people associate businesspeople or stocks and bonds with economics. That is correct because businesspeople are trying to make the most out of their company's resources, while stock and bond traders are trying to maximize their returns—but economics is so much more than that. Whenever a person, a firm, or a nation tries to make the most of its resources, it is practicing economics.
- Remember that the next time you have to decide between studying and watching TV. There's nothing wrong with watching TV. But you should realize that there is a cost to watching TV that goes beyond the cost of the electricity. The opportunity cost of watching TV is the study time you sacrifice. If you think it's worth it, then go for the TV, especially if you have a headache and wouldn't get much out of studying anyway. It's not just businesspeople and Wall Street players who make economic decisions.
- The idea that something must be sacrificed in order to pursue an alternative is captured in the concepts of opportunity cost and the productions possibilities frontier. The law of increasing costs suggests that the production possibilities frontier will be bowed and concave to the origin as opposed to a straight line.

TERMS

Absolute Advantage the ability to produce something more efficiently

Capital productive equipment or machinery

Comparative Advantage the ability to produce something with a lower opportunity cost

Economics a social science that studies how resources are used and is often concerned with how resources can be used to their fullest potential

Efficiency using resources to their maximum potential

Labor all human activity that is productive

Land all natural resources

Law of Increasing Costs law that states that when more of a product is initially being produced, the higher the opportunity cost will be to produce still more

Macroeconomics economic problems encountered by the nation as a whole

Microeconomics economic problems faced by individual units within the overall economy

Normative Economics economics involving value judgments

Opportunity Cost the amount of one good that must be sacrificed to obtain an alternative good

$$\text{Opportunity cost of Good X} = \frac{\text{Change in Good Y production}}{\text{Change in Good X production}}$$

Positive Economics economic analysis that draws conclusions based on logical deduction or induction; value judgments are avoided

Production Possibilities Frontier the combinations of two goods that can be produced if the economy uses all of its resources fully and efficiently

Resource anything that can be used to produce a good or service

Terms of Trade the amount of one good a country is willing and able to trade for another

MULTIPLE-CHOICE REVIEW QUESTIONS

1. Economics is a social science that
   (A) is primarily concerned with money.
   (B) is primarily concerned with how resources are used.
   (C) relies solely on the scientific method for analysis.
   (D) is primarily concerned with maximizing spiritual well-being.
   (E) is purely normative.

2. Macroeconomics focuses on

   (A) government and its laws that affect commerce.
   (B) individuals and their resource use.
   (C) corporations and their production levels.
   (D) the resource use of the entire nation.
   (E) money.

3. Given the table below what is the opportunity cost of wheat in France?

Country	Labor hours needed to produce a unit of:	
	Wheat	Cloth
France	5	10
England	20	60

   (A) $1/2$ cloth.
   (B) $1/2$ wheat.
   (C) 2 cloth.
   (D) 2 wheat.
   (E) $1/4$ cloth.

4. Given the table below, which statement is true?

Country	Labor hours needed to produce a unit of:	
	Wheat	Cloth
France	5	10
England	20	20

   (A) England has the absolute advantage in both products.
   (B) France should specialize in and export wheat while England should specialize in and export cloth.
   (C) France has the comparative advantage in cloth.
   (D) England has the comparative advantage in wheat.
   (E) France has the absolute advantage in wheat while England has the absolute advantage in cloth.

5. Which of the following statements is positive?

   (A) An economy that produces more butter than guns is better off than an economy that produces more guns than butter.
   (B) Nations should concentrate their resources on producing wholesome consumer goods as opposed to the weapons of war.
   (C) The production possibilities frontier is concave to the origin because of the law of increasing costs.
   (D) Nations ought to devote at least some of their resources to national defense.
   (E) Nations would do better by producing toward the middle of their production possibilities frontiers as opposed to the extreme points near the axes.

6. The primary focus of microeconomics is

(A) families and how they make money.
(B) firms and how they make profits.
(C) individual units within the overall economy.
(D) government.
(E) small countries.

7. Economists use the term "capital" to mean

(A) money.
(B) plant and equipment.
(C) where the central government is located.
(D) the center of the economy.
(E) a major idea.

8. Land refers to

(A) all productive resources.
(B) all natural resources.
(C) farmland only.
(D) real estate.
(E) chattels.

9. What you give up to pursue another alternative is known as

(A) capital.
(B) land.
(C) money cost.
(D) the price of the product.
(E) opportunity cost.

10. Given the following table,

(combinations that can be produced using resources fully and efficiently)

Apples	Oranges
0	20
7	10
14	0

the opportunity cost of apples is

(A) $^{10}/_7$ oranges.
(B) $^{7}/_{10}$ oranges.
(C) $^{10}/_7$ apples.
(D) $^{7}/_{10}$ apples.
(E) 70 percent.

11. Given the following table,

(combinations that can be produced using resources fully and efficiently)

Soup	Nuts
0	15
1	10
2	5

the opportunity cost of soup is

(A) 5 nuts.
(B) 5 soup.
(C) 20 percent.
(D) 500 percent.
(E) constant.

12. Production possibilities frontiers are concave to the origin because

(A) of inefficiencies in the economy.
(B) of opportunity cost.
(C) of the law of increasing costs.
(D) of constant opportunity costs.
(E) the extreme points are not as well established.

13. When opportunity cost is constant across all production levels, the productions possibilities frontier is

(A) concave to the origin.
(B) convex to the origin.
(C) undefined.
(D) shifted.
(E) a straight diagonal line sloping downward from left to right.

14. When an economy produces a combination of goods that lies on the production possibilities frontier,

(A) resources are being used fully and efficiently.
(B) prices are constant.
(C) opportunity cost is constant.
(D) resources will never be depleted.
(E) prices will rise.

15. The law of increasing costs

(A) does not apply to guns and butter.
(B) is the result of resources not being perfectly adaptable between the production of two goods.
(C) implies that prices will rise when the costs of making a good rise.
(D) causes the production possibilities frontier to be a straight line.
(E) implies that opportunity costs will rise as production levels fall.

Multiple-Choice Review Answers

1. **(B)**	4. **(B)**	7. **(B)**	10. **(A)**	13. **(E)**
2. **(D)**	5. **(C)**	8. **(B)**	11. **(A)**	14. **(A)**
3. **(A)**	6. **(C)**	9. **(E)**	12. **(C)**	15. **(B)**

FREE-RESPONSE REVIEW QUESTIONS

I. The law of increasing costs states that the opportunity cost of producing a good will rise as more of the good is initially being produced. Explain why this is so.

II. Select two goods for which the law of increasing costs might not apply. Explain why the law would not apply in this case.

III. Select two goods for which it is clear the law of increasing costs would definitely apply. Explain why the law is definitely applicable in this case.

Free-Response Review Answers

I. The law of increasing costs indicates that the opportunity cost of producing a good will be higher when more of the good is being produced. This is because when the economy is devoting a significant amount of its resources toward the production of a particular product, all the resources that are proficient in the production of the good are already being used to produce it. If more of the good is to be produced, resources that are not as proficient will have to be drawn into the production process. You won't get much more production of this good but production of other goods will fall significantly. This means the opportunity cost of producing more of the good is high. The situation is reversed when production levels of the good are low to begin with.

II. The law of increasing costs would not apply to refrigerators and freezers because the resources required for the production of these two goods are essentially the same. Since the resources are perfectly adaptable between the two goods, we always have to give up the same amount of refrigerators to produce one more freezer, regardless of how many freezers we are producing to begin with.

III. The law of increasing costs would most likely apply to milk and computers. Most of the resources required to produce milk are not very useful in computer production. Therefore, when most of the economy's resources are already being used to produce computers, only cows, farmland, tractors, and farmers are left producing milk. In order to produce still more computers you will have to take these resources off the farm and use them to make computers. You will have to give up quite a bit of milk just to produce one more computer.

Economic Systems

CHAPTER 3

- Command economy
- Capitalism
- Allocative efficiency

- Mixed economy
- Circular flow diagram

FUNDAMENTAL ECONOMIC ISSUES

In every nation there are a variety of issues that demand attention: What can be done about poverty and unemployment? Pollution? The national debt? Inflation? And so on. Yet before these questions can be addressed—indeed, before these problems even crop up—there are some fundamental economic questions that each and every country will have to contend with.

Even Robinson Crusoe had to deal with economic issues on his deserted island. What resources were on hand to provide food and shelter? Was clothing necessary? Crusoe had to decide how to best employ his meager resources to ensure his survival. In the same manner, each nation must decide what is the best way to use the resources at its disposal.

Would it be wise for Crusoe to spend all his time keeping a signal fire burning and searching the horizon for a rescue ship? Or should the same wood that might be used in the signal fire be used to build a shelter? Should the United States use its resources to explore Mars or to build low-income housing? One of the most fundamental questions any economy will have to address, whether it is one man trapped on an island or a highly industrialized nation, is what should be produced given its resources.

In Cuba it is virtually impossible to get cosmetic surgery, while the United States devotes a significant amount of its resources to this. Part of the reason why this is so has to do with the fact that the United States has so many resources compared to Cuba, but another reason why Cuba spends hardly any resources on plastic surgery is because of the way the decision is made about what will be produced in Cuba.

Opportunity Costs

Before exploring further the differences in the way economic decisions are undertaken in Cuba versus in the United States, let us consider some other fundamental economic questions. Once it is decided to produce a certain set of goods and services, how much of each item should be produced? The concept of opportunity cost comes into play here. If it is decided to produce more than one item, then some amount of another item must be sacrificed.

Not only that, but many goods and services are related to one another. For instance, if it is decided to produce more wheat, this will require an increase in the production of tractors, seed, fertilizer, and other products needed to produce wheat. Considering opportunity costs and the fact that many products are related, the decision of how much to produce of each good and service becomes an extremely complex issue.

WHO GETS WHAT?

After having decided what and how much of each item is to be produced, there is still another basic question: Who is going to get how much of each good and service? In the United States, a medical doctor can obtain more and higher-quality goods and services than a schoolteacher. In Cuba doctors and teachers have roughly equal living standards. Certainly a person's income is important in determining how many goods and services can be obtained. But why do doctors receive so much more income than teachers in the United States and not in Cuba? The answer to that question involves how each economy responds to the basic economic issue of "who gets what?"

So there are two fundamental economic questions that any society will have to address:

1. How much, if any, of each good and service should be produced?
2. Who will get how much of each good and service?

In order to appreciate the complexity of these questions, imagine yourself shipwrecked on a desert island with 11 other people. It is possible to produce only a limited number of items with the resources on hand. The necessities of life will have to be produced: food, clothing, and shelter.

Should you attempt to build a boat large enough to take 12 people back to civilization? Or is a signal fire more logical? It would be possible to provide haircuts, and makeup could be manufactured, however crude. Exactly what should be produced?

If the production of cosmetics and haircuts is forsaken in order to produce more food, it will be necessary to produce more tools for working the land and harvesting the crops.

Who will get how much of each item produced? Should the doctor get more than the food production manager? Should the sick people get more or less than the others?

Now try and imagine coping with these questions when there are 290 million people and the array of goods and service encompasses everything from rubber bands to space shuttles. The organization of large economies is a mind-boggling task. How is it accomplished?

STRATEGIES FOR ADDRESSING ECONOMIC QUESTIONS

There are three basic ways to address the economic questions that are imposed upon a society: (1) government commands, (2) capitalism, and (3) a blend of government commands and capitalism.

The Command Economy

A command economy is one in which the central government dictates what will or will not be produced. The government also stipulates how much of each item is to be produced and finally, who is to get how many of the final products. Cuba and North Korea are examples of nations that rely heavily on the command system. The terms *communism* and *socialism* are sometimes used to describe economies that use central commands to address the fundamental economic questions.

Cosmetic surgery is not available in Cuba because the central government does not allow resources to be used on this service. Through the use of quotas and production plans, the Cuban government dictates how much of each good and service will be available. This is no simple task since thousands of items are produced.

Moreover, the production levels of the various goods and services must be coordinated so that if more sugar is to be produced, then more arable land, fertilizer, farm labor, and so on must be provided.

Finally, by setting the prices on almost all goods and services, and by setting the wage rates for almost all citizens, the Cuban government can dictate who gets what share of these products.

Setting prices and wages and stipulating how much of each item is to be produced for the whole economy are Herculean tasks. It is done with the help of computers by a large bureaucracy. Often, mistakes are made. The quota of sugar cannot be met because not enough tractors are available. Without sugar, the rum quota cannot be met.

On the other hand, the command system has some commendable features. Wages can be set so that there is no lower class. However, if everyone makes about the same income, incentives to work hard and develop new lines of business are discouraged. Still, the price of alcohol can be set high to curtail alcoholism, while the price of textbooks can be established artificially low to encourage education.

The Cuban economy is not a pure command economy. There is some experimentation with households and firms being allowed to sell their excess production in markets where prices are not fixed by the government. And there are many transactions between households that the government cannot control. Some products and a variety of services are provided on the "black market."

Capitalism

Capitalism has been defined by different writers in remarkably different ways. Some point to the importance of private property in capitalist economies, while others note the emphasis on risk-taking and entrepreneurial skills. The best definition of capitalism, however, is in regard to how the basic economic questions are addressed. Capitalism is an economic system where supply and demand determine prices. These prices coordinate the economy by resolving what and how much will be produced. Supply and demand will also determine a person's income and therefore how much of the production the person can obtain for his or her own use.

In this type of system, the government does not run the economy but, instead, attempts to create an environment where prices can be determined in free markets. Amazingly, these prices coordinate the economy.

In a capitalist economy, prices determine how much of each item will be produced. If consumers want more baggy, pleated pants instead of blue jeans, then the price of baggy, pleated pants increases and the price of jeans falls. Producers, with an eye on profit possibilities, then manufacture more baggy, pleated pants and fewer jeans. In fact, textile manufacturers who do not respond to the price changes could go out of business.

Consumers, not the government, determine how much of each item will be produced. They do this by purchasing the products they like. When consumers demand and purchase products, they are voting for those products. The prices of consumers' favorite products rise and this sends a signal to suppliers to provide more of that product.

An individual's income determines how much of the production he can obtain and enjoy, but income is largely determined by the wages an individual receives. And the wage rate is just another price in the economy: the price of labor.

Notice that the government does not have to get involved in setting prices and wages in capitalist economies. Prices and wages are determined in free markets and these prices serve to coordinate the economy and answer the basic economic questions. Prices govern the behavior of consumers and producers who seek to make the most out of their respective resources. Just the right goods and services are produced in just the right amounts. This is known as "allocative efficiency" in economic jargon.

Price Determination

Prices in capitalist economies are determined by supply and demand. The Law of Demand states that when the price of a product increases the quantity demanded decreases, *ceteris paribus*. *Ceteris paribus* (pronounced KET-er-us PAR-i-bus) is Latin for "all other things remaining unchanged." The Law of Demand can also be stated conversely: When the price of a product falls, the quantity demanded will increase, *ceteris paribus*.

It is common sense that higher prices will result in fewer units being demanded by consumers, but we may observe prices rising and consumers buying even more units of the product if something else changes simultaneously. For instance, the income of consumers may have increased along with the prices and this explains why more units of the product are demanded. The Law of Demand stipulates the relationship between the price of the product and the quantity demanded when all other factors remain constant.

If we were to graph the demand for a product, say corn, then a high price of corn would be associated with a rather low demand. When the price of corn fell, the quantity demanded would rise. This results in a demand curve that slopes downward from left to right. See Figure 3.1.

Notice that by tradition the price of the product is measured on the vertical axis and the quantity demanded on the horizontal axis. Demand curves can be steeply sloped or more flat, but they will always slope downward in order to conform with the Law of Demand. A demand curve that sloped upward would imply that when the price of the product increased, the quantity demanded would increase. That could happen only if the *ceteris paribus* assumption of the Law of Demand was violated.

Fig. 3.1 A Demand Curve

The price of any given product is determined by the demand for it relative to the supply. The Law of Supply states that when the price of a product increases the quantity supplied increases, *ceteris paribus.* This law may also be stated conversely: when the price of a product falls the quantity supplied falls, *ceteris paribus.*

The graph of the supply of corn slopes upward from left to right in order to conform with the Law of Supply. See Figure 3.2.

Fig. 3.2 A Supply Curve

Notice that the graph of the supply curve has the same axes as that of the demand curve. We can put both curves on the same graph.

Fig. 3.3 A Supply and Demand

Equilibrium Price

The intersection of the supply and demand curves is known as the *equilibrium point*. A line drawn from the equilibrium point to the vertical axis determines the equilibrium price. The equilibrium price is the price that will prevail in a free market. A line drawn from the equilibrium point to the horizontal axis determines the equilibrium quantity, which is the amount of the product that will be bought and sold in a free market.

If the price of corn is not the equilibrium price, it will be shortly, because when the price of corn is above its equilibrium, it will be driven down. It will be driven down because a surplus of corn will emerge when the price is *above* its equilibrium. When the price of corn is *below* its equilibrium value, it will be driven up because a shortage of corn will emerge when the price is below its equilibrium.

Equilibrium is a state of balance between opposing forces. In this case the opposing forces are surpluses and shortages. When the price of corn is above the equilibrium price, consumers will cut back on their demand, but suppliers are induced to bring more to market. This results in a surplus of corn. The surplus of corn induces suppliers to lower the price.

Just the opposite occurs when the price of corn is below the equilibrium price. Consumers will have a brisk demand for corn because the price is relatively low. Suppliers, however, are not motivated to provide much corn when the price is relatively low. The result is a shortage and the shortage of corn drives the price higher.

Only at the equilibrium price will there be no shortage or surplus. This is how allocative efficiency is achieved: Just the right amount of corn is produced to satisfy the demand; there is no shortage or surplus.

The preceding analysis of how prices are determined makes it seem that the price of corn will stabilize at its equilibrium value. This is true, but the equilibrium value is constantly changing because the demand and supply curves are constantly shifting left and right.

For instance, an increase in consumers' incomes would increase the demand for corn. This would be reflected in a shift to the right of the demand curve. The new equilibrium price will be greater than before the increase in income. See Figure 3.4.

Fig. 3.4 **An Increase in Demand**

Demand Curve

A variety of things could cause the demand curve to shift:

1. Consumers' tastes could change and they may prefer some other vegetable to corn. This would cause the demand for corn to decrease and the demand curve to shift to the left.
2. If the prices of substitute products change, this will change the demand for corn. For example, an increase in the price of carrots would increase the demand for corn, shifting the demand curve to the right.
3. If the prices of complimentary products change, this will change the demand for corn. The example is the price of butter rising to exorbitant levels. Few people want to eat corn without butter, so the demand for corn decreases.
4. Finally, the expected future price of corn can affect the current demand for corn. If consumers expect the price of corn to be higher in the future, they will demand more right now. It is best to buy it before the price goes up. Table 3.1 lists the major determinants of demand.

The primary determinant of the demand for a given product is its own price. If the price of a product changes we would move from one point on its demand curve to another, but the demand curve would not shift. The demand curve shifts only when one of the other determinants of demand changes. Economists distinguish between these two situations by using, or not using, the word *quantity*.

TABLE 3.1

Determinants of Demand

Price of the product

Income

Consumer tastes

Prices of substitute products

Prices of complementary products

Expected future price of the product

When the price of a product decreases and we move from point A to point B on the demand curve, this is referred to as an "increase in the *quantity* demanded."

Fig. 3.5 An Increase in the Quantity Demanded

Fig. 3.6 An Increase in Demand

An increase in income would shift the demand curve to the right because more of the product is demanded at any price now that income has risen. This is referred to as an "increase in demand," dropping the word "quantity."

Supply Curve

The same principle applies to the supply curve. If the price of the product were to change, we would move from one point to another along a stable supply curve. This would be called a "change in the *quantity* supplied." However, if the supply curve shifted, this would be called a "change in supply."

The most important factor determining the supply of a given product is its price, but a change in the costs of inputs required to make the product would also affect supply. Specifically, if the cost of inputs required to produce corn, such as seed and fertilizer, increased, then the supply of corn would decrease.

Advances in technology and productivity would result in an increase in supply. Imagine that a new drought-resistant corn seed was developed. This would increase the supply of corn and be reflected by a shift to the right of the supply curve.

The expected future price of corn would affect its current supply. If the price of corn was expected to be higher next month, farmers would store their harvest till then. This would result in a decrease in the current supply. Table 3.2 lists the major determinants of supply.

TABLE 3.2

Determinants of Supply

Price of the product

Prices of inputs required to make the product

Technology and productivity

Expected future price of the product

END RESULT

Let us use what we have learned about supply and demand to determine how prices would react to different events in a capitalist economy. Suppose there was an increase in income and consumers demanded more corn. The demand curve for corn would shift to the right. The equilibrium price of corn would rise. The higher price of corn would induce farmers to supply more. The end result is a higher price for corn, while more is bought and sold. See Figure 3.7.

Suppose the cost of corn seeds rises. This would shift the supply curve to the left. The equilibrium price is now higher. The higher price of corn causes

 TIP

Students often think that supply affects demand or vice versa. This is not quite correct. If supply changed, say a shortage occurred, then the price of the product would go up. It is the increase in the product's price, not supply, that affects demand.

consumers to lower their quantity demanded. The new equilibrium point reflects a higher price and less corn being bought and sold. See Figure 3.8.

When the price system works it is truly an elegant system. Just the right items are provided in just the right proportions to satisfy society's wants. The economy is almost automatically coordinated. This stands in contrast to the command economy where a huge effort and bureaucracy are required to coordinate an economy that is usually far from being allocatively efficient. But the command economy can easily ensure that goods and services are distributed fairly or equally, while an unequal distribution is the norm in economies that rely on free markets.

Fig. 3.7 An Increase in the Demand for Corn

Fig. 3.8 A Decrease in the Supply of Corn

The Mixed Economy

All of the countries in the world today use a blend of government commands and capitalism to address the fundamental economic questions that arise. In the United States, capitalism is emphasized, but government commands are used when free markets break down. For instance, society benefits when people pursue education beyond high school. The government promotes higher education by providing scholarships, grants, and loans. Private colleges have competition from state schools. Our government doesn't trust the production of higher education to the market. It gets involved and increases the equilibrium quantity of college degrees granted.

Similarly, there is no pure command economy on the planet; even Cuba and North Korea have some free markets. It is best to view the economies of the world on a spectrum with pure capitalism on the right and pure command economies on the left. The United States is closer to pure capitalism than France, and France is closer to pure capitalism than China.

As we go forward we will focus on the fundamental macroeconomic concepts of capitalist economies such as the United States where the decentralized decision making of the price system predominates.

THE CIRCULAR FLOW DIAGRAM

In capitalist economies, most of the resources are owned by individuals and households. The government and business enterprises will own some resources in such a system, but not the lion's share. Moreover, since most of the large firms are owned by stockholders (individuals and households) and most government resources, such as Yosemite National Park, are considered to be jointly owned by everyone, it is fair to assume that all of the resources are owned by individuals and households.

The circular flow diagram portrayed in Figure 3.9 shows these resources (land, labor, and capital) flowing from households to firms. In return, households receive wages and profits. This exchange of resources for money is known as the market for resources.

Fig. 3.9 The Circular Flow Diagram

Households spend their money income to purchase the goods and services supplied by firms. This exchange of income for products is known as the *market for goods and services*.

The circular flow diagram shows how resources are used to produce goods and services and how these goods and services are distributed. Essentially, individuals and households sell their resources to firms that use the resources to produce goods and services. Individuals and households use the proceeds from the sale of their resources to purchase the output of the firms.

The circular flow diagram can be expanded to include the government and banks. There would be more boxes and more lines representing flows of money and products, but no matter how complicated or simple, the circular flow diagram shows how institutions in capitalist economies are tied together.

SUMMARY

Even if you drop out of society and go to live as a hermit on an isolated mountaintop, you will have to cope with the fundamental economic questions: What should be produced with the resources on hand and how much of each item should be produced? Hermits, however, do not have to deal with the other fundamental economic question: How much of the production should each member of society get?

- Government commands and capitalism are two general ways to address the fundamental economic questions. Each approach has its strengths and weaknesses. Basically, an economy organized by government commands can be more equitable while a market economy is more efficient.
- When supply and demand are allowed to determine prices, we argued that just the right amount of goods and services would be produced to satisfy society's wants. This is known as *allocative efficiency*. Resources are deployed in the production of the things society desires.
- No country in the world is purely capitalistic. Even in the United States the government does not allow free markets to determine all prices. Similarly, no nation is a pure command economy. Even Cuba has some free markets.

TERMS

Allocative Efficiency term for resources being deployed to produce just the right amount of each product to satisfy society's wants

Capitalism an economic system where supply and demand determine prices

Circular Flow Diagram diagram that shows how households and firms are related by the exchange of resources and products

Command Economy economy in which the central government dictates what will or will not be produced and who gets what

Law of Demand law that states that when the price of a product increases, the quantity demanded decreases, *ceteris paribus*

Law of Supply law that states that when the price of a product increases, the quantity supplied increases, *ceteris paribus*

Mixed Economy a blend of government commands and capitalism

MULTIPLE-CHOICE REVIEW QUESTIONS

1. Which of the following is a fundamental economic question?
   (A) Who will get how much of each good and service?
   (B) Who should pay taxes?
   (C) Who will work?
   (D) Who will make the economic decisions?
   (E) Who will be allowed into the economy?

2. In a command economy
   (A) the market dictates the answers to the fundamental economic questions.
   (B) competition helps answer the fundamental economic questions.
   (C) state and local governments respond to the fundamental economic questions.
   (D) the central government dictates the answers to the fundamental economic questions.
   (E) laws are set up to answer the fundamental economic questions.

3. Market economies
   (A) rely on markets to coordinate economic activity.
   (B) rely on the government to address the fundamental economic questions.
   (C) rely on elected officials to make the most important economic decisions.
   (D) rely on courts to ensure people and firms get what they deserve.
   (E) are more equitable than command economies.

4. Prices in capitalist economies are
   (A) unfair.
   (B) determined by supply and demand.
   (C) determined, in most cases, by the federal government.
   (D) a reflection of our basic values.
   (E) a means to achieve equality.

5. If people expect the price of a particular product to increase in the near future,
   (A) this will not affect the demand for the product right now.
   (B) this will decrease the demand for the product.
   (C) this will not affect the demand for the product now or later.
   (D) this will cause firms to expect the same thing.
   (E) this will increase the demand for the product.

6. A decrease in the price of a particular product will result in
   (A) an increase in demand.
   (B) a decrease in demand.
   (C) an increase in the quantity demanded.
   (D) a decrease in the quantity demanded.
   (E) a change in the expected future price.

7. If firms that make a particular product expect its price will be lower in the future,
   (A) this will cause the supply of the product to increase right now.
   (B) this will cause the supply of the product to decrease right now.
   (C) this will have no effect on the amount of the product supplied right now.
   (D) this will have no effect on the supply of the product now or later.
   (E) this will cause consumers to expect the price to be higher in the near future also.

8. What will happen to the equilibrium price and the equilibrium quantity of good Z when the price of good X, which is a close substitute for Z, rises?

    (A) The equilibrium price will rise and the equilibrium quantity will fall.
    (B) The equilibrium price will fall and the equilibrium quantity will rise.
    (C) The equilibrium price and the equilibrium quantity will both rise.
    (D) The equilibrium price and the equilibrium quantity will both fall.
    (E) There is not enough information to answer definitely.

9. What will happen to the equilibrium price and the equilibrium quantity of good A when producers of good A expect the price to be higher in the near future?

    (A) The equilibrium price will rise and the equilibrium quantity will fall.
    (B) The equilibrium price will fall and the equilibrium quantity will rise.
    (C) The equilibrium price and the equilibrium quantity will rise.
    (D) The equilibrium price and the equilibrium quantity will fall.
    (E) There is not enough information to answer definitely.

10. What will happen to the equilibrium price and the equilibrium quantity of corn when the prices of corn seed and fertilizer fall?

    (A) The equilibrium price will rise and the equilibrium quantity will fall.
    (B) The equilibrium price will fall and the equilibrium quantity will rise.
    (C) The equilibrium price and the equilibrium quantity will rise.
    (D) The equilibrium price and the equilibrium quantity will fall.
    (E) There is not enough information to answer definitely.

11. Suppose the demand for a particular product falls while the supply simultaneously increases. What will happen to the equilibrium price and the equilibrium quantity?

    (A) The equilibrium price will rise while the equilibrium quantity is indeterminate.
    (B) The equilibrium price will fall while the equilibrium quantity is indeterminate.
    (C) The equilibrium price is indeterminate while the equilibrium quantity will rise.
    (D) The equilibrium price is indeterminate while the equilibrium quantity will fall.
    (E) There is not enough information to answer definitely.

12. Suppose consumers expect the price of corn to be lower in the near future while the price of seed corn and fertilizer fall. What will happen to the equilibrium price and the equilibrium quantity?

    (A) The equilibrium price will rise while the equilibrium quantity is indeterminate.
    (B) The equilibrium price will fall while the equilibrium quantity is indeterminate.
    (C) The equilibrium price is indeterminate while the equilibrium quantity will rise.
    (D) The equilibrium price is indeterminate while the equilibrium quantity will fall.
    (E) There is not enough information to answer definitely.

13. Allocative efficiency

(A) means that no inferior products will be produced.

(B) implies that the economy's output is distributed evenly.

(C) means that those who work hardest will get more.

(D) implies that resources are used to produce the goods and services society desires in just the right amounts.

(E) can only occur in command economies.

14. The Law of Demand states that

(A) the quantity demanded of a product will fall when the price of the product falls.

(B) the quantity demanded of a product will fall when the price of the product rises.

(C) when the demand for a product falls, so will its price.

(D) when the demand for a product falls, its price will rise.

(E) a product's price and the quantity demanded of that product are positively related.

15. *Ceteris paribus*

(A) is Greek for "never changing."

(B) means anything can change at any time.

(C) is Latin for "everything else remains constant."

(D) means "when in equilibrium."

(E) is Latin for "holds true."

Multiple-Choice Review Answers

1. **(A)**	4. **(B)**	7. **(A)**	10. **(B)**	13. **(D)**
2. **(D)**	5. **(E)**	8. **(C)**	11. **(B)**	14. **(B)**
3. **(A)**	6. **(C)**	9. **(A)**	12. **(B)**	15. **(C)**

FREE-RESPONSE REVIEW QUESTIONS

I. What are the fundamental economic questions?

II. Contrast how the fundamental economic questions are addressed in command versus capitalist economies.

III. Cite the advantages and disadvantages of command economies.

Free-Response Review Answers

I. There are two fundamental economic questions that any society will have to address: (1) How much, if any, of each good and service should be produced? and (2) Who will get how much of each good and service?

II. In command economies the central government stipulates what and how much of most products will be produced. By setting prices and wages the central government can also dictate how much of the production is allotted to each household. In short, the central government controls production and income in command economies.

In capitalist economies free markets coordinate output and income. Supply and demand, which depend upon the decentralized decision making of all consumers and producers, determine what and how much will be produced. Supply and demand also determine incomes and, therefore, who gets how much of each good and service.

III. One disadvantage of command economies is that there can be a lack of incentive to work hard to get ahead. Since the government decides one's income level, it may not pay to put one's nose to the grindstone—the government may reward you all the same, anyway. One advantage of command economies is that prices can be set to achieve social goals. For example, the price of textbooks could be set low to promote education. Another advantage of command economies is that incomes can be set more equitably than capitalist economies.

Capitalist economies are typically more allocatively efficient than command economies; also, they do not require the large bureaucracy of command economies.

MICROECONOMICS

As you work toward achieving that 5 on your
AP Microeconomics exam, here are five essentials
that you **MUST** know above everything else:

1 **Characteristics of product markets.** You will be asked specific questions on these characteristics as well as questions about pricing, output, and the effects of government regulation. These questions may constitute as much as 25% of the multiple-choice questions and more than 50% of the free-response questions.
- You should know how the relationships of Price and Marginal Revenue, Price and Marginal Cost, Output and Price, Price and Average Cost differ among the product markets.
- Be sure to know how these markets differ on the degree of efficiency, price elasticity, barriers to entry, economic profits, availability of substitutes, the numbers of sellers, and the independence or interdependence (the latter as in Game Theory) in pricing strategy among sellers.
- Be sure to know how government regulation of monopolies affects prices, profits, and output.

2 **Basic relationships of costs and production and their application to output and price decisions.** Marginal analysis is central in this context.
- You should know the law of diminishing marginal productivity, the relationships between average and marginal costs and product curves, and the distinctions between the long and short run.
- Pay attention to economies of scale particularly in the adjustment from the short run to the long run in plant capacity.
- Be able to demonstrate the relationship of production to costs, e.g., the relationship of MPP and APP to AVC and MC.

3 **The applications of demand and supply to elasticity and consumer choice in economic decision making.**
- You should know the concept of diminishing marginal utility and the utility-maximizing rule. You will be expected to find the utility-maximizing combination of two goods given the constraints.
- You should be able to explain and graph consumer and producer surplus. Know the income and substitution effects of a downward sloping demand curve.
- Know the concepts and the formulas for price, cross price, and income elasticity of demand. Also, know the formulas for the numerical coefficient of elasticity and the price elasticity of supply.

4 **The connections between product markets and labor markets, as they frame the bases for many AP micro exam questions.** Know the relationships between costs, production and supply, and the relationships among prices, costs, and revenue as in Essentials points # 1 and #2 above.
- Know the laws and measurement of labor as a derived demand.
- Know cost minimization and profit maximization for hiring labor.
- Expect a question on MRP and MFC as in Table 13.1, and a question on the Lorenz Curve.

5 **Basic functions of government in a market-oriented economy.** The bases for government roles can be based on positive or normative considerations and involve the following concepts that appear in AP exams. Know these concepts and how to apply them.
- Market failure to produce desired outcomes.
- The presence of externalities, positive or negative.
- The nature and significance of public, quasi-public, and private goods.

Demand and Supply: The Basics

- Changes in demand and supply
- Price-takers
- Competition
- Price ceilings and price floors
- Functions of prices and markets
- Equilibrium, disequilibrium
- Changes in amounts demanded (supplied)

INTRODUCTION

This chapter is fundamental to the study of economics in general, and to the study of microeconomics in particular. Indeed, the trend in most colleges and universities is to place microeconomics first in the sequence of micro- and macro-economics. Many contemporary issues involve applications of supply and demand which are often at the base of more complex economic concepts. Microeconomics is sometimes called the economics of the firm or price theory. We are interested in the role of prices in decision making and in the allocation of scarce resources. How are markets and their price mechanisms designed to produce efficient outcomes? In order to address this question, we need to explore prices in terms of the basics of supply and demand.

THINGS TO KNOW

Based on the most frequently asked questions on previous advanced placement exams, the following are the most important concepts. In the balance of the chapter, we will expand on these and other concepts and examples.

1. Changes in demand (supply) vs. changes in quantity demanded (supplied). Changes in demand (supply) show how non-price variables cause a shift (change in) of demand (supply) to a new demand (supply) function or curve. Changes in quantity demanded (supplied) depend only on a change in the price of the particular good being analyzed.

2. The role of competitive markets. This setting allows us to see how prices could function according to the design of the system. Firms or sellers are *price-takers*.

3. Market Equilibrium. This is the level of output and price at which the quantity demanded equals the quantity supplied. This provides a reference point for discussion of shortages and surpluses as well as a base of government policies.
4. Non-price determinants of supply and demand. Examples follow in this chapter on what factors influence increases or decreases in demand (supply).
5. Simultaneous changes in demand and supply. Examples and a table will follow to illustrate this situation.
6. Government induced changes in the form of price ceilings and price floors. Examples and graphs will follow in this chapter.

COMPETITIVE MARKETS

With a competitive market, the sellers or firms are price-takers; in other words, any one firm or groups of firms cannot significantly alter the terms of exchange or transaction terms—the price. Put another way, there are too many sellers for any effective price conspiracy to take place. The seller or firm must sell at the market price, the price established by the interaction of all buyers and sellers in a market setting. Later, we will review what happens in the real world of imperfect competition. For now we will concentrate on the function of prices: disciplinarians (competitive pressures to keep prices down to the market norm of efficiency), signals (the what, when, how much, where, and for whom goods and services should be produced), and rationers (high prices encourage economizing of relatively scarce resources and goods; low prices encourage more use of relatively abundant resources and goods).

MARKET EQUILIBRIUM—DEMAND AND SUPPLY
Trial and Error

The establishment of prices in competitive settings comes about by trial and error—sellers initiating a price only to discover that a surplus or glut occurs; a lowering of this initial price reduces the surplus until it disappears at equilibrium. The converse holds with too low a price resulting in shortages; therefore, a distinction between relative and absolute prices is important. An absolute price is the price of a good as stated. A price is high or low relative to other prices or to a base-year price. Increases in the price reduce the shortage (buyers or consumers "bid" against one another) until it disappears at equilibrium. This equilibrium (illustrated below) has the following characteristics:

1. There is no tendency for change; the demand function and supply function stay the same or constant.
2. The amounts demanded equal the amounts supplied (at the intersection of supply and demand).
3. There is no surplus or shortage; the equilibrium price "clears" the market.

Equilibrium—The Illustration

Equilibrium occurs at E (Price = $5; quantities exchanged = 300), the intersection of SS and DD (supply and demand), where the quantities demanded = quantities supplied. The characteristics of equilibrium (above) apply.

Fig. 4.1 Market Equilibrium

Disequilibrium

If the price is $8, then there is disequilibrium since the quantities demanded at $8 would equal 100 and the quantities supplied would equal 350; therefore, there would be a surplus of 250. As the market (suppliers) react to the surplus, the price will drop until it equals $5 (equilibrium price) at which the market is "cleared" of the surplus. The converse holds, when the price is *below* the equilibrium, such as $3, when a shortage of 150 would develop. At $3, the quantities demanded exceed the quantities supplied (400 > 250) and the consumers (buyers) would bid the price up until it reaches $5 (equilibrium price) and the market is cleared of any shortage.

Demand and Amounts Demanded

There are important distinctions between these two terms; these distinctions are bound to be included in any AP test in economics. Amounts demanded refer to the amounts consumers are willing to buy of a particular good or service at varying prices of that good or service. Changes in amounts demanded refer to changes along a demand curve or function as a result *only* of a change in the price of that good, *ceteris paribus* (holding all other factors or conditions constant). Changes in demand occur when these *ceteris paribus* conditions or determinants change.

Ceteris Paribus Conditions or Determinants of Demand

- the number of consumers
- tastes and preferences of consumers
- prices of related goods—substitutes and complements
- consumers' income
- price expectations

We will consider the market for SUVs (Sport Utility Vehicles). For each of the above determinants (except for complements under "prices of related goods"), a positive change will cause an increase in demand that is a change (shift) to a new demand schedule for which there will be higher amounts demanded for each price. Thus, an increase in the population or in the number of consumers would mean more buyers of SUVs at the same prices. Similarly, if consumers' incomes increase, they can afford to buy more SUVs at the same price. This increase in demand would occur if SUVs are "normal goods"; that is, as consumers' income increases, demand for the goods increase. The consequence of this is that as income rises, consumers may demand a *smaller* quantity of inferior goods. If some people have preferences for SUVs, and can now afford them, they may buy fewer small-size vehicles. Recently, consumers have indicated an increase in preferences for sport utility vehicles over other vehicles, leading to an increase in demand for SUVs. If the prices of luxury sedans, a substitute for SUVs increases, then there will be an increase in demand for SUVs. If consumers expect that there will be a sharp increase in prices for SUVs in the near future, they may increase their demand now for SUVs to "beat the price increase." In each of these situations, one of the determinants of demand had a positive change leading to a shift (increase in demand) as illustrated on page 49.

The shift in demand is illustrated as the changes from A to A′, B to B′, and C to C′; in each case the quantities demanded at each price (44, 40, 36) increased with the event (for example, consumers' incomes increasing). Each of these changes is an increase in demand, a shift to a new demand function.

The converse holds for each of these same determinants if a negative event were to occur—if the prices of SUVs were expected to decrease in the near future or if the prices of luxury sedans, substitute good, decreased. We would have, for these changes in determinants, a decrease in demand to a new function or curve such as D″D″ (see Figure 4.2). However, if the prices of complement goods, such as 17-inch tires for the large SUVs *increase*, there would be a decrease in demand for SUVs.

However, a change from A to B on demand curve DD is a change in amounts demanded as a result of the price of SUVs *decreasing* from $44,000 to $40,000 with amounts demanded *increasing* from 200,000 to 300,000 SUVs. This is an example of an inverse relationship between the price of SUVs and the quantities demanded, or, as the price of SUVs decreases, the quantities demanded increase, *ceteris paribus* (the non-price determinants of demand remaining constant). Only in the case of a Giffen good can there be an upward-sloping demand curve.

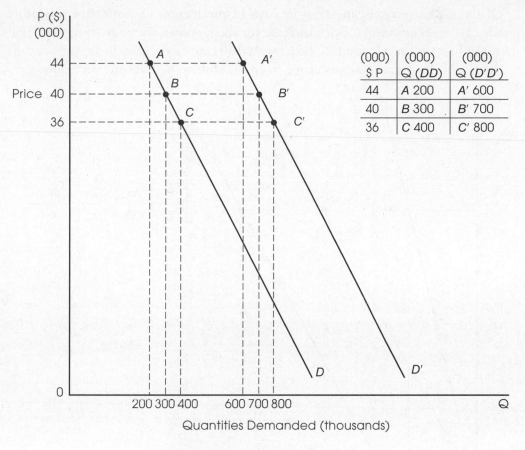

(000)	(000)	(000)
$ P	Q (*DD*)	Q (*D'D'*)
44	A 200	A' 600
40	B 300	B' 700
36	C 400	C' 800

Fig. 4.2 SUVs: Shift in Demand

Supply and Amounts Supplied

Similar distinctions apply here as they did with demand. Amounts supplied refer to the amounts suppliers or sellers (providers) are willing to provide of a particular good at varying prices of that good. This is a direct relationship (curve): As the price of the good *increases*, the amounts willing to be supplied increases (the converse holds). Changes in amounts supplied refer to changes along a supply curve or function as a result only of a change in the price of that good, *ceteris paribus*. Changes *in supply* occur when these *ceteris paribus* conditions or non-price determinants of supply change:

1. the number of sellers (providers, suppliers)
2. costs of resources or production
3. prices of substitute goods (goods that are also produced or could be using similar resources)
4. price expectations
5. technology
6. taxes/subsidies

Of these determinants, increases in costs of production (2), prices of substitute goods (3), expectation of a price increase for this good in the near future (4), and increases in taxes on this good (6, taxes) would all cause a decrease in supply—a shift to the left of the original supply curve, as in the shift to S'S', illustrated below:

P	Q SS	Q' S'S	Q" S'S"
5	1000	500	1500

Fig. 4.3 Shift in Supply

This would be lower than the amounts supplied of the good at each of the prices as compared with SS supply curve. For example, the change from A to A' is a change in supply (decrease) or a shift in supply as a result of a non-price determinant. For the determinants listed above, increases in the number of sellers (1), technology (improvement), and government subsidies would cause the supply function (SS) to shift (increase) to S"S", thus, the change from A to A" (500Q to 1,500Q) at price $5. However, the change from A to B is a change along a supply function (a decrease in amounts supplied from 1,000 to 400) as a result only of a price change for this good from $5 a unit to $2 a unit.

Changes in Equilibria

1. Demand and/or supply shifts will cause new equilibrium positions (new intersections of supply and demand). With supply given (constant), changes in the demand determinants (as explained above) would cause shifts in the demand function. These shifts would cause new equilibrium price and equilibrium quantity positions. For example, if there is an increased preference for SUVs, then the demand for SUVs would increase in the form of a shift in the demand function or curve (as illustrated):

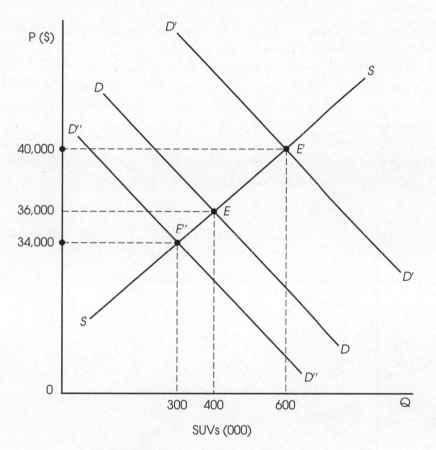

Fig. 4.4 Market for SUVs: Equilibria Changes

The demand function would shift (increase) from DD to D'D' (with supply constant at SS). As illustrated above, the new equilibrium is at E' with the equilibrium price of $40,000 (up from $36,000) and the equilibrium quantity at 600,000 SUVs (up from 400,000 SUVs). This same kind of effect would occur if one of the other determinants of demand changed in the same direction; for example, if there was a sharp increase in the number of buyers with very high incomes.

2. With supply again given at SS, and with the expectation that the prices of SUVs will decrease very soon since the market is becoming saturated with new models from competitors, demand for SUVs will now decrease as potential buyers wait for a better deal. This is illustrated (above) with a shift of DD to D″D″ and a new equilibrium at E″ (equilibrium price at $34,000, down from $36,000, and equilibrium quantity at 300,000, down from 400,000 SUVs).

   Useful Hint: With supply given or constant, an increase in demand will cause an increase in equilibrium price and equilibrium quantity. The converse holds: A decrease in demand leads to a decrease in equilibrium price and quantity.

3. In brief, we will now analyze shifts (increases or decreases) in supply with demand as given or constant.

   With demand constant or given, an increase in supply will lead to a decrease in equilibrium price and an increase in equilibrium quantity; conversely, a decrease in supply will lead to an increase in equilibrium price and a decrease in equilibrium quantity.

   Thus, if a producer of a particular form of steel faces increasing costs of coking coal (input in steel production), *ceteris paribus*, he will decrease his supply of steel. This is illustrated below.

Fig. 4.5 Steel Market

As a result of a supply shift (decrease) from SS to S'S', the equilibrium price increases to $350 a ton (from $300) and the equilibrium quantity decreases to 400 tons (from 600).

4. What happens if there are changes in demand and, simultaneously, in supply? The following is a schedule of which effects on price and quantities are determinable.

TABLE 4.1

Effects on Price and Quantities

Change in Demand	Change in Supply	Effect on Equilibrium Price	Effect on Equilibrium Quantity
Increase	Increase	Not Determinable	Increase
Decrease	Decrease	Not Determinable	Decrease
Increase	Decrease	Increase	Not Determinable
Decrease	Increase	Decrease	Not Determinable

Government-induced Changes— Price Ceilings and Price Floors

For varying reasons, a government may wish to establish a price ceiling, which prohibits prices to rise above a certain level as in rent (city-controlled prices or rents for apartments), or as in the establishment of a ceiling or interest rates for mortgage loans. In other situations, a government may wish to establish a price floor making it illegal, for example, to hire workers at a wage lower than the minimum wage. Thus, as illustrated in Figure 4.6, if the state government sets 6 percent as the maximum rate that can be charged on mortgage loans, and if the market equilibrium price would be 8 percent, the amount of mortgage loan funds actually exchanged would decrease to $15 million from $20 million.

This is an example of a price ceiling that would produce a shortage of mortgage funds relative to the amounts desired by borrowers.

A price floor might be instituted by the federal government for agricultural prices in order to support farmers who take losses under market prices and to maintain an adequate supply of agricultural products to the population. The floor would be established above the equilibrium or market price while a price ceiling would be established under the equilibrium or market price. See Figure 4.7. With the equilibrium price of $8,100 bushels of wheat are exchanged (the amounts demanded are equal to amounts supplied). At the price floor, by government, of $10, suppliers are willing to provide 140 bushels. Thus a surplus develops.

Fig. 4.6 Market for Mortgage Loans

Fig. 4.7 Wheat Market

SUMMARY

- The distinction between changes in quantity demanded (supplied) and changes in demand (supply) is significant in that the former refers only to a price change in a particular product in terms of movement along a demand (supply) curve and the latter refers to non-price factors that cause a shift (change) to a new demand (supply) curve.
- Equilibrium occurs in a market when:

  1. quantity demanded equals quantity supplied.
  2. no tendency for change given supply and demand.
  3. the equilibrium price "clears" the market of any surplus or shortage.

- Determinants of demand include the number of consumers, tastes and preferences, prices of related goods (substitutes and complements), consumer income and price expectations.
- Determinants of supply include the number of sellers, costs of production, technology, prices of substitutes, price expectations, taxes, and subsidies.
- Price ceilings are established under the equilibrium price when the equilibrium price is considered too high.
- Price floors are established over the equilibrium when the equilibrium price is considered too low.

TERMS

Market place where buyers and sellers meet to exchange goods and services

Quantity Demanded has an inverse relationship with changes in the price of a particular good

Quantity Supplied has a direct relationship with changes in the price of a particular good

Changes in Demand (Supply) shift in demand (supply) due to non-price factors or determinants

Equilibrium Price price at which quantity supplied equals quantity demanded

Price Ceiling established below the equilibrium price

Price Floor established above the equilibrium price

Normal Goods goods whose consumption increases as income increases

Inferior Goods goods whose consumption decreases as income increases

Giffen Good good for which there is an upward-sloping demand curve (theoretical)

Ceteris Paribus holding all other factors or conditions constant

MULTIPLE-CHOICE REVIEW QUESTIONS

1. A price ceiling is characterized by

(A) a price set below the current (or equilibrium) market price of the good.

(B) a price set above the current (or equilibrium) market price of the good.

(C) a shift of the demand curve (function).

(D) a shift of the supply curve.

2. For which of the following statements are both the price change and quantity change determinable (for a particular good)?

(A) Both the supply of and the demand for the good decrease.

(B) Both the supply of and the demand for the good increase.

(C) The supply increases and the demand for the good decreases.

(D) The supply decreases and the demand increases.

(E) None of the above.

3. If the government subsidizes the production of halogen headlights,

(A) the demand curve will shift to the left.

(B) the demand curve will shift to the right.

(C) the supply curve will shift to the left.

(D) the supply curve will shift to the right.

(E) the amounts demanded will increase along the demand curve.

4. If consumers are advised that multigrained bread will substantially lessen the risk of cancer, which of the following will happen in the market for multigrained bread?

(A) The demand curve will shift to the left, decreasing the price of multigrained bread.

(B) The supply curve will shift to the left, increasing the price of multigrained bread.

(C) The demand curve will shift to the right, increasing the price of multi-grained bread.

(D) The supply curve will shift to the right, decreasing the price of multi-grained bread.

(E) None of the above.

Multiple-Choice Review Answers

1. **(A)**   2. **(E)**   3. **(D)**   4. **(C)**

FREE-RESPONSE REVIEW QUESTIONS

I. For each of the following simultaneous changes in demand and in supply for a product, indicate the effect on equilibrium price *and* equilibrium quantity.
   A. increase in demand and an increase in supply
   B. decrease in demand and a decrease in supply
   C. increase in demand and a decrease in supply

II. How might a government establish a price ceiling or price floor to offset any one of the changes (A, B, C) above? Explain.

Free-Response Review Answers

I. A. An increase in demand and an increase in supply would result in an increase in equilibrium quantity; the effect on equilibrium price is not determinable.
   B. A decrease in demand and a decrease in supply will result in a decrease in equilibrium quantity, and the effect on equilibrium price is not determinable.
   C. An increase in demand and a decrease in supply would result in an increase in equilibrium price; the effect on equilibrium is not determinable.

II. B. If the government wants to offset the increase in equilibrium price in C above, it could establish a price ceiling below the new equilibrium price and/or subsidize the supplier to increase supply.

Applications of Demand and Supply—Elasticity

CHAPTER 5

- Price elasticity of demand and of supply
- Income elasticity of demand
- Cross price elasticity of demand
- Determinants of demand

- Applications to decision-making, marketing, and revenues of firms
- Burden of taxes on consumers and suppliers

INTRODUCTION

The application of elasticity to the basics of demand and supply lends itself well to the solution or resolution of many buyer and seller decision-making dilemmas in personal consumption, business finance, corporate finance, and societal or public finance settings. Elasticity, in the broad sense, relates to responsiveness to price changes. Normally we expect that as the price of a particular good increases, suppliers or producers will wish to increase the amounts they provide to the markets, *ceteris paribus*. On the other hand, consumers will reduce the amounts they wish to buy of the same product with its price increase, *ceteris paribus*. There are, of course, exceptions to this normality as we reviewed Giffen goods and inferior goods in Chapter 4. The *ceteris paribus* clause refers to no changes in the conditions underlying the demand and supply curves; they do not shift.

How sensitive are consumers to a price change in terms of the quantities they are willing to consume? Should they be expected to stop buying pizza when its price increases from \$8 to \$10 for a whole pizza? Should they be expected to continue buying pizza but less of it? If so, how much less? This appears as a consumer decision but it is also a producer's question. As a producer of pizza, what effect will the \$2 increase have on your sales and total revenue? To answer the latter question, the producer has to estimate the degree of sensitivity to price changes from the consumers. On the one hand, the producer will realize \$2 more from each pizza sold. However, the expected decrease in the number of pizzas sold could result in a greater decrease in quantity demanded than the increase in the per unit price of the pizza; therefore, the total revenue will decrease. Whether or not the total revenue decreases depends on the degree of sensitivity of the consumer to the price change.

THINGS TO KNOW

Based on the most frequently asked questions on previous AP exams, the following are the most important concepts. The balance of this chapter will include other concepts and examples.

Consider the following as a guide:

1. $P \times Q = TR$
   - Thus, if price (P) increases by 20 percent and quantity demanded (Q) decreases by 20 percent, total revenue (TR) will stay the same. This is called a *unit elastic* or *proportional change*.
   - If P increases by 20 percent and Q decreases by 25 percent, then TR will decrease. This is called an *elastic* or *greater than proportional change*.
   - If P increases by 20 percent and Q decreases by 10 percent, then TR will increase. This is called an *inelastic* or *less than proportional change*.

2. Price Elasticity of Demand $= \dfrac{\% \,\Delta \text{ Quantity Demanded}}{\% \,\Delta \text{ Price}}$

   (The percentage change in the quantity demanded of a particular good divided by the price of the same good, *ceteris paribus*.) Using the three examples above (number 1), in the first case, the value of the ratio = 1 since the percentage change (Δ) in quantities demanded equals the percentage change in price. This is called *unit elastic*. In the second case, the value of the ratio = 25/20 or 1.25. Since the change in Q is more than proportional to the change in P, the response is *elastic* or greater than 1. In the third case, the value of the ratio = 10/20 or .5. Since the change in Q is less than proportional to the change in P, the response is inelastic or a ratio value of less than 1.

3. If we want to measure the numerical coefficient of elasticity (E), we would rewrite the ratio in number 2 above to read as follows. (**Note:** This uses the average price and the average quantity or *ARC* elasticity to avoid biases when using beginning or ending prices.)

$$E_D = \frac{\Delta Q^*}{(Q_1 + Q_2)/2} \div \frac{\Delta P}{(P_1 + P_2)/2}$$

$$= \frac{\Delta Q^*}{(Q_1 + Q_2)/2} \times \frac{(P_1 + P_2)/2}{\Delta P}$$

*ΔQ refers here to change in Quantity Demanded.

4. Price elasticity of supply uses essentially the same formula except that as P increases, Q supplied also increases, rendering the total revenue check useless in the supply case. For Elasticity of Supply:

$$E_S = \frac{\Delta Q^{**}}{(Q_1 + Q_2)/2} \times \frac{(P_1 + P_2)/2}{\Delta P}$$

**ΔQ refers here to change in Quantity Supplied.

In brief, the relationship of price changes, elasticity, quantities demanded, and total revenue can be summarized as follows:

Price	Q Demanded	TR	Price Elasticity of Demand
increases	decreases	decreases	>1, elastic
increases	decreases	increases	<1, inelastic
increases	decreases	stays the same	=1, unit elastic
decreases	increases	increases	>1, elastic
decreases	increases	decreases	<1, inelastic
decreases	increases	stays the same	=1, unit elastic

Note: The negative sign is ignored so that the nature of the response—elastic, inelastic—will not be confused with a negative slope or inverse relationship.

PROBLEM TO SOLVE (FREE-RESPONSE QUESTION)

An out-of-state tourist uses a laundromat in Langley, Washington. A large, hand-written sign advises the users of this service that the owner was experiencing some economic difficulties including rising costs of water and propane gas. The monthly charge to the owner for water use was $2,225 and the cost for propane gas was $542 a month. Thus, the owner felt justified in increasing the price for the use of a washer from $1.50 to $1.75. The owner advised the users that her service represented a monopoly since it was the only laundromat on the southern end of the island. She claimed that she was not taking undue advantage of the customers but she wanted to be able to continue serving them while "making a living." Please answer the following:

1. What percentage of decrease in quantities demanded of the owner's services would allow her to maintain the same level of total revenue (given the increase in the price of use of a washer)?

2. What percentage of decrease in quantities demanded would realize an increase in total revenue?

3. What percentage of decrease in quantities demanded would result in a decrease in total revenue?

4. For numbers 1, 2, and 3 above, indicate whether the price elasticity of demand is elastic, inelastic, or unit elastic.

5. What are the connections between her increase in costs of providing the service and the price elasticity of supply? What are the connections between her increase in cost and the supply of her service?

Answers:
1. The increase in price is 16.67 percent (.25 on a basis of $1.50). Thus, the owner could experience the same (16.67 percent) decrease in quantities demanded to maintain the same level of total revenue $P \times Q = TR$ and

$$\text{Price elasticity of demand} = \frac{\% \, \Delta \, \text{Quantity Demanded}}{\% \, \Delta \, \text{Price}}$$

2. Less than 16.67 percent

3. More than 16.67 percent

4. For number 1, unit elastic; for number 2 inelastic; for number 3 elastic.

5. She must cover her costs; in other words, the higher the price/cost ratio, the more willing she is to supply more. Also, the closer she is to a monopolist, the more she can determine the price.

LIMITS AND DEGREES OF ELASTICITY

Perfectly elastic, coefficient of elasticity is infinity. This means that the buyer is so sensitive to price changes that if one seller raises his price, the buyer will switch to another seller. This situation implicitly assumes that there are many sellers so that no one seller or group of sellers can exercise any significant control over the terms of exchange: prices, quantities, market share, etc. Nowhere is this better exemplified than in the norm for competition in product markets, that is perfect competition (more on this later in Chapter 10). The seller is a "price taker," that is, the market of all buyers and sellers for a particular product determines the price that the seller must charge or lose business to other competitors who produce the identical product that becomes a perfect substitute. It is illustrated below in Figure 5.1.

Fig. 5.1 Perfectly Competitive Firm (Perfectly or Infinitely Elastic)

This is the only curve that can be called elastic, since it is *perfectly* elastic. As demand curves approach this horizontal function, they become relatively more elastic until they reach the horizontal shape. As demand curves approach the perfectly vertical function (*perfectly inelastic*), they become relatively more inelastic. Hence, the perfectly elastic and imperfectly elastic curves (functions) set the mathematical or graphical limits on elasticity. The perfectly inelastic demand function would be illustrated as follows:

Fig. 5.2

Price elasticity of demand can vary along a demand curve. The slope does not change along a linear curve but elasticity does change along a linear curve. This is illustrated by the following:

Fig. 5.3

Also, price elasticity of demand will vary between the short run and the long run. In the short run, buyers have more limited choices because of the relative scarcity of products and resources. Over the long run (when supply fully adjusts to changes in demand), the choice of products and resources becomes greater and hence, buyers are more resistant to price increases for any given product or resource.

Therefore, the long run demand function for any given product will be relatively more elastic than the demand function in the short run.

TIP

Remember, that as a demand curve approaches the perfectly horizontal shape (perfectly elastic), it becomes relatively more elastic.

Fig. 5.4

The degree of elasticity also depends on the competitive structure of the market as we have already noted for perfect competition and will observe in the chapters on market structures (Chapters 9–12).

Degrees of elasticity also depend upon the nature of the product. Goods that are considered luxuries will be relatively more sensitive to price increases than will goods that are considered necessities. For example, suppose that a blight on coffee plants causes the price in the market to increase. Which kind of coffee will reflect a higher elasticity among consumers: regular brands or the specialty (higher-priced brands)? One would more likely see some coffee drinkers substituting regular brands for the specialty brands; hence, the elasticity would be higher for the specialty brands since regular coffee can more readily substitute for the specialty kind than tea can substitute for coffee, in general.

SAMPLE QUESTION

As the price for regular grade (octane), unleaded gasoline increases from $3.00 to $3.25, and higher grade (octane) unleaded gasoline increases from $3.25 to $3.75, which is most likely to occur?

(A) Drivers using the regular grade gasoline will decrease their use of gasoline by a higher percentage than will the drivers using the high grade octane.
(B) Drivers using the high-grade gasoline will decrease their use of high-grade gasoline by a higher percentage than will the drivers using the regular-grade gasoline.
(C) Both the drivers using the high-grade gasoline and the drivers using the regular-grade gasoline will continue to use the same amount of gasoline.
(D) The drivers using the regular-grade gasoline will switch to the high-grade gasoline and the drivers using the high-grade gasoline will switch to the regular-grade gasoline.

(Answer: **B**.)

CROSS-ELASTICITY OF DEMAND

As abstract as this sounds, it is actually an important part of marketing decisions, merger or acquisition decisions, and antitrust court decisions. The essential question to which this concept is addressed is, "What effect on quantities demanded of one product will a price change in another product have?" The estimation or empirical evidence of the answer to this question will, in turn, give us clues to market share, the degree of competition that may extend from one market to another, and the related leverage a dominant product in one market may have on products in another market. First, the relationship in ratio form:

$$\text{Cross Price Elasticity of Demand} = \text{CPED}$$

$$\text{CPED} = \frac{\%\,\Delta\ \text{Quantity Demanded of Product Y}}{\%\,\Delta\ \text{Price of Product X}}$$

$$\left(\text{where } \Delta = \text{change in}\right)$$

Suppose that the price of plastic wrap increases by 20 percent, and the quantities demanded of waxed paper increased by 50 percent. What would that tell us about the ability to substitute waxed paper for plastic wrap? Are the two goods, plastic wrap and waxed paper, good substitutes or are they complements? They would be good substitutes because of the positive sign on the ratio that indicates substitutes: If the quantities demanded of waxed paper increase as the price of plastic wrap increases, *ceteris paribus,* substitution of waxed paper for plastic wrap is occurring. If instead, as the price of plastic wrap increases, the quantities of waxed paper decreases with the resultant negative sign on the ratio, the two goods are complements: both used for wrapping or storing different goods.

In summary form, the following are the determinants of price elasticity of demand:

Determinants of Price Elasticity of Demand

1. **The period of adjustment, or the long run versus the short run.** The short run is the time over which supply cannot fully adjust to changes in demand so that there is a relative scarcity of goods compared to the change in demand for the goods. Therefore, in the short run, prices act as rationers of the relatively scarce goods; in other words, the prices are "bid up" by the excess demand; there are more buyers willing to purchase these goods than there are goods available, the result being that the goods go to the highest bidders. In the 1970s fuel-efficient automobiles, produced mostly by the Japanese, were in high demand, particularly during the oil shortage crisis. Since the supply of these automobiles was limited relative to the demand, retail automobile dealers were able to charge prices well above the suggested list ("sticker") price rather than to charge prices at some typical discount. Over the long run, when more choices are available (supply having adjusted to the increase in demand), consumers have more choices and are more sensitive (higher

price elasticity of demand) to price changes. We illustrated this earlier with the long-run demand curve being more elastic (less steep) than the short-run demand curve.

2. **The ratio of the cost of a particular product to the total budget of the consumer:**

$$\frac{\$ \text{ Cost of Product A}}{\$ \text{ Total Budget}}$$

In general, the higher the value of this ratio, for a particular product, the more sensitive (more price elastic) the consumer will be to any price increases. Thus, a relatively small price increase for a home and/or its financing charge (mortgage loan interest rate) could cause a delay in the purchase of a house or cause a decision to move in with relatives or purchase a smaller house, rent an apartment, or postpone the purchase of a house. However, a small percentage increase in the price for many staples will have virtually no effect on the purchases of these products since their costs are low and constitute only a small portion of the consumer's budget.

3. **Competitive structure of the market and consumer choices.** The outcome of this determinant is similar to that of number 1. That is, the consumer will have more choices of products and substitutes the more competitive the product market. Thus, we can see that more competition among producers will develop over the long run (as in number 1), making the consumers more sensitive (more price elastic) to price changes. As in the fuel-efficient automobile example, more competitors in Japan and elsewhere will produce more automobiles (more choices) as time allows producers to adopt fuel-efficient technology.

INCOME ELASTICITY OF DEMAND

In addition to consumers being constrained by prices in their purchasing decisions, they are also constrained by their budgets or incomes. Thus, we consider consumers' sensitivity in terms of their responses to changes in both prices and incomes. Income elasticity of demand is defined as:

$$\frac{\text{Percentage (\%) Change (} \Delta \text{) in Consumption of a Good}}{\text{Percentage (\%) Change (} \Delta \text{) in Consumer Income (I)}}$$

$$\frac{\% \ \Delta \text{ Consumption of a Good}}{\% \ \Delta \text{ Consumer Income}}$$

This ratio for normal goods will have a positive sign, that is, as consumer income (I) increases, we expect that consumption of a normal good will also increase. If the increase in consumption is more than proportional to increase in income,* then the value of the ratio is greater than one (>1) and the response is more than proportional to the change in income, making the response elastic (>1). If the change in consumption is less than proportional to the change in income (ratio is <1), then the response is inelastic but still with a positive sign. If the change in consumption is exactly proportional to change in consumer income, then the value of the ratio is one and the response is unit elasticity (=1).

Income elasticity can explain some market phenomena that could not be explained entirely, if at all, by changes in prices. For example, the sale of automobiles continued to increase through the fifties, sixties, and seventies and at least until the increase in imports of foreign automobiles introduced some price competition into an oligopolistic industry. The earlier increases in sales seemed to contradict the downward sloping demand curve and any sensitivity to increases in prices.

PRICE ELASTICITY OF SUPPLY

The basic relationship of the degree of the response of quantities supplied to changes in prices is the same as that for quantities demanded. For supply, however, the normal reaction of suppliers to changes in the prices of their goods in the market is to increase amounts willing to be supplied as prices increase, a direct relationship as opposed to the inverse relationship with price elasticity of demand. In both cases we ignore whether the slope is positive or negative. We deal only with the degree of the response, such as >1, <1, or =1.

As prices increase for computers, suppliers are more willing to produce and sell more computers. The ratio for the determination of the coefficient for price elasticity of supply is:

$$\text{Price Elasticity of Supply} = \frac{\% \, \Delta \text{ Quantities Supplied}}{\% \, \Delta \text{ Price}}$$

INCIDENCE OF TAX ON SUPPLIERS AND CONSUMERS

If a government imposes a tax on a supplier, part of the burden can be in the form of an increase in the price that the consumer pays for the product and/or a burden on the supplier who can produce less (cost in the form of the tax) can result in less production. The degree to which the burden falls more on the consumer or the supplier is determined by the relative price elasticity of demand; the consumer may have a highly elastic response to any tax passed on to him or her by the supplier. This is illustrated in Figure 5.5.

Thus, the consumer facing relatively inelastic demand function D_1D_1 will take more of the incidence of the tax in the form of paying a higher price than will the supplier who has a relatively small reduction in quantities supplied ($P_1 + T$ compared to P_1; $Q_1 + T$ compared to Q_1). With a relatively more elastic demand function, D_2D_2, the supplier takes on the higher burden ($Q_2 + T$ compared to Q_2) than the consumers ($P_2 + T$ compared to P_2).

---

* (See Chapter 4.) A normal good increases in consumption with an increase in income. An inferior good decreases in consumption with an increase in income.

Fig. 5.5

SUMMARY

- Price elasticity of demand or the percentage of change in the quantity demanded of a particular good divided by the price of the same good demonstrates the sensitivity of consumers to price changes. $P \times Q = TR$ allows a revenue test, i.e., whether a price change will increase or decrease total revenue.
- Price elasticity of supply shows the sensitivity of producers or firms to price changes for their products.
- Price elasticity of demand or supply which has a numerical coefficient >1 is elastic, =1 is unit elastic or <1 is inelastic.
- Cross price elasticity of demand is the percentage change in the quantity demanded of one product in response to the percentage change in the price of a second product. If this ratio produces a positive sign, the two products are good substitutes. If this ratio produces a negative sign, then the two products are complements.
- The determinants of the price elasticity of demand are the period of adjustment, the ratio of the cost of a particular product to the total budget of the consumer and the competitive structure of the market.
- Income elasticity of demand measures the responsiveness of consumers to changes in their income.
- The incidence of a tax imposed on suppliers will have an impact on consumers in the form of price increases depending on the price elasticity of demand, i.e., the greater the elasticity, the smaller the impact on prices.

FORMULAS

Price Elasticity of Demand:

$$\frac{\% \, \Delta \text{ Quantity Demanded}}{\% \, \Delta \text{ Price}}$$

Numerical Coefficient of Elasticity:

$$\Delta Q \left(\frac{P_1 + P_2}{2} \right) \times \Delta P \left(\frac{Q_1 + Q_2}{2} \right)$$

Cross Price Elasticity of Demand:

$$\frac{\% \, \Delta \text{ Quantity Demanded of Product}}{\% \, \Delta \text{ Price of Product X}}$$

Income Elasticity of Demand:

$$\frac{\% \, \Delta \text{ Consumption of a Good}}{\% \, \Delta \text{ Consumer Income}}$$

Price Elasticity of Supply:

$$\frac{\% \, \Delta \text{ Quantity Supplied}}{\% \, \Delta \text{ Price}}$$

MULTIPLE-CHOICE REVIEW QUESTIONS

1. When price elasticity of demand is greater than 1, demand is

   (A) perfectly inelastic.
   (B) elastic.
   (C) inelastic.
   (D) unit elastic.
   (E) not measurable.

2. Price times quantity measures

   (A) the international trade gap.
   (B) the budget deficit.
   (C) total revenue.
   (D) price elasticity of demand.
   (E) price elasticity of supply.

3. A positive sign on cross price elasticity of demand indicates that the two products are

   (A) luxuries.
   (B) necessities.
   (C) substitutes.
   (D) complements.
   (E) independent.

4. The price elasticity of demand for a product is greater if

   (A) the proportion of the good of the consumer's budget is high.
   (B) the period of time to respond to a price change is short.
   (C) the number of substitute products is limited.
   (D) the product is a necessity.
   (E) imports decrease.

5. A tax imposed on a supplier will more likely be passed on to the consumer in the form of price increase if

   (A) price elasticity of demand is highly elastic.
   (B) price elasticity of demand is highly inelastic.
   (C) price elasticity of demand is unit elastic.
   (D) wage elasticity of demand is highly elastic.
   (E) wage elasticity of demand is highly inelastic.

Multiple-Choice Review Answers

1. **(B)**   2. **(C)**   3. **(C)**   4. **(A)**   5. **(B)**

FREE-RESPONSE REVIEW QUESTION

The Free-Response Question for this chapter appears on page 65.

Free-Response Review Answers

NOTE: The answers are on pages 65 and 66.

Theory of Consumer Choice or Behavior

CHAPTER **6**

- Basic tenets of consumer choice theory
- Diminishing marginal utility
- Maximizing utility or satisfaction
- Constraints of income and prices
- Income and substitution effects

INTRODUCTION

Economics is the study of choices involving decisions set in the context of scarcity limited by constraints. We buy a basket of goods knowing that we cannot buy as large a selection as we might want, given the constraints of prices and income. How do we make these choices? How does a consumer allocate a limited income among the many choices of goods and services?

THINGS TO KNOW

Based on the most frequently asked questions on previous advanced placement exams, the following are the most important concepts. For this chapter, there are only a few concepts that have appeared in question form on the exams. We identify these below and in the balance of this chapter, we will expand on these and other important concepts.

1. The basic tenets of the theory of **consumer choice**. This involves many sub-concepts, including the **law of diminishing marginal utility**. The student needs to identify this law as being associated with **consumer choice**, as opposed to the law of diminishing marginal productivity, which is associated with producers or suppliers.

2. **Consumer Surplus.** Students can count on one or two questions on consumer surplus. This concept is revisited in the chapter on monopoly; students can expect a related question on "dead-weight loss" which we deal with in the chapter on monopoly. With consumer surplus, the price in the market would favor consumers who placed a higher value on a product than the market price paid by all consumers. Often, there is a question on this concept.

BASIC TENETS OF THE THEORY OF CONSUMER CHOICE

1. **The consumer is rational.** The consumer wants to get the most satisfaction (utility) for the money expended on the products and services in the basket.

2. **The consumer can rank goods** in order of preference: "I prefer a new cell phone to a pair of running shoes."

3. **The consumer understands diminishing marginal utility.** As a consumer buys a hot dog, her utility (satisfaction) increases (from zero); as she consumes a second hot dog, her total utility (satisfaction) from the second hot dog is likely to be less than the satisfaction she derived from the first. That is, satisfaction derived from a continuing consumption of hot dogs is going to increase at a decreasing rate, or each additional hot dog is going to add less to total satisfaction than that of the previous hot dog. The *marginal utility* (the addition to total satisfaction) is decreasing, while the total satisfaction continues to increase up to the level of disutility when too many hot dogs lead to a point at which one more hot dog actually *decreases* total utility or satisfaction, that is, the marginal utility of the "one more hot dog" is negative. Diminishing marginal utility becomes a factor in a consumer's choice when comparing goods and their prices with a limited income. Diminishing marginal utility is also a factor in the determination of a pricing strategy for firms.

4. **The consumer faces constraints of prices and incomes.** The factors of rationality, preferences, and diminishing marginal utility are not sufficient in order for the consumer to make final decisions about what to buy and how much to buy. The consumer is constrained from buying every good or service that meets the first three tenets of consumer choice listed above. She can be effectively prevented from purchasing every item on the "list" by a limited income and the prices of the goods and services.

5. **The utility-maximizing rule.** Using the above four tenets of consumer choice, the consumer wants to make choices from a variety of goods and services that will maximize her total utility or satisfaction relative to the constraints of prices and income. To do that, the consumer will want to obtain as much extra satisfaction for one good per its price as will be obtained from any other good per its price, given the amount of income available for "N" number of goods. Thus,

$$\frac{MU_A}{P_A} = \frac{MU_B}{P_B} = \frac{MU_C}{P_C} \ \cdots \cdots \ \frac{MU_U}{P_U}$$

with as much income as is available being spent, given a discrete number of goods. In other words, whatever combination of two goods (for instance, four of good A and three of good B) that meets this condition with the available income will maximize the consumer's total utility. The consumer would be in equilibrium with this combination. There would be no tendency to change this combination of the two goods. There would be no other combination of units of Good A and Good B that would produce a greater total utility given the same prices of Goods A and B and the same income for the consumer. Different consumers are going to have different tastes and preferences and therefore, different utility-maximizing combinations of the same two goods with the same prices and the same income. This holds for a particular time period only.

SAMPLE QUESTION

TABLE 6.1
MARGINAL UTILITY AND UTILITY-MAXIMIZING COMBINATION

Units of J	MU_j	Units of K	MU_K
1	56	1	32
2	48	2	28
3	32	3	24
4	24	4	20
5	20	5	12
6	16	6	10
7	12	7	8

Given:

      Consumer income = $52
      Price of J   8
      Price of K   4

The consumer will maximize her utility by purchasing

(A) 3 units of J and 6 units of K
(B) 6 units of J and 3 units of K
(C) 4 units of J and 5 units of K
(D) 5 units of J and 5 units of K
(E) 2 units of J and 7 units of K

(Answer: **C.**)

Based on Table 6.1, 4 units of J and 5 units of K =

4J @ $8 = $32
   +
5K @ $4 = $20
         $52

TIP

For Table 6.1, first construct two additional columns: MU_j/P_j and MU_k/P_k. Next, find all the combination of units of J and units of K that satisfy the condition of $MU_j/P_j = MU_k/P_k$. The answer will be the combination that costs $52 or comes close to $52 without exceeding it.

CONSUMER SURPLUS

Even with diminishing marginal utility, the consumer may enjoy the situation in which the marginal utility is greater than the price charged for the good. Later (Chapter 11) we will review price-discriminating (*not* racial- or gender-discriminating) firms that would like to charge each buyer the maximum price each buyer would be willing to pay. For instance, each buyer would pay a different price based on each consumer's price elasticity of demand (perfect price discrimination) or at least, charge different groups of buyers different prices. However, in competitive markets, such as we are assuming here, sellers are often pricing their products at the going market price. Therefore, in competitive markets, and even in imperfectly competitive markets with less than full information, sellers face downward sloping demand curves in which sellers price at the last unit purchased with the effect that previous units were sold at prices *below* the values received, at the margin, by the consumers. To illustrate:

Fig. 6.1 Running Shoes

The consumer surplus is the area, ABC, that represents the amount of total utility the consumer receives (summation of MU for each unit, 1 through 7, or total utility under the demand curve up to the last unit, 7, consumed) minus the price paid by the consumer (OA) times the number of units or the area, OEBA. This surplus reveals the difference between what the consumer is willing to pay (based on marginal utility) for each good and the price actually paid (OA). Therefore, if a consumer is willing to pay $100 for a pair of running shoes, but the market price charged is $60 (price OA), the consumer has a bonus, or consumer surplus, of $40.

Since the firm selling the running shoes has imperfect information about consumers and faces a downward-sloping demand curve, the market price could favor consumers who place a higher value on the shoes than is charged by the market; these consumers would realize a bonus or *consumer surplus*. The negative effects of a monopoly on consumer surplus and the creation of a dead-weight loss are discussed and illustrated in Chapter 11 (Monopoly).

EXAMPLE

A farmer has such a surplus of apples that he drops the price from $10 a bushel to $4 a bushel. A consumer surplus would be evident in which of the following?

(A) A consumer buys the apples at $4 a bushel on the basis that at higher prices, she would not be willing to make a purchase.
(B) A consumer would have purchased the apples at $10 and buys them at the $4 price.
(C) The farmer's cost of production of the apples is $3 a bushel.
(D) A consumer prefers pears to apples but buys the apples at $4 a bushel.

(Answer: **B**.) The relationship of producer surplus and consumer surplus is illustrated and explained in Chapter 10, Figure 10.8 on page 128.

INCOME AND SUBSTITUTION EFFECTS

A brief discussion of income and substitution effects relative to the downward sloping demand curve is placed here in order to more fully explain the theory of consumer choice. In the discourse on the utility-maximizing rule (page 76), we referred to the combination of two goods that would maximize total utility. Diminishing marginal utility (DMU) helps explain the downward sloping demand curve. For example, as marginal utility decreases, the consumer may compare the MU of good A and its price with the MU of good B and its price. Thus, the income effect and the substitution effect also help explain the downward sloping demand curve. If we consider the market for apples, we assume that the price of oranges as a substitute good would remain constant. If the price of apples increases, *ceteris paribus*, the price ratio of apples to oranges would change so that oranges may be an attractive substitution for at least some of the purchases of apples. This would reinforce the notion that as the price of apples increases, *ceteris paribus*, the amounts demanded of apples would decrease. This is known as the *substitution effect*. Also, as the price of apples increases, *ceteris paribus*, the consumer can afford less of both apples and oranges, and thus will purchase fewer apples (the ratio of change between apples and oranges is dependent on other factors). This is known as *the income effect* and further reinforces the notion of a downward-sloping demand curve.

SUMMARY

- The basic tenets of the theory of consumer choice include consumers being rational, ranking goods in order of tastes and preferences, understanding diminishing marginal utility, facing constraints of prices and income and making choices of goods on the basis of the utility-maximizing rule.
- Consumer Surplus. This surplus of utility over cost (price paid) for the consumer is exemplified by consumers who place a higher value on the product than is charged by the market.
- Income and Substitution Effects. The income effect allows consumers to buy more products as the price of one product decreases. The substitution effect allows consumers to buy more of a product as its price decreases with the price of a substitute good remaining constant.

TERMS

Total Utility the total satisfaction a consumer receives from the consumption of a good or service

Diminishing Marginal Utility at some point in the consumption pattern of a good, each additional unit consumed yields less additional satisfaction (utility)

Income Effect as the price of a particular good decreases, a consumer can afford more of it and other goods

Substitution Effect as the price of a particular good decreases, a consumer may buy more of this good relative to the price of a substitute good

Consumer Surplus the difference between the utility gained and the price paid by the consumer. The utility gained would measure the value of the product to the consumer. The price paid by the consumer would be the market price

MULTIPLE-CHOICE REVIEW QUESTIONS

1. If the price of a product decreases with the price of a substitute product remaining constant such that the consumer buys more of this product, this is called the

   (A) income effect.
   (B) substitution effect.
   (C) marginal effect.
   (D) supply effect.
   (E) CPI effect.

2. If the price of a product decreases so that the consumer can buy more of it and other products, this is called the

   (A) income effect.
   (B) substitution effect.
   (C) marginal effect.
   (D) supply effect.
   (E) CPI effect.

3. Consumer surplus is

   (A) the price of a good divided by its marginal utility.
   (B) the marginal utility of the good divided by its price.
   (C) the total utility of the good.
   (D) the difference between the consumer's value and the market price.
   (E) consumers' annual savings.

4. The utility-maximizing rule is to choose the basket of goods that

   (A) has the highest marginal utility of each good in the basket.
   (B) has the lowest prices for the goods.
   (C) has the highest value of marginal utility to price for each good.
   (D) the marginal utility to price ratio equal for all goods in the basket.
   (E) the marginal utility to price ratio equal for all goods in the basket subject to the income constraint.

5. According to the principle of diminishing marginal utility,

   (A) marginal utility stays the same.
   (B) total utility stays the same.
   (D) marginal utility decreases with each additional unit of a good that is consumed.
   (D) marginal utility and total utility both decrease.
   (E) total utility declines.

Multiple-Choice Review Answers

1. **(B)**   2. **(A)**   3. **(D)**   4. **(E)**   5. **(C)**

FREE-RESPONSE REVIEW QUESTION

See question and answer on page 77.

Government and Public Sector: Market Failure, Rents, Externalities, Public Goods, Efficiency

---

- Externalities, negative and positive
- Social costs
- Public goods and private goods
- Efficiency and pareto optimality
- Bases for government interference

INTRODUCTION

This chapter flows from the knowledge of the function of the market system and its ability, at least in its design, to allocate resources efficiently. Indeed, most of the definitions of economic efficiency manifest themselves best, if not only, in competitive markets. However, not all people are satisfied, in normative judgments, with the outcomes of a market system. These outcomes include some differences among groups with respect to income and wealth distribution. Also, there is market failure when buyers and sellers do not come to terms, when the sale is not consummated, for instance. In other words, the market cannot determine the terms of exchange—price, quantity, location, service, financing, etc.—and/or one party is not willing or able to pay the price. The market fails. In both of these situations, we have possible functions for the government. Also, the presence of externalities, negative and positive, can be the basis of government taxation or subsidies to move the market to a more efficient or equitable position. With respect to the efficient position, remember the market role of efficiency—but if the market fails or there are externalities, the market will not be the vehicle for efficiency. The government may then intervene to promote a desirable social outcome.

THINGS TO KNOW

Based on the most frequently asked questions on previous Advanced Placement exams, the following are the most important concepts. In the balance of this chapter, we will expand on these and other concepts and examples.

1. **Externalities.** In an externality, either the buyer or the seller does not "capture" all of the benefits or costs of a transaction; that is, some of the benefits or costs accrue to the public as social costs or benefits. Often there will be questions asking how the government might react to a positive or to a negative externality.

   The right answer in terms of *positive externality* would be the granting of a *subsidy* to private producers in order to continue production for this positive externality.

   Conversely, there is a *negative externality*—the government might impose a tax to improve economic efficiency. This situation of a negative externality is often used in the context of a pollution by a firm. The purpose of the tax is to promote efficiency in the controlling of pollution. Often, the tax will vary directly as the pollution by the firm varies. Thus, the more the pollution and the subsequent tax rises, the greater the incentive by the firm to control pollution.

   Also, with respect to negative externalities, the private markets will determine a price that is relatively low; the relatively low price encourages more sales, more production, and more negative externalities. Here, a tax on the producer might be considered a factor or determinant of a shift to the left of supply (a decrease in supply), which would cause a higher price and reduce output or production of the good. Conversely, with respect to positive externalities, the price of the product would be relatively high. A government subsidy would cause an increase in supply (shift to the right of the supply curve), which would cause a lower price and increase output (see Figures 7.1 and 7.2 on pages 89 and 90).

2. **Social costs, private costs, and externalities.** Since externalities are, by definition, those costs *not* incurred by the buyer or the seller of a market transaction (the costs are incurred by the public, such as polluted waterways), then social costs are equal to private costs and the value of the externalities. Thus, we can distinguish marginal private costs (MPC or MC) from marginal social costs, knowing that MSC > MC (private) since marginal social costs incorporate marginal private costs. These distinctions will serve us well when we discuss the government, the market, and optional amounts of pollution. These definitions and distinctions support the knowledge of externalities, taxes, and subsidies identified above. For example, social costs will equal private costs when government either taxes negative externalities or subsidizes positive externalities by the amounts of the externalities. In this way, the government hopes to move the markets to some level of efficiency to compensate for market failure.

3. **Definitions and nature of efficiency.** Efficiency and its several implications take up much of advanced microeconomic analysis. For purposes of this review text, we will discuss only three definitions: *technological, allocative,* and *Pareto optimality* (sometimes used as a general definition of efficiency). A condition in society where any further improvement in well-being for some people will come at the expense of others is a point of efficiency or optimality. Details will follow later in this chapter.

4. **Public goods and private goods.** The two major distinctions between public goods and private goods are that private goods are exclusive and distributive and public goods are nonexclusive and nondistributive. These distinctions refer to pure public goods and pure private goods. One can be excluded from the benefits of private goods by not being willing or able to pay the price. Also, one more good for me means one less good for you. For public goods, I cannot be excluded from their benefits by refusing to pay for them, and the cost of one more unit of a public good does not result in one less unit available to someone else. A question sometimes asked on the Advanced Placement exam is on the marginal cost of one more unit of a pure public good. The answer is that the marginal cost in such a situation is equal to zero. In this chapter we will discuss other public goods, including congestible and price-excludable public goods. The reader might expect a question in the form of congestible public goods. For example, a bridge or tunnel leading to a city may be a public good (nonexclusive and nondistributive) until rush or commuting hours. At commuting time, the highway crowding takes the form of an externality, since one more car on the congested bridge means that much less space or slower traffic for other cars. (Correct answer for AP test.)

5. **Other roles of government.** You should be able to identify these on exam questions, for instance, antitrust for monopolies, provision of information, redistribution of income, etc.

PRIVATE GOODS AND PUBLIC GOODS

To extend the discussion above, the following are the definitions, uses, and examples of private and public goods. A *private good* is a good that has exclusion and distributive characteristics. That is, one who is unwilling or unable to purchase a good is denied its benefits. Thus, if I am unwilling to pay $20 to purchase a ticket to a major league baseball game, I am denied the fun of watching the game in person (the *exclusion* characteristics). Also, if there are 40,000 seats available, one more ticket for me means one less for someone else (the *distributive* characteristic). Private goods are divisible into discrete units such as the example of 40,000 baseball tickets. If private goods have externalities, then there is a less efficient or inefficient outcome. Externalities and the government use of taxes and subsidies are discussed later in this chapter.

MEASURES OF EFFICIENCY

As stated earlier, Pareto efficiency is the general measure of efficiency. First, we will define and explain two specific measures of efficiency. We will see how they are related and how they are subsumed under Pareto or general efficiency.

Technological Efficiency

The study of microeconomics or the economics of the firm is focused on the efficient allocation of resources. Technological efficiency is the identification of those inputs that have the greatest impact on outputs per dollar of input expenditure. In a simple engineering sense, output ÷ input. We discuss this in the chapter on costs, production, and supply, Chapter 8, in terms of economies of scale. Economists want to know which production process gets the most output per dollar cost of inputs. We could look at this as a given amount of output and which input or combination of inputs (resources) could produce the output at the least cost. The firm has an incentive to find the most cost-effective method of production since it can expand profit margins. Technological efficiency allows us a standard to achieve in terms of obtaining increasing returns to our technology. Any improvement in the value of the ratio of output to input will allow us to increase our productivity, or to make more efficient use of resources.

Allocative Efficiency

Ideally, every society would like to channel its resources (land, labor, capital, entrepreneurial ability) to their most productive and desired uses. Thus, the industries and firms that have the highest productivity are rewarded with higher profits; their profits are the motivation to continue to produce. If consumers are voting with their dollars, the firms will produce the products that consumers are willing and able to purchase.

Pareto Efficiency

Pareto efficiency has been identified earlier in this chapter. The general notion here is that there is an improvement for society as long as some people are gaining without others losing ground or benefits. Society reaches its optimal point or efficiency when any further improvement for some comes at the expense of others.

As indicated earlier, the competitive market economy, with its price mechanisms, is the best vehicle for efficiency. However, market failure, externalities, and other societal needs give rise to public goods and other forms of government intervention to recreate efficiency lost by market failure and externalities. Also, the government may attempt to create perceived need for equity by transferring payments for a redistribution of income.

Public Goods

Public goods lack the exclusion and distributive characteristics of private goods, and become public goods by default. Public goods have nonexclusion and nondistributive characteristics. A pure public good would be available for all regardless of any inability or unwillingness to pay. If a person does not approve of taxes being used for national defense and withholds the appropriate percentage of taxes used for that purpose (we would advise *against* this action to avoid problems with the law), that person would *not* be denied any of the benefits of national defense. Pure public goods are not marketable since benefits cannot be denied and because the units of a pure public good are not divisible. Thus, one more citizen who is qualified for a public good comes at zero marginal cost. One more unit of a public good does not come at the cost of one less for me. We cannot divide national defense into discrete units—and even if we could, who would be willing to buy shares of military defense in the marketplace?

Quasi-Public Goods

However, there are many public goods that have some private good characteristics that make them *quasi-public* goods. Sometimes, these goods are classified as public goods with some private goods attributes, such as *congestible public goods* and *price-excludable public goods.*

Congestible public goods occur when a public highway, bridge, or tunnel becomes acutely crowded at certain times, such as commuter rush hours. This might mean that at non-rush hours, one more car on the George Washington Bridge at say, 11:00 A.M. would not tie up traffic or in any way interfere with the normal speed of other vehicles on the bridge (one more car space for me does not mean, in this situation, one less car space for another person—the nondistributive, nondivisible principle). However, at around 4:30 to 5:00 P.M., the traffic begins to build so that, at least, until 7:00 to 7:30 P.M. there can be considerable delays in getting on the bridge (one-half hour to one hour) and once on the bridge, effective speed is lowered because of the very heavy traffic. This is a *negative externality.* Some economists have suggested that variable tolls be instituted at different times during the day, so that up to 6:30 or 7:00 A.M. and before 4:30 or 5:00 P.M., lower bridge fares would be in effect (this assumes tolls going both ways on the George Washington Bridge, for example). During the rush hours a higher toll would be in effect. These varying rates would more efficiently allocate scarce resources (time, space). Drivers, to a certain extent, would decide whether their time or their money is more important. Thus, the public bridge takes on the distributive characteristic of a private good as it becomes a contestable public good and therefore, officials can "bribe" enough drivers to travel at alternate times with a market mechanism, varying prices. Therefore, the city would effect a more efficient solution than that of a private good with externalities. Also, we can have public goods with a price-exclusion feature. For example, the government may make provision for medical insurance for the elderly, but the deductibles and co-payments may exclude some lower-income elderly from some or all of the benefits of medical insurance and the related medical care.

BASES FOR PUBLIC GOODS OR GOVERNMENT INTERFERENCE WITH MARKET OUTCOMES

The general case for some government action is a case for efficiency in the event of market failure rents, or externalities, or the case for equity in the event of an unequal distribution of income or wealth (normative judgment that unequal = inequitable).

Market Failure

In the most extreme form, market failure means that the buyer and seller are not able or willing to agree on the terms of the transaction—price, quantity, financing, etc. In the broad social sense, a desired social outcome does not occur. For example, individuals who have the HIV virus or AIDS may be unable to pay for health care or pay the health insurance premium; therefore, the market fails to "clear the market of any surplus or shortage" and there continues to be a demand greater than any willing suppliers of health care or health insurance. Market failure also refers to failure of the market mechanisms to achieve optimal or efficient outcomes. An efficient social outcome would be when marginal social benefits (MSB) equals marginal social costs (MSC). Therefore, market failure to produce efficient outcomes becomes a general basis for government intervention. A complete market failure to find MSB = MSC for certain goods is the case for a *public good* as discussed earlier in this chapter.

Externalities

Another form of market failure is the presence of externalities. Externalities are costs or benefits that are not "captured" by the price mechanisms. For example, a college student does not capture all of the benefits of a college education; some of the benefits would accrue to others in society who might benefit from a lab discovery or a work of art. Conversely, the producer of a product that causes pollution does not incur all of these costs; most of the costs are external to the producer.

The connection between externalities and social costs/benefits is through the relationship with private costs and benefits. The private market mechanisms have an equilibrium price, which is where private marginal benefits (MB$_P$) equal marginal social costs (MSC). However, in Figure 7.1, there is the presence of a positive externality associated with prenatal visits.

TIP ✏

In the case of a negative externality, such as pollution from industrial output, the government tax should be equal to the social cost of the pollution in order to internalize the cost to the polluting firm. This will cause less production (and less pollution). In the case of a positive externality, as in the case of the prenatal visits, the government subsidy should be equal to the value to society of the greater number of prenatal visits. The subsidy would cause more prenatal visits at a lower private cost.

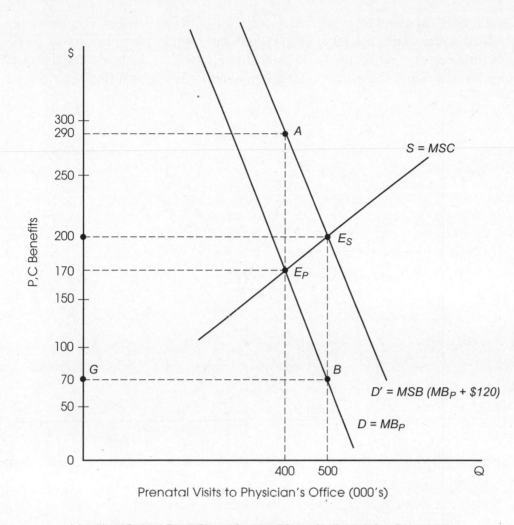

Marginal Social Benefits = Marginal Benefit (Private) + Externality
Positive Externalities Subsidy

Fig. 7.1 Positive Externalities and Related Subsidy

A positive externality means that benefits accrue to others as in the case of prenatal visits by women to a physician. In France, the government has allowed women these prenatal visits at zero cost. In addition, the women are paid a nominal sum when they do visit the physician. There is a social benefit of assuring the health of the mother and the fetus that is not captured in the market equilibrium price of $170. There is an externality of $120 (the difference between the marginal social benefits of $290—point A on the graph, and the equilibrium price of $170, the value of private marginal benefits). Therefore, the values of the externality are internalized in the price mechanisms as a subsidy. To sum up, marginal social benefits (MSB) equal private marginal benefits (MB_p) plus the externality. In this case, the subsidy is paid to the consumers in order to effectively lower the price. In a positive externality, the price is too high and the output is too low (too few prenatal visits at the market equilibrium of 400,000 visits). With the subsidy, the number of prenatal visits increases to 500,000 at which level, MSC = MSB or optimal (efficient output).

Government interference is justified so that this efficient level of output will be obtained. Otherwise, the level of 400,000 prenatal visits is below the optimal level.

With a negative externality (as illustrated in Figure 7.2) the market equilibrium price is too low and the market equilibrium quantity is too high (P_p, X_2).

T^* Tax per unit = Externality per unit
$P_S E'_S A P_{PC}$ = Total taxes = Total externality ($E'_S - A$) × X_1 units output
Social costs = Private costs + Externality value
Negative externality = Tax

Fig. 7.2 Negative Externalities and Related Tax

The use of a tax to correct for this situation reflects this negative externality. Further, the tax equals the value of the negative externality and thus corrects or internalizes this externality. With the tax correction, the optimal (efficient) outcome is achieved (P_s, X_1) at the level of output of the polluting firm, MSB = MSC. Thus, the price that was too low is now higher ($P_s > P_p$) and the output that was too high is now lower ($X_1 < X_2$). Remember, marginal social cost (MSC) = marginal cost private (MC_p) + tax (T). The tax (T) = value of negative externality.

This negative externality of pollution can also be illustrated in terms of a *tolerable level of pollution* or that level of water pollution at which MSB = MSC. This is illustrated in Figure 7.3, entitled, Pollution, Optimal Output, Social Costs.

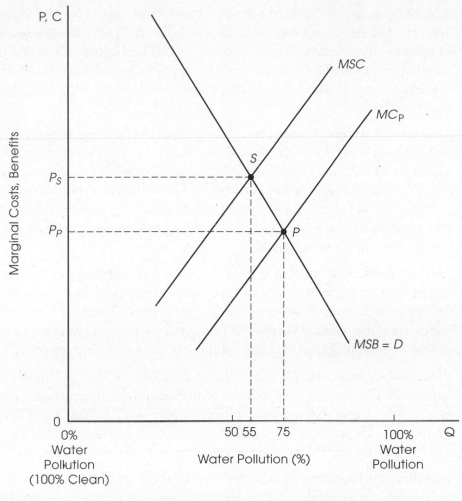

Fig. 7.3 **Pollution, Optimal Output, Social Costs**

The tolerable level of pollution would be 55 percent (MSB = MSC); however, the private market equilibrium level of pollution would be 75 percent pollution (where private marginal cost, MC_p, equals MSB). If the government wants to internalize this negative externality, it would tax this externality ($MSC - MC_p +$ tax, where the tax = negative externality). This tax will not end pollution but it would pass the external costs to the firm with the likely outcome of a lower level of pollution (55 percent versus 75 percent) and a decrease in supply (MC_p shifts to the left).

Other Bases for Government Interference

1. **Information.** Information might be considered a public good. Since the provision of full information about a good by its manufacturer would come at a cost to the manufacturer without a corresponding benefit at the margin of providing this information, we might expect that this full information will not be forthcoming. Since this information (nutritional content, fat content, additives, price per unit, etc.) is of social benefit, the government might require appropriate labeling, weights and measure control, price per unit information, warnings, etc. As you know, this information is now mandatory.

2. **Meritorious nature.** Richard Musgrave coined this phrase. Some goods and services may be of such a meritorious nature as to transcend any economic criteria in the determination of public goods. The United Kingdom (UK) has determined that health care services are public goods even though these services possess, to some degree, the private good characteristics of exclusion and distribution.

3. **Efficient allocation of resources.** If the ratio of Public Good Benefits/Public Good Costs is greater than 1 and if this public ratio is greater than Private Good Benefit/Private Good Cost, then the good should be produced or provided by public means; otherwise, Private Good Benefit/Private Good Cost > Public Good Benefit/Public Good Cost, the resources in the production of the good would be most efficiently used in private production, in other words, the case for privatization.

4. **Income redistribution.** The government may feel that the poor are deserving of help from the non-poor or that older citizens need more income distributed their way from the young population. These are normative judgments that manifest themselves in transfer payments such as social security retirement programs, the Earned Income Tax credit, and others.

5. **Competitive markets.** The government may use the Federal Trade Commission (FTC) to correct or penalize firms that provide deceptive sales techniques or practices that promote unfair competition. The Antitrust Division of the U.S. Department of Justice investigates monopolies or mergers that tend to substantially lessen competition or that tend to create monopolies.

6. **Stabilization programs.** On the macro side, there are government stabilization programs to stabilize prices (curb inflation) or to stabilize the business cycle (promote growth without serious or prolonged contraction or recession). In the United States, discretionary stabilization programs are fiscal and monetary. In the macro section of this book, you will find the details and analyses of stabilization programs.

SUMMARY

- Externalities become the basis for government taxes or subsidies. Any government action stems from the costs or benefits occurring to others than the market buyers and sellers.
- Appropriate government action would be to *tax* the polluter for the value of the *negative externality*. The outcome would be efficient level of output at which marginal social ben-efits (MSB) = marginal social costs (MSC). *Taxing a Negative Externality* raises "too low" market price and reduces "too high" market output.
- The government *subsidies* the amount of a *positive externality* such that the subsidy = value of the positive externality. The outcome would be an efficient level of output at which MSB = MSC and that the market price which was "too high" will be reduced and the market output which was "too low" will be increased.

- The study of microeconomics or the economics of the firm is focused on the efficient allocation of resources. Measures of efficiency include technological, allocative and pare to efficiency.
- Private goods have exclusion and distributive characteristics which, in competitive market settings, promote efficiency. Public goods lack these characteristics such that the marginal *cost* of one more unit of a *pure* public good is equal to *zero*. There are examples of price exclusive and congestible public (quasi) goods.
- With the presence of market failures, rents, externalities, inequity, non-optimal social outcomes and need for information, price stability, cyclical stability and competitive markets, there are bases for government interference in the market.

TERMS

Externalities either the buyer or the seller does not "capture" all of the benefits of a transaction

Social Costs those costs which are incurred by the public, i.e., polluted waterways; these are costs not captured by the market

Social Benefits those benefits which are realized by the public or outside the buyer/seller exchange

Pure Private Good a good that has exclusion and distributive characteristics

Technological Efficiency the identification of those inputs that have the greatest effect on output per $ of input expenditure

Allocative Efficiency the channeling of resources to their most productive and desired uses

Pareto Efficiency the optimal point (efficient point) for society when any *further* improvement for some comes at the expense of others

Pure Public Goods goods which have non-exclusion and non-distributive characteristics

Quasi-Public Goods goods which have some limited private good characteristics such as congestible public goods and price-excludable public goods

FORMULAS

Marginal Social Cost (MSC) = Private Marginal Cost (MC_p) + Negative Externality

$MSC = MC_p$ + Tax where tax = the value of the Negative Externality

Marginal Social Benefits (MSB) = Private Marginal Benefits (MB_p) + Positive Externality

MULTIPLE-CHOICE REVIEW QUESTIONS

1. Which of the following is true about the pure public good?

   (A) The marginal cost of providing an additional unit of the good to additional citizens is greater than zero.
   (B) Consumers can be excluded from its benefits by not paying for it.
   (C) One more unit of a public good for some consumers means one less unit for other consumers.
   (D) The good cannot be divided into discrete units.
   (E) It has a pure moral nature.

2. If there is a negative externality associated with the production of a private good, which of the following is an action by government that would most likely move the market to an efficient outcome?

   (A) Close the firm producing the good.
   (B) Subsidize the firm or its customers.
   (C) Tax the firm.
   (D) Appoint a commission.
   (E) Relocate the firm.

3. If there is a positive externality associated with the production of a private good, which of the following is an action of government that would most likely move the market to an efficient outcome?

   (A) Close the firm producing the good.
   (B) Subsidize the firm or its customers.
   (C) Tax the firm.
   (D) Appoint a commission.
   (E) Relocate the firm.

4. For a polluting steel company, a government action to most likely achieve an optimal or efficient outcome would produce what effect on the market equilibrium price and output?

   (A) Output would increase; no change in price.
   (B) Output would increase; price would decrease.
   (C) Output would increase; price would increase.
   (D) Output would decrease; price would decrease.
   (E) Output would decrease, price would increase.

5. Which of the following is true?

   (A) Marginal Social Costs = Private Marginal Costs + Negative Externality.
   (B) Marginal Social Costs = Private Marginal Costs + Subsidy.
   (C) Marginal Social Benefits = Private Marginal Benefits + Tax.
   (D) Tax = Positive Externality.
   (E) Subsidy = Negative Externality.

Multiple-Choice Review Answers

1. **(D)** 2. **(C)** 3. **(B)** 4. **(E)** 5. **(A)**

FREE-RESPONSE REVIEW QUESTION

I. With the use of a graph, illustrate and explain the following:

A. How a government might take action to correct a negative externality, i.e., either through the imposition of a tax or through the granting of a subsidy.

B. Explain what your answer in "a" above indicates about the equilibrium price (too low, too high) and about the equilibrium quantity.

C. Explain how the government action in "a" could result in a socially optimal outcome.

Free-Response Review Answer

The government would impose a tax to correct a negative externality. This would produce the optimal (efficient) outcome. The price that was too low to produce the optimal outcome is now higher. The output that was too high is now lower. Marginal Social Cost (MSC) = Marginal Private Cost (MPC) + tax.

The tax (T) = *value* of the negative externality.

Costs, Production, Supply

- Law of diminishing marginal productivity
- Production function
- Relationship of production curves to cost curves
- Long run vs. short run
- Economies of scale

- Implicit and explicit costs
- Opportunity Costs
- Economic costs/profits vs. accounting (business) costs/profits
- Average costs and marginal costs, fixed costs and variable costs
- Total costs and marginal cost

INTRODUCTION

All of the basic concepts of costs and production and their interrelationships upon which price and output decisions are made are the subject matter of this chapter. We are not able to fully analyze decisions on prices and outputs without the appropriate revenue data and the related market structure (perfect competition, monopoly, monopolistic competition, oligopoly). The following chapters on product markets will allow us to complete the analysis.

Production data alone provide us with the "engineering" information but fall short of what is necessary to determine cost-effectiveness or to identify the least cost combination of resources for a given level of output. For profit maximization, we will need price and revenue data as well.

THINGS TO KNOW

Based on the most frequently asked questions on previous Advanced Placement exams, the following are the most important concepts. In the balance of this chapter, we will expand on these and other concepts and examples.

1. **Law of diminishing marginal productivity or returns.** In the short run, as variable inputs are applied to fixed inputs, production first increases at an increasing rate; then, production increases at a decreasing rate (diminishing marginal returns or additions to total production become less and less at the margin). Later, there is actually a decrease in total production or output as successively equal increments of variable inputs are added. Examples, graphs, and explanations will follow in this chapter.

2. **Relationships among average and marginal cost and product curves.** Basically, marginal cost (MC) intersects both the average variable cost (AVC) and the average total cost (ATC) curves at their minimum points. This means that if MC > AVC, AVC must be rising (see Figure 8.2); if MC < AVC, AVC must be declining. Similarly, the marginal physical product curve (MPP) intersects the average physical product curve (APP) at the maximum point of the APP curve (see Figure 8.1(a)).

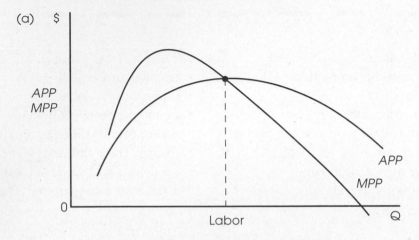

Fig. 8.1(a) Average Product, Marginal Product

3. **Economies of scale.** There are reductions in average cost per unit as production increases. *Constant, increasing,* and *decreasing* returns to scale (concepts, graphs, etc., will follow in this chapter). Briefly, if a firm triples its labor input and triples its output (constant returns); triples its labor and doubles its output (decreasing returns); triples its labor and quadruples its output (increasing returns).

4. **Relationships** among AFC, AVC, ATC, MC, and among average costs and *total costs; between MC and total costs.* You will progressively develop a cost table. Also, you will need to know the relationships between cost and product curve. See Figures 8.1(a) and (b).

Fig. 8.1(b) Average Cost, Marginal Cost

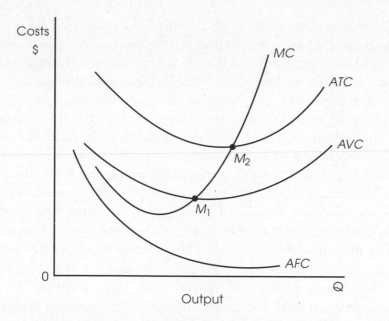

Fig. 8.2 Average Variable Cost, Average Fixed Cost,
Average Total Cost, and Marginal Cost

5. **Short run and long run cost curves.**

6. **Costs:** opportunity costs, economic costs versus accounting costs, economic profits versus accounting profits. (This will be covered at the end of this chapter.)

PRODUCTION

In the theory and practice of the firm, we start with the basic facts of the need of the firm to combine its resources into a product or a service. The resources are land, labor, and capital, and entrepreneurial ability. The latter suggests this task of combining resources with some "taking" or assuming of risks. The firm or entrepreneur needs to be innovative and able to adjust to changing technology, labor supply, and new sources of funding capital projects including venture capital. Microeconomics is really the economics of the firm, the theory of the firm, or price theory. Before a firm can engage resources in any effective manner, it needs to know basic production concepts such as the relationship between resources (also known as inputs, factors of production, or agents of production) and output. This is the basic production function or $X = F(a, b, c \ldots n)$ where X is output, F is function, and a, b, c, ... n are factors of production. So, output is a function of inputs a, b, c, up to n inputs.

Distinction Between Short Run and Long Run

The distinction between the short run and the long run is significant in economics. It is *not* the difference declared by a student; the student posited that a long run was any run over one mile in distance. In economics, the distinction is that in the short run, supply cannot fully adjust to changes in demand. In the long run, supply does fully adjust to changes in demand. The law of diminishing marginal productivity is a *short run phenomenon.* That is, when some inputs are fixed in number, what happens when another input or resources varies by successive equal increments? The law of diminishing returns explains how, at first, production increases at an increasing rate (the additions or marginal physical products—MPPs become increasingly larger). Then, at some point, production increases at a decreasing rate (the additions or MPPs becoming smaller with each successive equal increment of labor). Eventually, total production or output will actually decrease. In order for efficiency to develop, there has to be a sufficient quantity of fixed resources or inputs for the variable inputs. Thus, as the firm adds more variable inputs to a fixed quantity of other inputs, each added input has less fixed inputs with which to work. If grapes are to be pressed for juice with the use of workers' feet, and there is a fixed supply of grapes, one can imagine that increasing the number of workers will, initially, greatly increase the amount of pressed grapes. However, at some point, there will be a scramble among workers to find a suitable space for the pressing of grapes. An increasing number of workers are competing for space and need to share space leading to smaller and smaller increases in output or diminishing marginal returns.

Relationship of Production to Costs

In order to fully appreciate the nature of production and its relationship with costs, we need to define terms for production and then set forth the transition or connection between production and costs.

The relationship between average physical product (APP) and marginal physical product (MPP) is illustrated in Figure 8.2. You will note that when MPP is at its peak, APP intersects MPP. Also, when MPP is negative total physical product, TPP has just peaked. Any further additions of variable inputs will be associated only with decreasing total product or output. Therefore, there can be no economic rationale for hiring any additional units of labor since these units will have some cost. See Table 8.1.

TABLE 8.1

Product Curves and Schedules

No. of Grape Pressers	Total Output (Grape Juice)	Average Product	Marginal Product
1	60	60	60
2	160	80	100
3	250	83.3	90
4	330	82.5	80
5	400	80	70
6	460	76.67	60
7	510	72.86	50
8	550	68.75	40
9	580	64.44	30
10	600	60.00	20
11	610	55.45	10
12	610	50.83	0
13	600	46.15	−10

On this table you will see that if the firm hires a twelfth grape presser, output remains at 610. If the firm hires at thirteenth presser, there is an associated decrease in output to 600 costs. Average physical product (APP) is defined as the total product or output divided by the number of units of variable input, e.g., labor, and

$$APP^* = \frac{\text{total output}}{\text{variable input}}$$

$$MPP^* = \frac{\text{change in output}}{\text{change in input}}$$

where MPP = marginal physical product. Marginal physical product is the more significant meas-ure of these two. We need to know the impact of adding one more unit of input, such as labor, on output. As we identify costs and revenues later, we will be able to ascertain whether the additional cost of an additional unit of input relative to its marginal contribution to revenue is justified. We will reserve that analysis until the chapter on resource markets (Chapter 13). In this current chapter, and the chapters to follow on product markets, we will emphasize the various cost curves related to increases in product and their connection to prices and revenues.

TIP

Marginal analysis is crucial to economic decision-making. Decisions are made at the margin, not at the average. Firms want to know whether an additional unit of production adds more to total costs or more to total revenue.

COSTS

Relationship of MPP and APP to AVC and MC:

In Figure 8.1(a) and (b), there is an illustration of this relationship. It is as if we are in a maximum/minimum symmetry. That is, the relationship of marginal physical product (MPP) to average physical product (APP) is the converse of the relationship of marginal cost (MC) to average variable costs (AVC). In both cases, as the marginal (MPP, MC) is less than the average (APP, AVC), the average is declining. As the marginal (MPP, MC) is greater than the average (APP, AVC), the average is increasing. However, the MPP curve intersects the APP at the *maximum* point on APP, but the MC curve intersects the AVC curve at the minimum point on AVC. Thus, as MPP declines, each additional unit of labor adds less and less to total product (think of MPP as the addition to total product or the difference in total product as one more unit of labor is added). Regardless of the loss of an additional unit of labor, if each successive equal increment of labor adds less and less to total product, then MC will tend to rise as MPC decreases.

A WORD OF CAUTION

Simply because MPP is declining (diminishing marginal productivity) and MC is rising does *not* necessarily mean that the firm should discontinue production. We need to have the comparison of marginal revenue (MR) with marginal cost. We will look at this in the unit on product markets (Chapter 9). If MR > MC, then the firm

---

* We use marginal and average *physical* product in this chapter to distinguish these terms from average and marginal *revenue* product, which we use later.

will want to continue since it is adding more to revenue than to cost at the margin of producing an additional unit of output.

This relationship of cost to production will be extended to economies of scale later in this chapter. The different measures are AFC, AVC, ATC, MC, TFC, TVC, TC:

1. **Fixed costs:** Total fixed costs are those that, in total, do not vary with changes in output. At zero output, total costs = total fixed costs. Examples would be depreciation costs, capital costs or building and equipment, property taxes, mortgage interest, administrative salaries, and sometimes employee salaries or wages (all or a portion of, such as, tenured faculty, high percent of nurses' salaries, etc.). Average fixed costs (AFC) are total fixed costs divided by output or TFC ÷ Q. As you might expect, since total fixed costs are constant over varying output, then average fixed costs are going to decline as output increases. So, if TFC are constant or

$$\frac{TFC}{Q}$$

then as output increases, AFC decline.

$$\frac{(TFC)}{Q \uparrow} => AFC \downarrow$$

where Q = output. This AFC along with the other marginal and average cost curves are depicted in Figure 8.1.

2. **Variable costs.** Total variable costs are costs that, in total, vary as output changes. As we will see in the next section on economies of scale, these costs tend to decline initially, then reach a minimum, and then increase. Variable costs include the changes in number of employees, energy costs related to production changes, travel expenses, materials related to production, etc. Average Variable Costs (AVC) equal Total Variable Costs (TVC) divided by Q where Q equals the output level. AVC is illustrated in Figure 8.2.

3. **Total costs.** Total Costs = Total Fixed Costs + Total Variable Costs or TC = TFC + TVC. This relationship and the others identified in this section will become important as the readers will progressively complete a table of cost data; different columns will be blank in total or part on different tables. The correct or final table will appear in the chapter on perfect competition, Chapter 10; indeed, this final table will become the basis for a problem on best or optimal output in that chapter. Also, the total of the average costs is significant and necessary to know to complete the cost tables. Thus, ATC = AFC + AVC. As with TC = TFC + TVC, the above identity can be completed if one knows two of the three numbers or has progressively developed the necessary numbers. Thus, if one knows TC and TVC, one can determine TFC and so on. Before we expand the discussion to the long run, Figure 8.2 illustrates these cost curves (average and marginal) including their relation-

ships. The reader will note that MC intersects both the average variable cost curve (AVC) and the average total cost curve (ATC) at their respective minimum points (M_1, M_2). *This is important to know.* Also, as in our previous discussion, the AFC curve declines rapidly approaching zero level as Quantity (Q) of output increases with total fixed costs constant. The location or level of average variable costs (AVC) and average total costs (ATC) are significant as you will need to know the shut-down position (minimum AVC) and the relationship of price to ATC at best output (P > ATC, profits; P < ATC, losses) under perfect competition (Chapter 10).

Costs: The Long Run and Economies of Scale (And the Associated Adjustment From the Short Run)

First, we might need a refresher on the differences between the long run and the short run. When we looked at diminishing marginal productivity, we were considering the short run since we held some input (resources) constant, such as land or capital, to see the effect of adding successive equal increments of a variable input, such as labor (grape pressers) on the output (grape juice). In the short run, not all of the inputs have sufficient time to adjust to the changes in demand. In this section, we will consider the variability of all inputs and therefore, the long run.

I – ATC plant capacity of 1000 units ATC curve
II – ATC plant capacity of 1500 units ATC curve
III – ATC plant capacity of 2200 units ATC curve
IV – ATC plant capacity of 2500 units ATC curve
V – ATC plant capacity of 3000 units ATC curve
Where ATC = Average Total Cost

Fig. 8.3 Adjustment in Plant Size (capacity) From Short Run to Long Run Cost Curves

Economies of scale are those savings in average cost of production per unit that are realized as the firm increases production of its goods. In Figure 8.3, we have illustrated hypothetical plant size (capacity) for different "runs" of production. That is, the firm has an average total cost (ATC) curve I for production up to 1,000 units, ATC curve II for up to 1,500 units, and so on. The decision comes at production of 800 units whether to stay with plant size I and its related ATC curve or to expand capacity to plant size II. The advantage of expanding the plant size at this juncture would be to enjoy the economies of scale evident in II ATC. That is, at 800 units the firm could produce more efficiently on curve II ATC since it is downward sloping—lower per unit average costs, while curve I ATC is upper sloping at 800 units to its limit of 1,000 units. Thus, the firm could produce 800 to 1,000 units more cheaply with plant size II than with plant size I. However, the caveat is that demand for the firm's production will be sufficient to justify the move to a plant size (capacity) of 1,500. Much of this decision will rest on the ability to know the market, use forecasting tools, and to have some confidence in the general economy, including but not limited to the expected level of consumer income and the expected actions of the government (regulation, antitrust, and so on) and the monetary authorities. A firm may conclude that the demand increase is only temporary and might be better supplied by outsourcing. For example, when the Great Atlantic and Pacific Tea Company (the A&P) owned its brand name (Ann Page Foods) factory in Big Flats, New York, it took orders from other name brand companies to produce their products with their names according to the brand name companies' own specifications. On a visit to the factory in New York State, one might have encountered the production of a name brand pasta complete with the brand name packages. Since the pasta company had excess orders from industries that were one-time-only orders, it figured that it would be foolish to expand its plant capacity and, instead, to have Ann Page Foods produce their order.

Similarly, when Ford Motor Company and General Motors faced an increase in demand for diesel engines for passenger cars, they took different paths in their decision making. Ford hired the services of experienced diesel engine manufacturers in Germany in order to meet its demand, while at the same time to determine whether this was simply a temporary situation. General Motors undertook a major investment in changing piston engines to diesel engines and had to adjust and expand its production capacity.

Thus, if the demand increase seems long term and sufficient to justify increased plant capacity, and the related utilization of that capacity, the firm would move to the next-larger plant size when the ATC curve of one size intersected the ATC curve of the next-larger size (e.g., when ATC I intersects ATC II at 800 units of production rather than waiting until production reaches 1,000). The extent to which this becomes an on-going process, the long run average total cost curve becomes the envelope curve that touches base with these decision points—800, 1,300, 2,000, and 2,400 units.

Thus far, we have explained the nature of economies of scale, which implies that as output or production increases, there are some savings in per unit average cost of production. The sources of these savings or economies are of two types: external economies of scale and internal economies of scale. With respect to internal economies, there are those economies that derive from specialization and those that derive from efficiency gains with large size.

VALUE OF A LARGE-SIZE FIRM

The value of having a large-size firm is that it can hire specialists in finance, marketing, distribution, public relations, corporate communications, information technology, and even economics! The sole proprietorship or "Mom and Pop" operation has to be "Jack and Jill of everything"—all those specialized areas listed above—and "master of none." Thus, the larger firm can become more efficient than the small firm simply on the basis of being able to hire more expertise. The other general internal efficiency is the gain that comes from the increase in volume that allows fixed costs to be spread over a larger output of goods and services lending to a decrease in average per unit costs (ATC).

In the chapter on imperfect competition, Chapter 12, we cite the case of too many gasoline stations at a busy intersection. The volume of sales, gallons of gasoline, is too low in total to provide any basis for economies of scale for any of the four gasoline stations. It is a classic example of underutilization or excess capacity as the major source of inefficiency in the long run under monopolistic competition. This situation could be illustrated with the graph in Figure 8.4(c). You will see the economies of scale (ATC declining) being very quickly exhausted and then a long range of diseconomies of scale (the longer, upward sloping portion of the ATC curve). Each station simply cannot pump enough gallons of gasoline over which to spread its fixed costs. Figure 8.4(c) illustrates a relatively small firm. Conversely, a very large firm such as an automobile manufacturing company can enjoy an ATC curve as illustrated in Figure 8.4(b) since it can cover its fixed costs over a very large number (millions) of its output or automobiles. This ATC curve has a long downward declining shape with economies of scale. Also, the company can use the most modern technology that would be, in many cases, too expensive for smaller firms or the smaller firms would have to purchase smaller technology. This smaller technology would be more expensive per unit produced. For example, a machine with 1,000 horsepower would not cost twice as much as one with 500 horsepower.

External economies of scale do not depend upon the efficient operation of a firm but rather derive from the large-scale advanced industrial economy. It is going to be much more efficient (less costly) to build a steel company in Germany or the United States than it is to build one in Afghanistan, which lacks the infrastructure of the more advanced industrial countries. Infrastructure would include a highly trained, educated, and experienced labor force; a well-developed telecommunications system; an advanced computer technology; a ready-made source of supplies, and retail/wholesale buyers of products. Given an advanced industrial economy like the German economy, there will be many companies that rely on steel products for part or all of their production. These are external economies of scale.

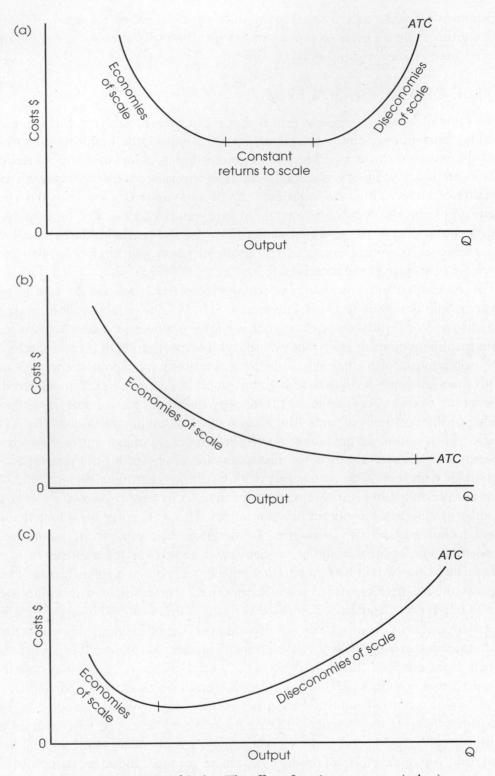

Fig. 8.4 **Economies of Scale—The effect of varying cost curves (a, b, c)**

Economic Costs

There is a particular definition of economic costs that is at variance with the definition of business or accounting costs. Further, this particular definition will help explain the distinction between economic profits and accounting or business profits. Economic profits involve opportunity or implicit costs as well as the explicit costs of accounting.

In economics we reason that the cost of producing one good or service or engaging in a parti-cular activity is measured in terms of what other goods or services could have been produced or what other activity could have been undertaken using the same resources, including time. For example, if an F-16 fighter plane costs $16 million (hypothetically), how many automobiles, air conditioners, or computers could have been produced with the same amount of resources for $16 million? So, the production of what a fighter plane *costs* us (consumers) is what we could have had available in the form of these other products. Also, we could say that that economic cost is what must be paid, at minimum, to maintain or attract production of the goods and services that we are demanding.

Economic costs include the implicit cost of what could have been earned elsewhere with the same resources that are employed in the current business. For example, if Mom and Pop spend $100,000 on a building and equipment to open a restaurant, what might be included as implicit costs? If the $100,000 were invested in a similar risk mutual fund and the return on the investment was nine percent compared to a six percent return on one capital investment in the restaurant, the *implicit* cost would be three percent or $3,000*, or the amount that could be earned elsewhere compared to the investment in the restaurant. Similarly, if Mom and Pop paid themselves $40,000 each as salary and, with the same number of hours they could have earned $50,000 each working for some other restaurant, their *implicit* cost would be $20,000* ($100,000 − $80,000). We add these implicit costs to the explicit costs in order to determine the economic feasibility of going into the restaurant business. To illustrate this, review the hypothetical data below (assume no other implicit costs):

Sales (Income) for restaurant	$900,000
- explicit (accounting) costs	−600,000
accounting business profit	300,000
- implicit (economic) costs*	−23,000*
economic profit	$277,000

* Opportunity cost ($23,000) of operating their own business versus "hiring out" their resources result from subtracting explicit *and* implicit (opportunity costs of resources in alternative uses) costs from income or revenue. These implicit costs of $23,000 result from the $3,000 and $20,000 described in the preceding paragraph.

SUMMARY

- Law of Diminishing Marginal Productivity. This is the range of output over which production increases at a decreasing rate, i.e., the additional units of production become smaller and smaller.
- Relationships Among Average Cost (AC, AVC, ATC), Marginal Cost (MC), Average Product (AP) and marginal Product (MP) Curves. The MP curve *always* intersects the AP curve at the maximum point of the AP curve. The MC curve *always* intersects the Average Cost Curve (AVC, ATC) at their minimum points.
- Economies of Scale. These reductions in average cost per unit of output as production increases may be in the form of constant, increasing or decreasing returns to scale.
- Economic Profits vs. Accounting Profits. Accounting profits result from subtracting explicit costs from income or revenue. Economic profits produce a return which is less than a return of an alternative activity using the same resources (implicit costs).
- Economic Profits. Income or revenue minus explicit *and* implicit costs.
- Accounting Profits. Income or revenue minus explicit costs.

TERMS

Law of Diminishing Marginal Productivity the range of output over which smaller and smaller additional units of output are produced as successive equal increments of a variable input are added to fixed quantities of other inputs in the short run

Economies of Scale savings in per unit costs of production as output increases

Short Run period of time over which supply cannot fully adjust to changes in demand

Long Run period of time over which supply can fully adjust to changes in demand

Opportunity Costs the cost incurred when resources engaged in one activity are not as productive as they would have been in a forgone activity

FORMULAS

Total Costs (TC) = Total Variable Costs (TVC) + Total Fixed Costs (TFC)

Average Total Costs (ATC) = Average Variable Costs + Average Fixed Costs (AFC)

Marginal Costs = the change is total costs with one additional unit of output

$$\frac{TFC}{Q} = AFC; \ \frac{TVC}{Q} = AVC; \ \frac{TC}{Q} = ATC$$

MULTIPLE-CHOICE REVIEW QUESTIONS

1. Which of the following is true?

    (A) TC = (AVC + AFC) Q.
    (B) TFC = TC at all levels of output.
    (C) AVC + AFC = TC.
    (D) MC = TC − TFC.
    (E) ATC = AVC + MC.

2. Opportunity costs or implicit costs of a "Mom & Pop"–owned business are:

    (A) equal to accounting costs.
    (B) equal to accounting profits.
    (C) equal to earnings or profits that could have occurred using resources elsewhere.
    (D) equal to earnings or profits that occurred for Mom & Pop's business.
    (E) equal to earnings or profits of other Mom & Pop businesses.

3. With capital fixed at one unit with 1, 2, 3 units of labor added in equal successive units, production of the output increases from 300 (1 unit of labor), to 350 (2 units of labor) to 375 (3 units of labor). Which of the following is a correct interpretation?

    (A) This is long run increasing returns to scale.
    (B) This is long run decreasing returns to scale.
    (C) This is long run constant returns to scale.
    (D) This is short run diminishing marginal productivity.
    (E) This is short run increasing marginal productivity.

4. Which of the following is *not correct* about economies of scale?

    (A) Economies of scale are associated with increases in production of output.
    (B) Economies of scale are associated with the rising or increasing portion of an average total cost (ATC) curve.
    (C) Economies of scale are associated with the declining or decreasing portions of the ATC curve.
    (D) Economies of scale result in decreases in per unit average cost.
    (E) Economies of scale may be associated with the ability to use more specialists in business.

5. Marginal cost (MC) is equal to average variable cost (AVC) and average total cost (ATC) when:

    (A) marginal cost (MC) intersects AVC and ATC at their maximum points.
    (B) AVC and ATC intersect MC at its maximum point.
    (C) MC intersects AVC and ATC at their minimum points.
    (D) AVC and ATC intersect MC at its minimum point.
    (E) the economy is in the recovery phase of the business cycle.

Multiple-Choice Review Answers

1. **(A)**   2. **(C)**   3. **(D)**   4. **(B)**   5. **(C)**

FREE-RESPONSE REVIEW QUESTION

I. A. Complete the table below.

Output	TC	AFC	AVC	ATC	MC
1		$400	$100		$100
2		200	75		
3		133	70		
4		100	73		
5		80	80		
6		67	90		
7		57	103		
8		50	119		
9		44	138		
10		40	160		

B. Determine what total costs (TC) would be for zero output.

HINT: Total fixed costs (TFC) are constant. They *do not vary* with output. Also, remember that AFC × Q (output) = TFC and again, TFC is the same at every level of output, including zero output.

Free-Response Review Answer

I. A.

Output	TC	AFC	AVC	ATC	MC
1	$500	$400	$100	$500	$100
2	550	200	75	275	50
3	610	133	70	203	60
4	690	100	73	173	80
5	800	80	80	160	110
6	940	67	90	157	140
7	1,120	57	103	160	180
8	1,350	50	119	169	230
9	1,640	44	138	182	290
10	2,000	40	160	200	360

B. At zero output, TC = $400.

Product Markets: Types, Characteristics, Pricing Strategies

CHAPTER 9

- Perfect competition, monopolistic competition, oligopoly, monopoly
- Efficiency
- Barriers to entry/exit
- Pricing policies
- Elasticity and product markets
- Availability of substitutes, similarity of products, number of sellers
- Price-takers and price-makers

INTRODUCTION

This section on product markets, and this introductory chapter relate to the production of goods and services and their costs and prices in differently structured markets ranging from the theoretical model of perfect competition through the imperfectly competitive real-world models of monopolistic competition and oligopoly to monopoly. For each of these product markets, there is a set of characteristics that provides guidance in explaining different costs, efficiencies and pricing strategies.

THINGS TO KNOW

Based on the most frequently asked questions on previous Advanced Placement exams, the following table of the characteristics of the different market structures provides the best overall reference guide.

PRODUCT MARKETS: DEFINITIONS

Perfect Competition

Perfect competition is characterized by a large number of sellers so that no one seller or group of sellers can have a significant effect on the terms of exchange (or transaction terms). These terms include prices, quantity, share of market, type of product, distribution, innovation, service/warranty/guarantee, etc. Prices for each firm in this perfectly competitive environment are determined in the market where all firms (sellers) compete for the buyers of the same (homogeneous) product. That is, the price is set in this market and each firm must charge the "going price"; to

TABLE 9.1

Product Market Characteristics

Characteristics	Perfect Competition	Monopolistic Competition	Oligopoly	Monopoly
1. Numbers of Sellers	Many (they are pricetakers from the market).	Fewer than perfect competition, more than oligopoly/monopoly (some price-makers).	Few sellers who have some control of market share; interdependence.	One seller for whom there are no close substitutes.
2. Availability of Substitutes	One product type available (fully substitutable) available from all sellers.	Imperfect substitutions.	Fewer substitutes available = market pricing power.	No close substitutes available.
3. Degree of Elasticity	Perfectly elastic.	Imperfect elasticity. Depends on degree of innovation.	Varies. Greater elasticity at high prices. Lower elasticity at lower prices.	Generally inelastic but still elastic at higher prices.
4. Similarity of Products	Homogeneous products from all sellers.	Heterogeneous.	Some markets— homogeneous for specialty products. Other markets heterogeneous products.	Follows from #1–3 above. Heterogeneous since there are no close substitutes.
5. Pricing Policy/ Strategy High value	No pricing policy or strategy. Price at market price, price-takers.	Mostly non-price competition; some independent pricing.	Much interdependence in pricing. Some evidence of monopoly pricing policy	Monopoly pricing power. High value to ratio: $\frac{P - MC}{P}$
6. Barriers to Entry/Exit	No barriers to entry/exit.	Weak barriers to entry/exit.	Formidable barriers to entry/exit.	Complete barriers to entry by definition.
7. Efficiency/* Rent-Seeking	Efficient. Each seller prices at cost. No rents. Only transfer earnings.	Inefficiency, excess capacity since P = AC (but not at minimum).	Monopoly pricing power leads to waste/inefficiency. Some economies of scale.	Dead-weight loss of monopoly (loss to society beyond monopoly profits and reduced consumer surplus).
8. Eco. Profits* P, AC	Zero economic profits. Price = Minimum AC.	P = AC; tendency for LR zero economic profits.	Tendency for existence of LR economic profits.	Empirical evidence of LR economic profits.
9. P, MC*	Ideal social pricing P = MC	P > MC	P > MC	P > MC
10. P, MR*	P = MR	P > MR	P > MR	P > MR

* Long run tendencies at equilibrium.

charge more would result in loss of sales to other firms that produce the identical product. As a result, these firms are price-takers; each firm sells at the price set in the market or at the intersection of demand and supply.

Fig. 9.1 Perfect Competition

To illustrate, under perfect competition, there are no barriers to entry for firms that want to enter the market—no technological secrets, no financial barriers, no legal or regulatory constraints, etc. Also, there are no barriers to exit, such as government subsidies, tax relief, import quotas, or high tariffs. In other words, efficiency is maintained or rewarded and inefficiency is reduced by new entrants. Perfect competition is also characterized by homogeneous (identical) product; firms must use the currently available technology and fully utilize plant and equipment to maintain the competitive norm of costs and hence, be efficient. We will discover in Chapter 10 that in long run equilibrium under pure competition, Price (P) = Minimum Average Cost (AC); Price (P) = Marginal Cost (MC) and Price (P) = Marginal Revenue. Since the products produced under perfect competition are identical (homogeneous), they are perfect substitutes and have to be priced at the market (firms as price-takers). That would also mean that Price (P) = Marginal Revenue (see Figure 9.1) since each unit sells for the same price regardless of the quantity produced.

Under perfect competition, there is no pricing strategy. The price elasticity of demand for each firm (see Chapter 5) is perfectly elastic, a horizontal function indicating that the products are perfect substitutes. Each firm must produce and price at minimum cost or lose sales to the other firms. Each customer buys a product at its minimum average cost. Thus, the more substitutes available, the more competitive the industry structure and the more elastic the response to price changes. The perfectly competitive model is one of price-takers with no pricing strategy or power independent of the market.

Monopoly

There are many forms that monopoly can take (see Chapter 11). It is important to note that we are on the opposite end of market structures than that of perfect competition. That is, monopolies are characterized as one seller of a product for which there are no close substitutes; therefore, we would expect the demand of the consumer to be less elastic than in a perfectly competitive market. However, the monopoly demand curve will *not* be perfectly inelastic since the buyers can be influenced by price changes, or, as the price decreases, they may wish to buy more. This, in turn, explains why the marginal revenue function will differ from the demand function as the price is lowered; the addition to total revenue becomes less and less.

Thus, under monopoly, the downward sloping demand curve implies a pricing strategy, even a pricing power. The strategy is to change prices and outputs (to have a significant effect on the terms of exchange or transaction terms) in order to maximize revenue and profits. Barriers to entry allow monopolists to increase prices and limit output; hence, no available close substitutes leads to lack of competition and the demand curve is less elastic than that of perfect competition. There are several types of monopolies and pricing strategies that we will review in later chapters.

Fig. 9.2 Monopoly. Firm = Market (Industry)

Monopolistic Competition

This market structure is the setting for many firms in the United States and other Western countries. It is characterized by many medium-sized firms that need to be innovative and differentiate their products in ways other than price. That is to say, a firm in monopolistic competition can take sales away from a rival with a variety of "price-distracting" products and services. For example, a food supermarket might develop a huge store complete with bakery, sandwich shop, restaurant, dry cleaner, specialty and take-home meals, film processing, drugstore, magazine and newspaper section, bulk foods, etc. This store could then price its regular and stable goods higher than its rival stores, thus, a strategy that is based on product differentiation and innovation that reduces competition. With few substitutes, the competition is reduced, and the demand curve becomes less elastic. The firms charge above marginal cost and above minimum average cost, in the long run. The firms are less efficient than perfect competition since they tend to have zero economic profits but price above minimum average cost. There will be a full explanation about this in Chapter 12. See the illustration which follows.

Fig. 9.3 Monopolistic Competition*

* Long run *tendency* to zero economic profits.

Oligopoly

There are relatively few sellers (specific measurements indices in Chapter 12) who act *interdependently* and/or collusively to be price-makers in order to control markets and the terms of exchange, for example, price, quantity sold, geographic markets, specialized markets, service terms, etc. There are very strong barriers to entry (technology, financial, legal, etc.). The goods produced can be both homogeneous and heterogeneous, in other words, similar as in a product specialization such as structural steel where firms compete with each other in the *same* product market. In heterogeneous competition, firms differentiate their products to gain in revenue; for example, one firm may provide a complete line of hardware products, including some products that sell at a loss, in order to compete against firms that sell only those lines that produce profits. In the latter case, firms can increase their prices to the extent that there are fewer substitutes reflected in lower price elasticity of demand. Again, fewer substitutes, lower price elasticity of demand, and more pricing power are highly interrelated. There are more price-makers. (See more on oligopoly in Chapter 12.)

PRICE-TAKERS VS. PRICE-MAKERS

Price-takers act at the direction of the market; they must charge the going price or face possible elimination. Price-makers are able to control or manipulate some markets; they can charge a price that is in excess of marginal costs that maximizes profits.

SUMMARY

This chapter provides an overview of the different market structures which include perfect competition, monopoly, monopolistic competition, and oligopoly.

The basic reference guide to these market structures is in Table 9.1. This table compares the structures by numbers of sellers, availability of substitutes, degree of price elasticity of demand, similarity of products, pricing policy, barriers to entry/exit, efficiency/rent-seeking, economic profits, price related to marginal cost, and price related to marginal revenue. One might observe that as entry is easier, products more similar, availability of substitutes is greater and the number of sellers is larger, markets are more competitive (closer to the perfect competition model) and price elasticity of demand is greater.

TERMS

Perfect Competition this structure is characterized by a larger number of sellers with a homogeneous product, infinitely elastic demand, and no barriers to entry or exit (a price-taker)

Monopoly one firm constitutes the market (industry) selling a product for which there are no close substitutes (a price-maker)

Monopolistic Competition this structure is characterized by many medium-sized firms who need to be innovative and differentiate their products in price and non-price ways

Oligopoly this market structure is characterized by relatively few sellers who act interdependently and/or collusively to be price-makers and to control markets

MULTIPLE-CHOICE REVIEW QUESTIONS

1. For which of the following market structures are the most substitutes available for consumers?

    (A) Perfect competition.
    (B) Monopolistic competition.
    (C) Oligopoly.
    (D) Monopoly.
    (E) All of the above.

2. Which of the following market structures has the greatest degree of elasticity?

    (A) Perfect competition.
    (B) Monopolistic competition.
    (C) Oligopoly.
    (D) Monopoly.
    (E) All of the above.

3. Which of the following market structures has the largest number of sellers?

    (A) Perfect competition.
    (B) Monopolistic competition.
    (C) Oligopoly.
    (D) Monopoly.
    (E) All of the above.

4. Which of the following market structures is *not* a price maker?

    (A) Perfect competition.
    (B) Monopolistic competition.
    (C) Oligopoly.
    (D) Monopoly.
    (E) All of the above.

Multiple-Choice Review Answers

1. **(A)**   2. **(A)**   3. **(A)**   4. **(A)**

Perfect Competition

- Market demand curve and firm's demand curve
- Long run equilibrium
- Price-takers
- Price and marginal costs
- Strategies for profit maximization and loss minimization

- Optimal output and efficiency
- Evaluation of perfect competition in the long run
- Adjustment from short run to long run equilibrium
- Consumer and producer surplus

INTRODUCTION

Based on the most frequently asked questions on previous Advanced Placement exams, the following are the most important concepts. In the balance of the chapter, we will expand on these and other concepts and examples.

THINGS TO KNOW

Fig. 10.1 and 10.3 Perfect Competition

Note the following:

1. Demand curve of *market* (or *industry*—all firms selling some product) is downward sloping to the right but the demand curve of the firm is *horizontal* (implies perfectly elastic demand function).
2. Since the demand curve of the individual firm is horizontal, P = MR for the firm.

119

3. If we take this figure to be that of long run (LR) equilibrium, each firm will take its price from the market (price-taker). Thus, regardless of the quantity produced and sold, the price for the firm remains constant with the only decision being the optimal quantity to produce given a price.

4. Also, if Figure 10.1 represents LR equilibrium, you will note that P = MR, P = MC and P = minimum average cost. P = MR implies that there is no pricing strategy (firms are price-takers); the demand function is horizontal. P = MC implies that the price of the product (the "value" to the consumer) is equal to the extra cost incurred by the seller in producing the marginal or extra unit of production. P = Minimum Average Cost implies that firms are operating at zero economic profits (see Chapter 8 for explanation of economic versus accounting profits). This also means that efficiency has been attained; in other words, each increase in the cost of an extra unit of production equals the price that the consumer is willing to pay. We will discover later that, in contrast, monopolistic competition has a degree of inefficiency due largely to excess capacity by producing at average cost but not at minimum cost.

5. If we refer to the short run (SR), price as reflected by the demand function remains horizontal but can increase or decrease in the short run; therefore, there can be profits or losses in the short run. The firm wants to maximize profits or minimize losses by producing the optimal output—the level of output at which MR = MC (with perfect competition, MR = P). Thus, if you are given a graph, a table, or a set of output and price levels, you need to find the location of the optimizing output in the short run. For example, if Price is $14, find the optimal output in the diagram below:

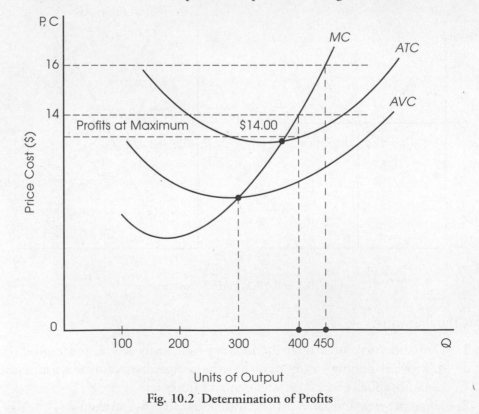

Fig. 10.2 Determination of Profits

*Note that MC intersects both AC curves (AVC and ATC) at their minimum levels.
**Note that, in the short run, P = MR.

If P = MR, then the optimal output would be at the level at which MC = MR. Follow the horizontal demand function over to where the price of $14 (MR) = MC (intersection of the MC function with Price or Demand). Drop a line perpendicular to the horizontal axis and the output of 400 would be the optimal output, the output level at which profits would be maximized or the level at which MR = MC. We will more fully develop this concept later as we look at shut-down, maximum profit, minimum loss levels of output and the criteria for best output in each of these situations. As a follow-up question, what would the firm do if the price increased to $16? (Again, refer to Figure 10.2). Would the firm produce at 300, 350, 400, 450, or 525 units of output? To determine the answer, follow the general criterion of best output @ MC = MR (remember that, in the short run, P = MR). Thus, with a price (MR) of $16, MR = MC at an output level of 450. Hence, the best (optimal) output level will be 450. If there is no level at which MR = MC, select the highest level of output at which MR > MC.

6. As mentioned in the chapter on costs (see Chapter 8) and as illustrated in point 5 above, ATC = MC when ATC is at its minimum point and AVC = MC when AVC is at its minimum point. That is, MC always intersects ATC and AVC at their minimum points. When MC > ATC, ATC must be rising since the additions to total cost (marginal costs) are greater than average costs. The converse holds with MC < ATC.

7. The following are conditions that are correct about firms operating under perfect competition:
   At *long-run* equilibrium,
   a. P = MR. No pricing strategy. Firms are price-takers.
   b. P = MC. Price at which product sells (at "market") equals the extra cost incurred.
   c. P = minimum average cost.
   d. Firms realize zero economic profit or *normal* profits.
   e. Firms have no incentive to price their goods and services below the market price.
   f. The demand function for each firm is horizontal.
   g. Products are homogeneous; therefore, no purpose for advertising.

8. Profits and competition. LR equilibrium under perfect competition leads to normal profits (zero economic profits). Profits less than normal = economic losses. Economic profits > zero or normal profits.

9. The conditions (criteria) for continuing production, shut-down, profits, losses in the short run under perfect competition (expanded coverage later in this chapter). For each price (P = MR), in the short run:
   a. If P < AVC, firm should shut down and its total losses = total fixed cost (TFC). If P ≥ AVC, firm should continue production.
   b. If P > AVC, firm continues to produce as long as MR > MC up to the level of output profits are maximized or losses minimized—level at which MR = MC. (Determination of profits or losses discussed later in this chapter.)

10. Under perfect competition, price elasticity of supply is greater in the long run than in the short run since there are more opportunities for substitution of inputs.

EXPANDED CONCEPTS

1. The individual firm as a price-taker (see Figure 10.1/10.3):
   The firm is a price-taker, that is, the price for the homogeneous (same) product is determined in the market, where all buyers and sellers meet, and "dictate" to each individual firm. Since there is a sufficiently large number of firms under perfect competition, no one firm or group of firms can determine its own price. The firms must sell at the market-determined price for two basic reasons: (1) If a firm increases its price above the market price, customers will buy the identical product from another seller at the market price; and, (2) If a firm lowers its price below the market price, it will incur losses and not increase its sales significantly, if at all, since each firm has a very small share of a very large number of sellers. (For more characteristics of perfect competition, see the introductory section of Chapter 9.)

2. Criteria and output strategies for profit-maximizing (and loss-minimizing) firms in the short run under perfect competition.

   • For the appropriate context, firms may incur some losses in the short run* as long as they are covering average variable costs (those costs that increase as output increases) with the market price. Unless a firm can cover (equal to or greater than) average variable costs with its price, it is more economical to shut down production and simply incur fixed costs (those costs that, in total, do not vary with output changes); rather than incurring the fixed costs plus the variable costs, the latter is not covered by the price. The context here is the short run only.

   • The decision-making process to determine best (optimal) output, that is, the output level that maximizes total profits or minimizes total losses.
     a. The firm should produce if P > Average Variable Cost (AVC). It should continue to produce as long as Marginal Revenue (MR) > Marginal Cost (MC). This means that the firm is adding more to its revenue than it is adding to its costs at the margin of producing one additional unit. Therefore, as long as MR > MC, the firm would, necessarily, be adding more to its profits or, in the situation of losses, be reducing losses. At the level of output at which MR = MC, profits would be maximized or losses minimized; hence, the optimal output would occur at MR = MC. In some cases (often used on examination questions), there will be no level of output at which MR = MC. To determine the optimal output, in such cases, select the highest level of output at which MR > MC. If the firm produced one more unit of output beyond this level, then the MC > MR, which would not lead to minimizing losses or maximizing profits.

---

*The short run is when supply cannot fully adjust to changes in demand.

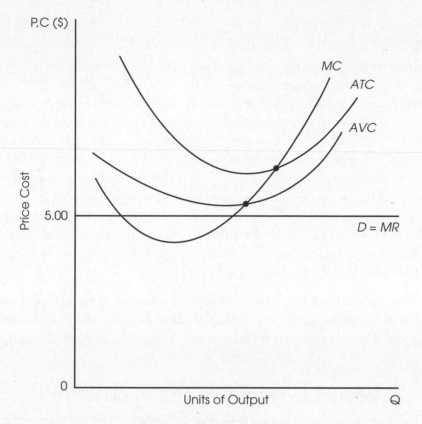

P,C ($)

Price Cost

5.00

MC
ATC
AVC

D = MR

0

Units of Output   Q

Fig. 10.4 Shut-Down Case

b. To determine the total profits or total losses at the optimal level of output, use the following: Optimal level of output X (P − ATC) or total profits = Q(P − ATC) where Q = optimal level of output. If at the optimal output, P > ATC, then the firm would be realizing profits, in other words, P > ATC with the difference being a per unit profit. Thus, if the optimal output is 10 units with a price of $38 and average total cost of $29, total profits would be $90 (Total Profits = Q(P − ATC) or 10 (38 − 29) = 10 × $9) = or $90. If, at the best output of 10 units with a price of $38 and average total cost at $40, losses would occur (ATC > P); total losses would be = Q(ATC − P) or 10(40 − 38) = $20.

TIP

This is the exception to the general rule that the optimal (best) output occurs at the level at which MC = MR. Whenever price is less than average variable cost (AVC), zero output is optimal in the short run. In Figure 10.4, the price of $5 is less than AVC at all levels of output. The firm shuts down and takes its total fixed costs at zero output as its losses (minimizes total losses).

In summary, to determine best (optimal) output, use the following steps (for *each* price) Remember P = MR for the firm in perfect competition:

1. Compare the price with AVC; go down the AVC column to see if P = AVC or P > AVC. If so, the firm continues to produce as long as MR > MC up to the level of output at which MR = MC or the highest level of output at which MR > MC. This would be the optimal output. If AVC > P, then the firm would shut down and take at its losses, total fixed costs. The MR = MC criterion would not apply here—the best (optimal) output is zero units of output.

2. If the firm continues to produce (P > AVC), then the best output is where MR = MC or the highest level of output at which MR > MC.

3. To determine total profits or losses, first determine whether at best output P > ATC or ATC > P. In the former case, profits are realized. In the latter case, losses are incurred. If Q is the optimal output then for total profits, Q(P − ATC); for total losses, Q(ATC − P).

There is a problem to solve, using hypothetical cost data, at the end of this chapter. You may wish to pause with your further reading of this chapter and take on the problem now. The table of costs is taken from Chapter 8, Costs, Production, Supply.

DECISION MAKING FOR THREE SITUATIONS

1. Shut-down case (see Figure 10.4). (P < AVC, therefore, shut down; total losses = TFC) At the market price of $5, the average variable cost is higher than price at every level of output. Therefore, the firm should shut down (at least temporarily) since its cost of continuing production is greater than its revenue. It has no revenue to apply to fixed costs and cannot recover its variable costs at the price of $5 per unit. Its optimal or best output is zero and its minimal total costs are equal to its total fixed costs.

2. Profit maximization case P > AVC, which suggests that the firm should continue to produce as long as MR > MC up to the level of output at which MR = MC; this level of output will maximize profits.

    At the market price of $9, the firm covers its AC (P > AVC) and thus, continues to produce as long as MR > MC up to the level of output at which MR = MC (or if there is no level of output at which MR = MC, the highest level of output at which MR > MC would be the optimal output. In this case MR = MC at the $7 units of output. The optimal (best) output is 7 at which profits are maximized. Total profits at 7 units of output would be Q*(P − ATC) = total profits. Profits are maximized when the Q* is the optimal level of output (MR = MC). So, Q*(P − ATC) becomes 7(9 − 7.75) = 8.75.

3. Loss minimization. P > AVC, which suggests that the firm, in the short run, will continue to produce as long as MR > MC up to the level of output at which MR = MC even if there are losses, then we want the level of output at which we minimize the total losses (MR = MC).

    At a market price of $6 per unit this level would be at 5 units of output (MR = MC). Total losses would be Q*(ATC − P) where Q* is the optimal or best output, that is, total losses are minimized. Thus, Q*(ATC − P) becomes 5(7.60 − 6) = 8.00. This is the rectangular area in the graph above, noted as "losses" (loss permit at best output, x number of units).

Fig. 10.5 Profit Maximization

Fig. 10.6 Loss Minimization

EVALUATION OF PERFECT COMPETITION

Some of this evaluation is reflected in our summary table in Chapter 9 and in this chapter. However, the following are areas from which questions are drawn for the Advanced Placement exams.

- In the short run, the supply curve is identified as that portion of the marginal cost (MC) curve above its intersection with the average variable cost (AVC) curve; the firm is only willing to supply its products or services if the given market price is greater than its average variable costs.
- We have efficiency with consumers buying the products and services they want at prices they pay that are equal to the minimum average cost and marginal cost of production. The producers gain (producer's surplus) from the difference between the price they are willing to supply goods and the price they receive in the market.
- With competitive market exchange and firms as price-takers, there is no "rent seeking"; firms cannot extract from the market any more than they contribute to the market at the margin of any transaction. Price = minimum average cost, which leads to zero economic profits in the long run.

THE LONG RUN

One of the frequently asked questions on the Advanced Placement exam deals with the adjustment of firms from the short run (when supply cannot fully adjust to changes in demand) to the long run when supply fully adjusts to changes in demand. Sometimes, this question appears in the free-response (or essay) section of the exam; at other times it appears as objective, multiple-choice questions.

The following is what you have to know in order to do well on this long run adjustment process.

1. We assume that the only adjustment made, as demand changes, is that new firms enter (as demand increases leading to short run profits). The other type of adjustment is that the present firms increase production. We are not using this adjustment in order to simplify the process.
2. We also assume that the firms' average cost curves are identical and that these cost curves are unaffected by the adjustment process.
3. We assume that new firms enter with the same cost curves as the present firms and that the new firms are attracted by the short run profits in the industry. Also, we assume that firms will exit from the industry when demand decreases, leading to short run losses.

To illustrate this adjustment process, two graphs are provided in Figure 10.7; the one on the left (a) represents the individual firms, and the one of the right (b) represents the industry or market where all buyers and sellers of the same product meet.

We start at an equilibrium position with the price at P_E and quantity at X_E (think of the scale of (b) being 1/100 as compared to (a) and 10 firms in the industry). For the firm (a), note that at equilibrium, P = minimum AC, P = MR, P = MC, and that the demand curve for the individual firm is horizontal. So, at equilibrium the firm "takes" the price from the market and produces at X_E for the optimal output. There is no tendency for change from this optimal output. If the firm produces more, the average cost and MC will exceed the price; if the firm produces less, the AC > price. Now, if the demand for the industry's product increases (DD shifts to D'D') as profits appear, we might expect the adjustment process to begin, that is, demand increases (DD shifts to D'D'); then, a profit appears as a result of demand > supply leading to the demand curve for the firm increasing horizontally (from D to D'), which means the new price (P'_E) is greater than average costs (AC) with the consequent profits. In the short run, supply cannot immediately or fully adjust to the increase in demand. However, with short run profits appearing, new firms are attracted into the industry. Thus, as a second step in the adjustment process, supply increases (SS to S'S') as new firms enter the market. Figure 10.7b is deliberately drawn to show an excess of the new supply relative to the increase in demand. Remember, this is a trial-and-error process much as is our speculation as to the future share prices in the high-tech stock markets. Thus, the excess of supply (S'S' relative to D'D') leads to price decreasing to P''_E, which is lower than average cost, which translates into losses. Then, as a third step, some firms realizing losses will exit from the market and eventually, the new equilibrium (shown as E''') will reflect this decrease in supply (from S' to S'') resulting in the same equilibrium of P_E and X_E as in the original equilibrium.

Perfect Competition Adjustment to LR

Fig. 10.7

This process of adjustment means that efficiency is produced in the long run under conditions of perfect competition. Microeconomics or price theory or the economics of the firm has as its major focus the allocation of resources to their most preferred and productive uses. Perfect competition, although only a model, creates the conditions and the pressures for this allocation process. Thus, in the long run (when supply fully adjusts to changes in demand) efficiency is attained. At the beginning of this chapter, there is reference to efficiency. At equilibrium, in the long run,

P = minimum average cost, P = MR and P = MC. Each firm operates at this level of output, each firm is a price-taker (the market dictates the price), which means there is no rent seeking or other distortions of the market efficiency. With P = minimum average cost, the firm has zero economic profits with just the return on investment that it could receive elsewhere at a similar level of risk. This means we, as consumers, pay the minimum price (considering the firm's opportunity or implicit costs) to maintain the firm producing the goods and services that we desire with P = MC; the consumer pays a price exactly equal to the extra cost incurred by the firm.

The supply curve for the firm is more elastic in the long run (LR) than in the short run (SR). The basis for this is that the firm has more possibilities for substituting among input choices, i.e., labor substituting for capital and vice versa, the longer the time period.

CONSUMER AND PRODUCER SURPLUS

Fig. 10.8

The consumer surplus and the producer surplus provide benefits that result directly from a perfectly competitive market. In Chapter 6, Figure 6.1, consumer surplus was demonstrated in the form of a consumer's willingness to buy running shoes. In Figure 10.8 above, consumer surplus is compared with producer surplus. The consumer is willing to pay $100 a pair for two pairs of shoes, or $80 a pair for four pairs, but the market equilibrium price of $60 a pair is what the consumer pays. The gain in utility or satisfaction over costs is the consumer surplus, as measured by the area of the triangle ABE. The total utility is the area under the demand curve up to the six pairs of shoes at the exchange or equilibrium price of $60 a pair. This is the area AOFE. The total cost of six pairs of shoes at $60 a pair, $360, is measured on Figure 6.1 as the area BOFE. Thus, the area of total utility for the consumer (AOFE) minus the area of total cost (BOFE) results in the consumer surplus of the triangular area of ABE. This represents the gain in utility or satisfaction from the purchase of running shoes at a price less than the price the consumer was willing to pay. This is *consumer surplus*.

Consumer surplus is measured graphically in this section. The reader would be advised to see how it is measured in terms of marginal utility *and* total utility in Chapter 6, Figure 6.1. This consumer surplus can be significantly reduced under imperfectly competitive conditions, particularly under monopoly. This reduction in the consumer surplus is accompanied by a dead-weight loss; that is, a misallocation of resources such that part of the reduction is the result of profits extracted by the monopolist and the rest of the reduction accrues to no one. This is explained in Chapter 11, Figure 11.2.

The producer surplus is demonstrated on the supply curve. The supplier or producer is willing to accept $20 a pair for each of the first two pairs of shoes and $40 a pair for each of four pairs. However, the market equilibrium price pays the supplier $60 a pair. In other words, the market is willing to pay the supplier *more* than (s)he is willing to accept. Remember that the supply curve indicates how much, at minimum, the supplier is willing to receive or accept in payment for additional units of a good. The producer surplus, BOE, is the bonus the supplier receives in payment in excess of the amount (s)he would be willing to accept. The producer is the beneficiary of a competitive market in an exchange between buyers and sellers.

SUMMARY

The perfectly competitive market is characterized by a large number of sellers, availability of perfect substitutes, perfectly elastic demand function, price-takers, no barriers to entry or exit, efficiency, normal (zero) economic profits, and pricing at marginal cost and at minimum average cost in the long run.

- The major criterion for determining the optimal (best) output for the firm operating under perfect competition, in the short run, is to produce that level of output at which MR = MC. The specific criteria and steps to determine the best output are:

  1. The firm will produce, in the short run, as long as price is greater than or equal to average variable cost (AVC). If price is less than AVC, the firm should shut down and take as losses its total fixed costs.
  2. The firm (if number 1 is satisfied), will produce up to the level of output at which MR = MC. This will either maximize profits or minimize losses.

- The evaluation of perfect competition in the long run would reveal that firms are operating efficiently by utilizing the available technology with zero economic profits, price equal to minimum average cost and price equal to marginal cost (socially efficient pricing). Firms are directed by the market in their pricing (price-takers).
- The adjustment of firms from the short run to the long run is accommodated by absence of barriers to entry or exit. The entry of new firms attracted by short run profits and exit of firms discouraged by losses ultimately results in the restoration of market equilibrium with the ensuing results described in the previous paragraph.

TERMS

Economic Efficiency the allocation of resources to most productive and desired uses

Profit Maximizing (Loss Minimizing) Criterion the level of output at which marginal revenue (MR) equals marginal cost (MC)

Shut-Down Criterion in the short run, the firm should shut down when price does not cover average variable cost (AVC)

FORMULAS

P < AVC firms shut down in the short run

P = MR perfectly competitive firm's demand function

MR = MC profit maximizing criterion

P = MC socially optimal price (under perfect competition in the long run); efficiency

P = minimum average cost in the long run for a perfectly competitive firm

MULTIPLE-CHOICE REVIEW QUESTIONS

1. The individual firm, operating under perfect competition, is characterized as:

   (A) a price-maker.
   (B) one of a few sellers.
   (C) a price strategist.
   (D) a price-taker.
   (E) interdependent.

2. Firms maximize their profits by producing a level of output at which

   (A) MC = AFC.
   (B) MC = MR.
   (C) P = ATC.
   (D) MR = AVC.
   (E) P = AVC.

3. In the short run, the shut down price is equal to

   (A) minimum point on average total cost.
   (B) maximum point on average total cost.
   (C) minimum point on average variable cost.
   (D) maximum point on average variable cost.
   (E) minimum point on marginal cost.

4. The demand curve for the firm operating under perfect competition is

   (A) upward sloping to the right.
   (B) downward sloping to the right.
   (C) perfectly vertical line.
   (D) perfectly horizontal function.
   (E) concave to origin.

5. Which of the following is not correct for the perfectly competitive firm, in the long run?

   (A) price = minimum average cost.
   (B) price = marginal revenue.
   (C) price = minimum average variable cost.
   (D) price = marginal cost.
   (E) normal profits.

Multiple-Choice Review Answers

1. **(D)**   2. **(B)**   3. **(C)**   4. **(D)**   5. **(C)**

FREE-RESPONSE REVIEW QUESTIONS

1. Using the table below (this table was developed progressively in the chapter on costs (Chapter 8, Tables 8.2, a & b)) and assuming that these cost data are for a firm in perfect competition for the short run, determine the best (optimal) output *and* the total amount of profits or losses at that output for *each* of the following prices:

   Hint: P = MR for each price

Price	Best Output	Total Profits or Losses
a. $60.00		
b. $130.00		
c. $230.00		

Output	TC	AFC	AVC	ATC	MC
1	$ 500	$400	$100	$500	$100
2	550	200	75	275	50
3	610	133	70	203	60
4	690	100	73	173	80
5	800	80	80	160	110
6	940	67	90	157	140
7	1,120	57	103	160	180
8	1,350	50	119	169	230
9	1,640	44	138	182	290
10	2,000	40	160	200	360

2. Perfect Competition Questions:
   By Reference to Figure 10.8 and Symbols

   Fig. 10.8

A. What is the effect of the shift of DD to D'D' on:
   1) profits
   2) entry/exit of firms
B. What is the effect of the shift of SS to S'S' on:
   1) profits
   2) entry/exit of firms
C. At LR equilibrium, what is the:
   1) significance of P = minimum AC
   2) significance of P = MC
D. Where would you place (draw on graph) supply curve S'' such that the original equilibrium price, P_E would be restored?

Free-Response Review Answers

1. A. Zero output, P < AVC. Total losses = $400 = TC @ zero output
   B. Five. Highest level with MR > MC. Total losses = $150 Q(ATC − P) or 5(160 − 130) = $150.
   C. Eight. Total profits = Q(P − ATC) or 8(230 − 169) = $488 (or $490.00); TR − TC = $1840 − 1350. Differences are due to rounding.

2. A. The shift from DD to D'D' increases profits and encourages entry of new firms.
   B. The shift from SS to S'S' decreases profits or incurs losses for some firms. It would encourage firms to exit.
   C. The significance of P = minimum AC is that there is efficiency, i.e., lowest price consistent with zero economic profits. P = MC is the optimal or socially efficient price.
   D. The supply curve S'' would be drawn in between and parallel to SS and SS' and intersect point E'''.

Monopoly

CHAPTER 11

- Monopoly pricing policy
- Price-makers
- Misallocation of resources
- Inefficiency and dead-weight loss
- Evaluation of monopoly
- Price discrimination
- Regulation of monopolies

INTRODUCTION

While it is important to know monopoly in terms of a definition—a market structure where one firm constitutes an industry and where no close substitutes exist for consumers, it is also important to know that a potential monopoly power can be found under oligopoly and monopolistic competition. Thus, firms can acquire power in imperfectly competitive markets if they can consistently price their goods in excess of marginal costs. Indeed, the Lerner Index (P − MC)/P is one method that economists use to ascertain this pricing power (the greater the value of the index, the greater the market power), including its duration and how the ratio compares among firms we distinguish as "price-takers" in perfect competition from the "price-makers" in imperfect competition who are exemplified by monopoly pricing power. Alternatively, economists use the *Herfindahl Index*, the sum of the squares of the market shares of firms in a particular market or industry, to measure the concentrated power or power generated by shares of the market. In turn, these forms of monopoly reflect the characteristics of monopoly as illustrated in Table 9.1 in Chapter 9.

THINGS TO KNOW

Even though we will examine the major concepts in some detail as we progress through this chapter, the following are important things to know as evidenced on previous AP exams:

1. The monopolist faces a downward sloping demand function that implies that price is greater than marginal revenue, which implies a pricing policy (in contrast to the perfect competition) that could actually lead to a lowering of price by the monopolist in order to induce more sales in a relatively elastic (demand) market (see Fig. 11.1 in this chapter).

2. What follows from number 1 above is the notion that the monopolist maximizes profits at the optimal (best) level of output (MC = MR). By definition, the monopolist does control the supply of a product for which there are no close substitutes. However, the monopolist does not control the demand for the product but can exercise some influence on the amounts demanded by

lowering or raising the price relative to price elasticity of demand. Also, the consumer can decide not to buy any of the monopolist's products. In other words, the monopolist can charge "what the traffic will bear."

3. Unregulated monopoly (see Figure 11.3) may lead to
   a. higher than competitive prices
   b. lower than competitive output
   c. misallocation of resources, inefficiency, and dead-weight loss
   d. rent seeking
4. Regulated monopoly (Figure 11.3) can lead to
   a. move toward outputs that are more efficient (as under competitive markets) through subsidies that rise as output rises.
   b. "fair" rate of return (as would prevail under competitive markets); P = ATC
   c. a socially optimal price and output, P = MC, which would require subsidies
5. It is important to know how to distinguish the various forms of monopoly regulated and unregulated, on a graph (see Figure 11.3), particularly in reference to the Basic Concepts listed here.
6. It is important to know the characteristics of monopoly. You may make reference to these characteristics in Chapter 9 on the introduction to product markets. The rest of this chapter on monopoly is primarily devoted to the development of these characteristics and their significance.

THE NATURE OF MONOPOLY AND ITS TYPES

Monopoly can be identified by its definition and, more importantly, by its power. By definition, a monopoly is both an industry and a firm; that is, a single firm sells a product for which there are no close substitutes. Thus, the firm *is* the industry (product market). This definition is significant in theory and also in practice as one end of the market structure spectrum. As we know the perfectly competitive firm as the most competitive market structure, we know monopoly as the other end of the market structure spectrum (as indicated in Chapter 9 on the introduction of product markets) or as the very antithesis of a competitive market structure.

In policy settings, such as antitrust cases, we know that a potential merger between two large firms could move the industry to be "less competitive" or to have a "tendency toward monopoly" with perfect competition and monopoly serving as "bookends" of market structure. A purely structural approach to antitrust policy would suggest that the above-cited merger be prevented. More importantly, monopoly can exert itself as a pricing power and/or as a determinant of output restrictions. This monopoly power need not exist only in definitional monopoly, i.e., monopoly pricing power can and does take place in other imperfectly competitive structures such as oligopoly and monopolistic competition. Two forms of monopoly power, pricing and market share, are measured in the Lerner Index and the Herfindahl Index, respectively, as identified at the beginning of this chapter. We discuss this pricing power more extensively in the following chapter.

The demand curve facing the monopolist is downward sloping to the right implying that P > MR and a pricing strategy ensues. The monopolist determines price and output (optimal or best) at the intersection of MR and MC.

Fig. 11.1 Firm/Market*

* One firm constitutes the market

If a vertical line is drawn at the intersection of MR and MC (point A) and extended up to the demand function (point C) and then horizontally to the vertical or price axis (point G), we find the price to be P_G and if a line is dropped perpendicular from A to the horizontal axis we find the optimal output to be X_G. Profits are maximized at P_G, X_G and are measured as the rectangular area, HGCB (P-ATC)Q. The per unit profit at the optimal output of X_G is C-B or the per unit price minus the per unit cost. Total profits would be price per unit minus average total cost times the number of units of output.

In contrast to perfect competition, the monopolist is likely to realize economic profits and be able to set a price where MC = MR and P > MC, the latter being symptomatic of monopoly pricing power. Also, output is restricted as compared to perfect competition. The price is higher and the output is lower than the competitive counterpart leading to a misallocation of resources; the monopolist extracts a profit and restricts output that leads to a reduction of consumer surplus. Consumers receive fewer goods at higher prices and the monopolist receives a rent; he receives more than he contributes to production at the margin of the effort of the monopolist. Part of the reduction of consumer surplus accrues not to the monopolist as profits but the other part of the reduction accrues to no one or to a *dead-weight loss*, which is another form of resource misallocation in which resources could have been utilized to produce goods and services and are, instead, totally wasted. We measure this loss in terms of the loss of those goods and services that could have been produced. All of this is illustrated in Figure 11.2. This graph assumes, for simplicity, that for the relevant range of costs, MC = AC.

Fig. 11.2 Dead-Weight Loss

In the graph above:

1. The original consumer surplus is ABF (formed by the amount of total utility area under the demand curve up to the amount of output consumed, OE, at price OF). This would occur in competitive markets.

2. Enter the monopolist who seeks economic profits. The monopolist will maximize profits with the optimal or best output. This level of output (OX) occurs at MC = MR (J). The line XH connects the intersection of MC and MR (J) with X, and H of this line XH is perpendicular to the horizontal axis at X (output OX) and connects with the demand function at H. Drawing a horizontal line from H to the vertical axis identifies OG as the monopolist's price. Therefore, the profit area is FGHJ, which is taken from the consumer surplus, leaving triangle JHB as an area that represents a further reduction in the consumer surplus but accrues to no one, not even the monopolist. Thus, the triangle JHB is a dead-weight loss representing neither a transfer to the monopolist from the consumer or a gain for society. It does represent resources that could have increased profits or that could have produced additional goods and services. There is an efficiency loss and a misallocation of resources.

3. Adverse effects of monopolists. As discussed earlier, the contrast can be made between perfect competition and monopoly with use of this same graph, namely:

	Perfect Competition	**Monopoly**
Price	Lower (*OF*)	Higher (*OG*)
Output	Higher (*OE*)	Lower (*OX*)

and the dead-weight loss to society of monopoly.

4. Thus, monopolies are likely to show some inefficiency relative to the efficient model of perfect competition.

PRICE DISCRIMINATION

If a monopoly or any imperfectly competitive firm had its way, it would charge each customer exactly the maximum price that each customer would be willing to pay. As a practical matter, this would be very difficult or impossible to do since the firm would not know the maximum price for each customer (the costs of identifying these differences would be high relative to any information revealed) and the policy would likely fall victim to some customers discovering they had paid more than others for the same product. Perhaps, you should not ask other passengers on an airline what they paid for their tickets unless you got a very good price.

Since the above suggests perfect price discrimination with perfect information about each consumer, we can still find many examples of price discrimination. For example, movie theaters may charge less for an afternoon (matinee) movie than for a movie in a more popular time such as evening or night. Senior citizens may be charged lower prices for lodging, museum attendance, and transportation. Some discounts simply promote better allocation of scarce commodities such as space on highways at commuter rush times or one's time. Price discrimination works best if the following conditions are operative:

1. Separate markets for consumers based on different price elasticities of demand. This really means that customers with higher price elasticities of demand have more choices of substitute products. Customers with lower price elasticities have less sensitivity to price of a particular product since they have fewer substitute choices.
2. There must not be opportunities for the resale of the product.
3. The price differences are not based on cost differences.
4. The firm is a price-maker—it has a pricing strategy that looks to charge a higher price and realize more profits.

QUICK CHECK QUESTION

Suppose that a private university has six colleges in the areas of liberal arts, veterinary medicine, business, education, law, and music. Also suppose that the college of veterinary medicine is one of only 16 in the entire United States and that the college of business competes with only three other business schools for its students. The liberal arts college competes with 1,000 other colleges in its standing in the nation. The college of music is ranked among the top three music schools. The colleges of education, law, and liberal arts are consistently undersubscribed, while the colleges of business, veterinary medicine, and music are consistently oversubscribed with many highly qualified students rejected.

What might you suggest as a pricing (tuition) policy for these six schools of the university. Explain. Is there any other additional information that you may wish to know? Why?

Answer: See Free-Response Review Answer, page 142.

TIP

You should be able to see the connection with tuition pricing and the relative degrees of price elasticity (and inelasticity) of demand. The greater the price elasticity (fewer substitutes), all other factors being equal, the better the opportunity to charge a higher price. (See the table in Chapter 5 on page 65).

TYPES OF MONOPOLIES AND THEIR POTENTIAL REGULATION

1. Natural monopoly
2. Unregulated monopoly
3. Regulated monopolies
   a. "fair" rate of return
   b. optimal pricing
   c. subsidized

Natural Monopoly

The original theory was that certain industries could best operate as monopolies, since to require or allow competition would negate the major economies of scale inherent in the nature (hence, natural) of these industries. For example, the electrical industry requires massive generating plants and a complex network of transmitting and distributing electrical energy. Therefore, smaller competitive firms would be less efficient and more costly. There would be unnecessary duplication of terminal facilities, electrical lines causing inefficiency. The traditional public policy for these natural monopolies was to create a power authority and/or a public service commission in each state that would approve the creation of a monopoly to an electrical generating private company for a particular region or city, but the company would yield the right to price its services without public utility commission approval. Recently, states have been experimenting with deregulation of the electric industry with respect to the generating function. The transmission and distribution functions would remain under control of a power or public authority.

Regulated Monopoly

In Figure 11.3 on page 139, the traditional regulation of a natural monopoly would be to allow prices that offer a "fair rate of return," which would allow a price of P_B (at the intersection of average cost with demand at point B). This price would be approximately the price of the perfectly competitive firm; it would "cover" average costs, including implicit costs that represent what would have been earned elsewhere with the same resources; so, the notion of a "fair return" follows. The utility firm needs to get a return on its investment at least equal to what investors could receive elsewhere at the same level of risk.

You will observe that as a result of this regulation, the price of P_B is lower than that of unregulated monopolist (P_A) but higher than that of a competitive firm (P_C). The output of the regulated monopolist (X_B) is less than that of the competitive firm (X_C) but greater than that of the unregulated monopolist (X_A). Thus, the regulation of the natural monopoly increases output and reduces price. However, in practice, the costs of the regulated electric utility were higher than expected with all sorts of inefficiencies present leading to calls for deregulation of the electrical generation function.

Fig. 11.3 Monopoly

Unregulated Monopoly

Again with reference to the same graph (Figure 11.3), we can see the different price and output effects of the unregulated monopolist. This monopolist is a profit maximizer. A profit maximizer prices and determines output at the level of output where MC = MR. This produces a price of P_A (higher than the competitive price of P_C) and an output of X_A, which is lower than that of the perfect competitor X_C. The profits of the monopolist are HP_AAG. Note then, the "fair return" price of P_B has zero economic profits.

Other Regulated Monopolies

Another possibility, at least in theory, would be to price at C (P_C), which is the price that is equal to MC. This would be the socially optimal price. When P = MC, as it does under perfect competition, the producer is having the extra cost incurred in producing one more unit "valued" at that cost by the consumer who is able to "coax" this extra unit from the producer or supplier. This represents efficiency at the margin of providing an additional unit of a good. Indeed, in antitrust cases, the question is often asked about the ability of the firm to consistently price goods *above* MC as an indication of monopoly power. However, if a producer sold goods at P_D with an output of X_C, the firm would incur a loss of (K-C) per unit of production times OX_C units of output. Since no profit-seeking firm would price at this level of losses, the government could provide subsidies for increasing units of output until the desired level of output (X_C) was attained.

Generally speaking, there is a tendency for less efficiency under monopoly since output is lower and price is higher as compared to perfect competition. Also, monopoly leads to dead-weight loss and resource misallocation.

TABLE 11.1

Characteristics of Monopolies*

Type	Price	Quantity	Comment
Unregulated Monopoly	P_A (Profit Max. Prices)	X_A	Price highest output, lowest economic profits.
Regulation of Natural Monopoly	P_B (Pricing for "fair return")	X_B Unregulated	Lower prices than monopolist. Higher output than unregulated monopolist. More efficient.
Regulation (subsidized)	P_C (Socially optimal price)	X_C	Lowest price, highest output of three types. Would require subsidy to move output to X_C with P_C.

*For price and quantity symbols, see Figure 11.3 on page 139.

TERMS

Herfindahl Index the sum of the squares of market shares of firms in a particular market or industry; used to measure the level of concentrated power of firms in an industry

Monopoly one firm constitutes the market or industry where there are no close substitutes available for consumers; a monopolist is a price-maker

Dead-Weight Loss the loss to society in the form of a reduction of consumer surplus from a competitive norm beyond any surplus reduction from a monopoly profit

Price-Discrimination this practice charges different customers with different prices for the same product

Natural Monopolies these are monopolies for which competition would prevent the benefits of economies of scale

FORMULAS

$$MR = MC, \text{ profit maximizing level of output}$$

$$\text{Lerner Index} = (P - MC)/P$$

Regulated Monopolies (pricing at):
  a. Fair Rate of Return:

  Price = average cost (at intersection of demand curve and average cost curve)

  b. Socially optimal price:

  Price = marginal cost (at the intersection of demand curve and marginal cost curve)

MULTIPLE-CHOICE REVIEW QUESTIONS

One firm constitutes the market

Fig. 11.4

For Fig. 11.4, answer Questions 1 and 2.

1. The total profits for this monopolist are identified by

(A) CEFL.
(B) ABJK.
(C) BCLF.
(D) CEHG.
(E) BEFJ.

2. The total costs for the monopolist are identified by

(A) CEFL.
(B) CEHG.
(C) ABJK.
(D) EOX_1F.
(E) BOX_1J.

Fig. 11.5

For Fig. 11.5, answer Questions 3, 4, and 5.

3. The socially optimal price would be

(A) P_3.
(B) P_2.
(C) P_1.
(D) P_4.
(E) None of the above.

4. The unregulated monopolist's price would be

(A) P_3.
(B) P_2.
(C) P_1.
(D) P_4.
(E) None of the above.

5. The "fair return" price of the regulated monopolist would be

(A) P_3.
(B) P_2.
(C) P_1.
(D) P_4.
(E) None of the above.

Fig. 11.6

For Fig. 11.6, answer questions 6, 7, and 8.

6. The original consumer surplus is

(A) ABG.
(B) ACF.
(C) BCEF.
(D) COKF.
(E) GEF.

7. After the monopolist enters, the consumer surplus is

(A) ABG.
(B) ACF.
(C) BCEG.
(D) COKF.
(E) GEF.

8. The dead-weight loss is

(A) ABG.
(B) ACF.
(C) BCEG.
(D) COKF.
(E) GEF.

Multiple-Choice Review Answers

| 1. **(B)** | 3. **(A)** | 5. **(B)** | 7. **(A)** |
| 2. **(E)** | 4. **(C)** | 6. **(B)** | 8. **(E)** |

FREE-RESPONSE REVIEW QUESTION

The free response question for this chapter is found inside the chapter. The question is based on price discrimination, page 137.

Free-Response Review Answers

Because of the greater number of choices for students and the consequent undersubscription in education, law, and liberal arts schools, and the converse for business, veterinary, and music schools, one might infer lower price elasticity of demand (relatively inelastic), for the latter group because of few good substitutes. Thus, we might apply the economics of price discrimination to charge higher tuition for the colleges of business, veterinary medicine, and music. We might want to know tuition rates at competing universities.

Imperfect Competition: Monopolistic Competition, Oligopoly

CHAPTER

- Monopolistic competition and non-price competition
- Differentiated products
- Inefficiency
- Price > marginal cost
- Barriers to entry and exit
- Oligopolies and interdependence
- Excess profits and price-makers
- Game theory and strategies on prices/output
- Nash equilibrium

INTRODUCTION

In the two previous chapters, we have reviewed the "bookends" of market structure: perfect competition and monopoly. Even though we have identified different forms of monopoly, monopoly is most importantly characterized for its monopoly pricing power (its sustainability of maintaining price over marginal cost) and its inefficiency compared to perfect competition. That is, the monopolist charges a higher price and restricts output to maximize profits as compared to the perfect competitor. Also, these restrictive actions of the monopolist as "price-maker" result in a "dead-weight" loss to society. The monopolist is the prototype of a rent seeker causing misallocation of resources away from more productive uses.

Monopoly is the very antithesis of perfect competition. You are advised to refer to the comparative characteristics of different market structures in Chapter 9 on market structures. Perfect competition provides a theoretical model. Firms and industries become more or less competitive as their behavior approaches or departs from the competitive model. Perfect competition sets the standard for efficiency. Thus, oligopolies and monopolistic competitors are inefficient since they are imperfect competitors. Monopolistic competition develops or fosters excess capacity in which there is underutilization of resources or inefficiency. Oligopolies, collusive and noncollusive, tend to set prices in such a way that P > MC, which is the standard identification and measure of monopoly pricing and rent seeking.

This chapter on monopolistic competition and oligopoly provides more real-world models and examples in between the bookends of perfect competition and monopoly. There are many more monopolistic competitors than there are oligopolies but oligopolies represent the most dominant industries in terms of market share, assets and control over prices, outputs, and allocation of resources. They are the best examples of "price-makers" and "rent seekers."

THINGS TO KNOW

Based on the most frequently asked questions on previous Advanced Placement exams, the following are the most important concepts. In the balance of this chapter, we will expand on these and other concepts and examples.

1. In the long run, monopolistic competition will be inefficient mainly due to excess capacity.
2. There is a long run tendency under monopolistic competition for zero economic profits. However, zero economic profits do not imply the efficiency of perfect competition (long run). The monopolistic competitor has zero economic profits when average total cost (ATC) equals price at the profit maximizing level of output but not at minimum average total cost, implying the inefficiency due to excess capacity as identified in number one above.
3. Inefficiency (allocative inefficiency) of monopolistic competition is also identified by price > marginal cost (P > MC). Unlike perfect competition, there is a tendency to price goods and services at a higher level than the costs to produce additional units.
4. Monopolistic competition is also inefficient compared to perfect competition since the monopolistically competitive firm restricts output level in order to maximize profits. In other words, optimal output is at the level at which MR = MC, which results in a higher price and less output as compared to perfect competition in the long run.
5. While the barriers to entry in the industry are not as formidable under monopolistic competition as under oligopoly, barriers to entry become a device for some monopolistic competitors to earn economic profits in the long run. Remember, as in number 2 above, there is a tendency for profits to be zero in the long run.
6. Monopolistic competition is characterized by non-price competition (advertising, unique products, warranties, coupons, appeal to brand or store name, etc.), differentiated products, innovation, large number of buyers and sellers, few barriers to entry and exit.
7. The profit-maximizing output and price for a firm under monopolistic competition is that level at which MR = MC. Also, unique to monopolistic competition is the long run tendency for zero economic profits but with the ATC curve tangent to the demand function at the level of output at which MR = MC. However, ATC is higher than the minimum average cost (see Figure 12.2).

8. Under oligopoly, there is more likely to be *interdependence* of the firms as contrasted to the price-takers of perfectly competitive markets and the price-makers of monopoly power. This, at least, holds for the noncollusive model of oligopoly. It maintains itself by rivals matching decreases in prices but not matching price increases. Even the collusive oligopolists are somewhat constrained in price-making by the interdependence of the market.

9. Oligopolists, like other imperfect competitors, may charge higher prices than needed to maximize profits. This is often reflected in monopoly pricing power or pricing where P > MC.

10. When merger activity increases, the structure, behavior (conduct), and performance of oligopolists comes into play on policy decisions. Refer to Chapter 11 on monopoly for pricing power and rent seeking.

11. Oligopolists can be noncollusive or collusive. In both models, an action of one rival is interdependent on the action of other rivals.

MONOPOLISTIC COMPETITION

There are many sellers and buyers under monopolistic competition; thus, it is difficult for any firms to emerge as price-makers or to seek rents. In order for a firm to gain an advantage in a market, it is often necessary to innovate or otherwise find a niche in the market. In other words, if a monopolistic competitor is able to distinguish its products or services from rivals, the firm will be successful. Most of any success for monopolistic competitors derives from non-price competition, such as brand name, store name, shoppers' cards, rewards for frequent customers, special amenities in lodging, etc. Wegman's Food Markets, a large and highly successful chain of stores in upstate New York, is known for its ability to attract customers on the basis of its varied and attractive displays of food and merchandise. The customers are not interested only in prices but almost everything else. Since the barriers to entry are relatively weak, rivals must continuously innovate to survive. There are many other fine supermarkets in upstate New York, including Tops, P&C, Price Chopper, A&P, and others. There is a highly competitive atmosphere with customers quite sensitive to prices since there are many good substitutes available and a relative ease of entry into the industry. Thus, each of these fine competitors has to find ways to distract the customers from prices and attract them to specialty features such as in-store brands of high quality, in-store bakeries, bulk food, etc.

These firms have downward sloping demand curves and they are characterized, as in monopolies, by price > marginal revenue and price > marginal cost.

Short Run

In the short run, there are dynamic shifts in demand in an intense competitive environment. Thus, we can expect that some firms will realize profits as demand for their products increases, sometimes at the expense of rival firms, some of which will incur losses even to the extent of leaving the industry. Thus, in the short run, we can illustrate both situations with the following graphs:

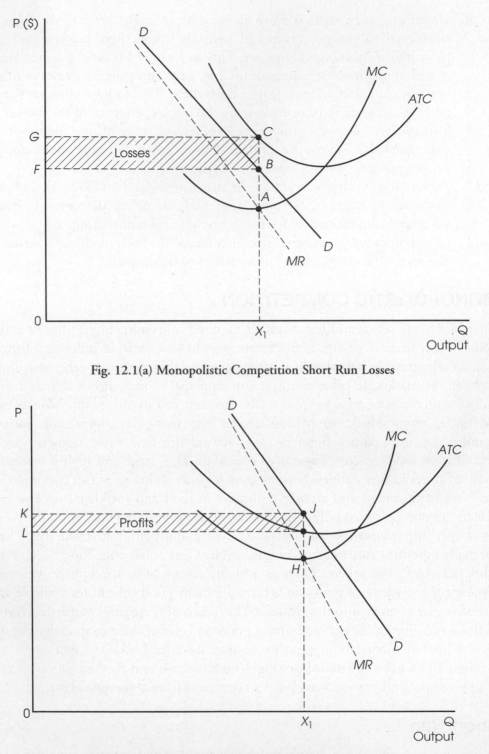

Fig. 12.1(a) Monopolistic Competition Short Run Losses

Fig. 12.1(b) Monopolistic Competition Short Run Profits

In Figure 12.1(a), the firm incurs losses in the short run; in contrast, the firm realizes profits in the short run in Figure 12.1(b). The reader may wish to infer that the difference is in the location of the demand (DD) function with the assumption that the cost functions (MC, ATC) are identical in both graphs. That is, as demand increases for a firm's product, the demand function shifts so that the juxtaposition of the new demand curve and average total cost (ATC) produces a profit as in Figure 12.1(b). Conversely, in Figure 12.1(a), a rival firm enters the industry (weak barriers to entry) and "takes" sales from the firm illustrated with the result of losses, in other words, the demand curve shifts down (decrease in demand) with the result of losses.

Monopolistic competition is very dynamic. An example would be the many competing e-commerce firms in recent years. Initially, the firms and their stockholders were reaping enormous profits. More recently, a number of these firms were forced to leave the industry; they were simply crowded out by other firms. Think of the losing firms being represented by Figure 12.1(a) and the successful firms by Figure 12.1(b). Also, understand that the normal or traditional way of illustrating these situations does not fully apply to e-commerce. Many e-commerce firms, except for those with exciting initial public offerings (IPOs), were not realizing profits or had very high price/earnings ratio, yet investors were interested in their stocks because of their potential or the sense that their stock prices would continue to soar to new highs.

Usually, on AP exams you will be asked to identify (on a graph) the presence of profits or losses and which rectangular area is the measure of total losses or profits at the optimal (best) output level. The best output level is that output at which MR = MC. Thus, in Figure 12.1(a), there are losses at the best output, OX_1, or the output at which total losses are minimized in the short run. The total loss rectangle is identified on the graph as GCBF. The distance, CB, is the measure of the per unit loss at OX_1 or C-B. The per unit loss times the number of units of output, OX_1, yields the total loss rectangle. In Figure 12.1(b), there are profits at the best output, OX_1 (the ATC curve is below the demand function at the level of output, OX_1), which is the output level at which MR = MC. This is the output that would maximize total profits. It is measured by the rectangle KJIL. The best output and its price, OL, are located by first finding the intersection of MR and MC, which is identified on Figure 12.1(b) as "H". From H, a line is drawn perpendicular to the horizontal axis at OX_1 (best output). From H, also, a vertical line is drawn to the intersection of the ATC curve (I) and to the intersection of the demand function at J. Drawing a horizontal line from J to the vertical axis identifies the price (OK) as the price at best output. The related per unit cost is OL (distance between J and I). Thus, the reader needs to know that MR = MC is the level of best or optimal output and how to identify losses or profits at that level of output.

Long Run Equilibrium—Monopolistic Competition

Since the nature of monopolistic competition is one of constant change, it is quite difficult to attain the status of long run equilibrium in practice, if not also in theory. However, a long run tendency emerges that allows us some ability to have a standard against which we can compare and contrast monopolistic competition with other forms of market structure, particularly perfect competition, which is definable in theory. We can then say that there is some inefficiency in monopolistic competition when compared to efficiency in perfect competition. This comparison has many applications in practice, such as, antitrust, market concentration, and innovation versus barriers to entry, etc.

There is a long run tendency for monopolistic competition to produce at zero or normal economic profits but not at minimum average total cost. This is an indication of some inefficiency in monopolistic competition as compared to perfect competition where long run equilibrium is at the efficient level—price equals minimum average total cost. The basic difference is that producing at less than minimum average total cost reveals inefficiency mainly in the form of excess capacity or underutilization of resources. One might visualize four gasoline stations on the four corners of a busy highway, an intersection. The total demand, on average, for gasoline is considerably less than the available supply; therefore, each station is not able to utilize all of its pump capacity. Each station does not sell enough gasoline to spread its high fixed costs over the gallons of gasoline sold, so the stations quickly exhaust any economies of scale and do not reach minimum average total costs. This is a classic case of underutilization or excess capacity. Suppose that two gasoline stations would have the right capacity to handle the demand. They could then spend the fixed costs over a greater number of gallons and achieve some efficiency. With easy entry, there tend to be too many competitors given a certain demand. This is illustrated in Figure 12.2 below.

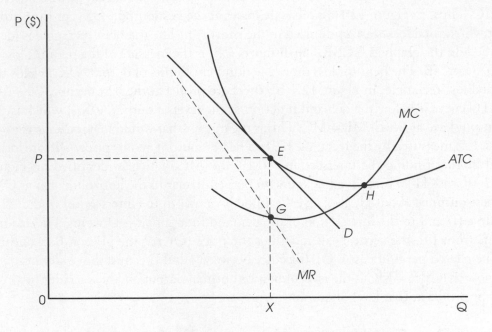

Fig. 12.2 Monopolistic Competition* Long Run Tendency
*Long run tendency to zero economic profits

In this graph, the best or optimal output is at OX_{mc} where $MR = MC$. Economic profits are zero or normal since the point of tangency of ATC and the demand curve (D) at E coincides with the level of best output ($MR = MC$). However, this point of tangency is higher on the demand curve than the minimum level of ATC at H. Therefore, the monopolistic competition is not achieving efficiency. The comparable point of efficiency for a perfect competitor would be at H with a higher output and a lower price. Also, observe that $P > MC$ and $P > MR$. These are indications that there is some monopoly pricing power ($P > MC$) and some pricing strategy or policy ($P > MR$). To summarize the differences between monopolistic competition and perfect competition, review the table that follows.

TABLE 12.1

Long Run Equilibrium

	Pure Competition	Monopolistic Competition
Profits (Economic)	Zero; Price = Minimum ATC	Zero; Price = ATC (*not* at minimum)
Efficiency/Inefficiency	Efficient = Market prices weed out the inefficient firms	Inefficient (excess capacity, underutilization of capacity)
Product Differentiation	None. Products are homogeneous (identical in each product market)	Differentiation is necessary for survival.
Price/Non-Price Competition	*Only price* competition. Firms are "price-takers."	Non-price competition is common.
P and MC	P = MC (socially optimal) efficient allocation of resources. Price (consumers) = MC (produces at extra cost)	P > MC. Allocatively inefficient. Consumer pays more than extra cost of production.
P and MR	P = MR. No pricing strategy. All firms take prices from the market.	P > MR. Pricing strategy. Some extent of price making.

SUMMARY: MONOPOLISTIC COMPETITION

1. Relatively easy entry
2. Differentiated products
3. Advertising, non-price competition
4. Inefficient, excess capacity
5. Large number of buyers and sellers
6. Long run equilibrium: zero economic profits
7. Allocatively inefficient: price > MC
8. P > MR: pricing strategy, price-makers
9. The most common (but not most dominant) type of market structure in the United States

OLIGOPOLY: THE NON-COLLUSIVE MODEL

The key to understanding oligopoly is the "interdependence" of rival oligopolists. This defining characteristic of oligopoly can be manifest in collusive as well as in noncollusive markets. In non-collusive markets rivals may base their strategies, in part, on the anticipated reactions of other firms. For example, one firm may want to raise its prices in order to increase profits. However, if a second firm is expected to lower its prices to undercut the sales of the first firm, then the first firm may not raise its prices in the first place. The second firm may employ a similar strategy depending on the anticipated reactions of the first firm. This noncollusive interdependence may actually lead to lower prices or, at least, no increases in prices. It may be apparent to the reader that the firms would want to have an understanding that both firms would increase prices to maximize their profits. However, one firm could cheat on the agreement and corner more profits for itself. The firms could have a "price war" in which there would be the possibility of both firms being worse off, even to the extent of substantial losses. However, if one firm raises its prices, the rival firm may not match the price increase so that it could capture market share from the other firm. Thus, it is assumed for noncollusive oligopolists that, often, rivals will follow (match) price decreases by a firm but not follow (match) price increases.

Other Oligopoly Models

Theoretically, business may be defined as Nobel Prize economist George Stigler described it "as the whole set of activities designed to overcome barriers to profits." The following are examples of other models of oligopoly that are evidenced by structure and behavior of oligopolistic markets:

1. Price leadership. If there is a price leader or dominant firm among other oligopolists, the leader can "set" price to maximize profits and the other firms simply price at the same level since they are virtually unable to gain market share by maintaining their previous prices. The other firms in the oligopoly market face smaller profits given their lower volume of production.
2. Cooperative noncollusive activities. Here there are tacit understandings about the value of limited advertising, promotion, etc. Much of this is based on the *interdependence* of oligopolists.
3. Collusive oligopolies. These oligopolists may decide that if "you can't beat them competitively, you might join them." That is, rivals may divide markets among themselves according to regional areas (you cover the Northeast; I'll cover the Southwest, etc.), or product specializations. Collusive activities also include agreements to charge the same or higher prices. An airline may enter a contract with an airplane producer if the airplane producer agrees *not* to produce airplanes for other airlines or to charge them higher prices. Many such collusive activities are illegal in the United States. Cartels, such as OPEC (Organization of Petroleum Exporting Countries) may have production limits or price agreements among its members in an effort to set or control prices. These agreements can be maintained most easily if there are few members and if the cartel controls a major share of the supply of the product. Cartels are clearly price-makers and not price-takers.

OLIGOPOLY: GAME THEORY

The interdependence of oligopolists can be illustrated in the context of a game in which the rivals attempt to maximize their profits. However, any particular strategy employed by one of the players may result in lower profits depending upon the strategy used by the other player. On the other hand, one firm finds that it can develop a dominant strategy that will increase its profits regardless of what the competitive firm does. For example, in the competition between the top two American based automobile firms, General Motors (GM) makes a special offer to sell its vehicles to the general public at the special discount prices enjoyed by its employees for a limited time. Will the strategy become dominant? That is, will GM profits be increased regardless of whether the Ford Motor Company follows suit? Or will GM's strategy be successful only if Ford does *not* offer similar discounts? This is *not* an empirically determined solution.

The following are hypothetical numbers which represent profits in a payoff matrix.

General Motors (GM)

	Discount	No Discount
Discount	GM 210 F 240	GM 120 F 300
No Discount	GM 300 F 150	GM 240 F 270

Ford (F)

The dominant strategy for GM is to offer the discount. If GM gives the discount and Ford also offers a similar discount, GM has a profit of 210. If GM does not discount the price of its vehicles and Ford does discount, GM's profits are only 120 (210 > 120 GM discount). If Ford does *not* use the discount strategy, then GM records 300 as a profit with the discount strategy but only 240 if GM chooses not to use the discount (300 > 240 GM uses discount strategy).

Therefore, General Motors would use the strategy of a discount whether or not Ford provides the same discount. General Motors has a dominant strategy, that of providing the employee discount to all its employers. A similar outcome would be realized if Ford also provided the employee discount for buyers of its cars. For example, if Ford discounts and GM follows suit, Ford earns 240 but if Ford does not discount its vehicles while GM does discount, Ford's profits are only 150. Since 240 > 150 Ford uses discount strategy, regardless of what GM does. Ford has a dominant strategy also. A *Nash equilibrium* represents a different kind of game theory in which the strategy of each player is the best choice based on the strategy of the other player. This was named after John Nash, a mathematician, who developed the theory and later received the Nobel Prize in *economics* (1994) for it. The life of John Nash was popularized in the movie "A Beautiful Mind."

In the matrix below, the number representing profits for Ford (F) in the lower right-hand corner has been changed from $270 to $340 as compared to the previous matrix. This change indicates that Ford no longer has a dominant strategy but rather bases its decision to discount or not to discount its vehicles on the strategy of General Motors (GM). In both matrices, if GM discounts and Ford follows suit, Ford profits of $240 are greater than the $150 in profits it would have earned if the corporation had not offered a discount. So if GM offers a discount, Ford's strategy

TIP

For a less complicated way to interpret the changes in the pay-off matrix, follow the profits for Ford by reading vertically down the matrix. For example, Ford's profits decrease from $240 to $150 as it moves from a discount policy while GM maintains a discount policy. You can follow the profits for GM by reading horizontally across the matrix. For example, GM's profits decrease from $210 to $120 while Ford maintains a discount policy.

would be to offer a discount. However, this strategy would change if GM adopts a "no discount" policy. If Ford had a dominant strategy of offering a discount regardless of what strategy GM pursues, it would decrease its profits if GM offered no discount. Ford's profits would be $300 instead of the $340 it would have earned if it had based its strategy on following the policy of GM. The failure of a player to have a dominant strategy results in a *Nash equilibrium*, where a player's best choice is based on the strategy of another player. In this case, if GM discounted, Ford would discount, and if GM did not offer a discount, Ford would follow suit. In following suit in each situation, Ford would improve its profits as opposed to following a policy of only offering a discount. GM's dominant strategy of discounting would remain as in the matrix on page 151.

		General Motors (GM)			
		Discount		No Discount	
Ford (F)	Discount	GM	210	GM	120
		F	240	F	300
	No Discount	GM	300	GM	240
		F	150	F	340

SUMMARY: OLIGOPOLY

1. Formidable barriers to entry
2. Differentiated or similar product
3. Interdependence
4. Few firms, controlling major shares of market
5. Allocatively inefficient: price > marginal cost, excess profits
6. Price > marginal revenue indicating pricing strategy and non-price competition
7. Price-makers
8. Collusive activities and cooperative arrangements
9. The dominant type of market structure in U.S. industry
10. An oligopolist's actions may be influenced by the likely actions of rivals. Also, firms are more likely to follow a price decrease but *not* follow a price increase.

TERMS

Monopolistic Competition this form of market structure is characterized by many medium-sized firms that need to innovate and differentiate their products in both price and non-price competition

Oligopoly this form of market structure is characterized by relatively few sellers who act interdependently and/or collusively to be price-makers. There are strong barriers to entry and exit

Inefficiency this is the expected outcome of monopolistic competition derived from underutilizing capacity

Game Theory this theory involves choices made by players based on the reaction expected by opponents as in oligopolies

Nash Equilibrium game theory in which the best choice for a player is based on the strategy of another player

FORMULAS

MR = MC profit maximizing criterion for monopolistic competition and oligopoly

P > MC relationship between price (P) and marginal cost (MC) for both monopolistic competition and oligopoly

P = average cost tendency for monopolistic competition in the long run

MULTIPLE-CHOICE REVIEW QUESTIONS

1. Which of the following is a characteristic of monopolistic competition?

   (A) P > MC.
   (B) Efficiency.
   (C) Mostly price competition.
   (D) P = MR.
   (E) Homogenous or similar products.

2. Which of the following is *not* a characteristic of oligopoly?

   (A) P = MC.
   (B) Price-maker.
   (C) Strong barriers to entry.
   (D) Few firms.
   (E) P > MR.

3. Which of the following is a characteristic of monopolistic competition?

   (A) Economically efficient in the long run.
   (B) Pricing at minimum ATC in long run.
   (C) Excess capacity.
   (D) Very few competitors.
   (E) Most dominant market structure in United States.

4. Which of the following illustrates the demand curve facing an oligopolist when rival firms follow a price decrease but *not* a price increase?

   (A) Perfectly horizontal demand curve.
   (B) Highly inelastic demand curve.
   (C) Highly elastic demand curve.
   (D) A demand curve that is tangent to the average total cost curve.
   (E) A demand curve consisting of two discontinuous segments.

Multiple-Choice Review Answers

1. **(A)**   2. **(A)**   3. **(C)**   4. **(E)**

FREE-RESPONSE REVIEW QUESTION

1. Compare perfect competition to monopolistic competition in terms of efficiency.

Free-Response Review Answer

1. In the long run under perfect competition, the firm demonstrates efficiency in the following ways:

   A. price is at minimum average cost which means the consumer obtains goods and services at the lowest costs of production. It also means the producer must sell at this low price or not be able to compete with other firms who sell at this market price. This demonstrates efficiency.

   B. Zero economic profits or normal profits. These profits include the implicit costs or that the producer (firm) is being paid the value of its resources if they were employed elsewhere. This is just a minimum payment to the firm to ensure continuing service.

   C. Price is equal to marginal cost. This is the socially optimal price. The consumer is able to coax out one or more units of a good from the producer at exactly the marginal cost of producing that unit.

2. In the long run under monopolistic competition, the firm is inefficient compared to the perfect competitor in the following ways:

   A. Price is at average cost but *not* at minimum average cost. This is an indication of inefficiency resulting from under-utilization of capacity or excess capacity.

   B. Price is greater than marginal cost; thus, socially optimal (efficient) pricing $(P = MC)$ is not attained.

Resource Markets with Applications to Labor

- Product markets and resource markets: the connections
- Marginal revenue product
- Derived demand
- Wage and income inequality
- Market imperfections

- Rents and transfer earnings
- Monopsony vs. competitive labor markets
- Determination of wages and compensating wage differentials
- Backward bending supply curve

CONNECTIONS BETWEEN PRODUCT MARKETS AND RESOURCE MARKETS

There is a symmetry between product markets and resource markets; further, there are direct connections between the two markets. In Chapter 8, Costs, Production, Supply, we discussed total physical product, average physical product, and marginal physical product (TPP, APP, MPP) in addition to their relationship to costs, especially for APP and MPP compared to AC and MC (see Figure 8.1 in Chapter 8 for the symmetry). The product markets and the resource markets are most directly linked by derived demand. For example, the demand for shoemakers (resource/labor market) is derived from the demand for shoes (product/shoe market). This relationship is significant since it ties together (not necessarily in a proportional manner) the elasticity of product markets with that of resource markets. Theoretically, it sets limits on the demand for pay increases by labor. Moreover, income distribution to labor depends on labor's contribution to increases in productivity—increases in marginal physical productivity became the basis for wage or salary increases. Of course, there are many other factors that can distort this basis for income distribution, including imperfect markets, discrimination, changes in product markets (including pay for workers), investment in human capital, etc. These factors will be discussed in this chapter as we apply the basic economic concepts of resource markets to labor.

Much of the material of resource markets is somewhat mechanical if not abstract. That is, the basic concepts can be explained in equations and graphs. The good side of this approach is that the student can condense much of what has to be learned into a few important relationships. The applications seem to flow easily from the knowledge of these basic concepts. For example, many of the questions on resource markets from past AP exams require the knowledge of marginal revenue product

(MRP) as equal to marginal physical product times the marginal revenue or price of the product. The firm wants to pay labor no more than it contributes to the value of the product at the margin of adding one more unit of labor. So, if either the productivity of labor (MPP) increases, or the price of any good produced by labor increases, the MRP will increase. If we know that MRP equals the demand for labor, then with the increase of the MPP or the price of the product, the demand curve will shift to the right (an increase). Thus, the basic relationship of the marginal productivity of labor to the price of the good produced is important.

THINGS TO KNOW

Based on the most frequently asked questions on previous AP exams, the following are the most important concepts. In the balance of this chapter, we will expand on these and other concepts and examples.

1. Extending the knowledge of production, costs, and supply of Chapter 8, we need to know that marginal revenue product (MRP) of a resource such as labor represents the demand for labor. It is a downward sloping demand curve that tells the firm hiring labor what labor contributes to the revenue of the firm at the margin of each unit of labor (L) added. Thus, $MRP_L = MPP_L \times MR_x$ (or P_x in perfectly competitive product markets), where x = product produced. If product price is constant at all levels of output, we know that it is a perfectly competitive market.

2. Number 1 above tells us what labor contributes to the revenue of the firm; now, we need to know the related cost of labor. Essentially, marginal factor cost (MFC) is the cost of each additional unit of labor hired by the firm. In perfectly competitive labor markets, the price of labor is constant and MFC = price of labor, average cost of labor or the wage rate. $MFC = P_L, AC_L$ or W_L.

3. If demand for labor is the marginal revenue productivity (MRP) of labor, and if the cost of hiring additional units of labor is the marginal factor cost (MFC) of labor, then the firm maximizes its profits in the hire of labor by continuing to hire labor as long as MRP > MFC up to the level of hiring at which MRP = MFC. This is the summary of the criterion for profit maximization for the hiring of one resource such as labor.

4. Criterion for profit maximization in the hire of more than one resource:

$$\frac{MRP_L}{MFC_L} = \frac{MRP_K}{MFC_K} \cdots \frac{MRP_N}{MFC_N} = 1$$

P_L or wage rate can substitute for MFC if there is a perfectly competitive resource market. (L = labor; K = capital; N = number of resources).

5. Criterion for cost minimization (least-cost) for more than one resource:

$$\frac{MPP_L}{MFC_L} = \frac{MPP_K}{MFC_K} \cdots \frac{MPP_N}{MFC_N}$$

P_L or wage rate can be substituted for MFC if there is a perfectly competitive resource market.

6. Derived demand. The demand for a resource is derived from the demand for the product produced, in part, by the resource. This concept, in turn, assists us in determining the wage elasticity of demand for labor. We will extend this discussion later in this chapter.

7. Government and market imperfections or interference with resource markets. This is about price ceilings and price floors; also, we examine the effects of trade unions and buyers of labor in a single market for labor. By name, these are imperfections in resource markets, including monopsonies that lower wage rates and hire fewer workers than competitive markets.

8. The bases for wage inequality. There are usually a few questions about this on the Advanced Placement exam. The factors responsible include risk (some jobs, such as skyscraper repair, carry higher levels of risk), attractiveness of job, human capital investment, discrimination, immobility, etc. We will discuss these factors in this chapter. Additionally, we will discuss "rents," those payments received by workers that are in excess of what they could have earned elsewhere or what would minimally be necessary to attract or maintain workers. When workers receive in pay what they could have earned elsewhere, they are paid the value of the market or transfer earnings.

9. Factors that cause shifts in demand and supply for resources. For example, an increase in wage rates by a firm could attract more workers to that firm.

DERIVED DEMAND: WAGE ELASTICITY OF DEMAND

As noted above, the demand for labor (resource) is derived from the demand for the product that labor helped produce. The three laws of derived demand are based on the definition of wage elasticity of demand:

$$\frac{\%\Delta \text{ Quantity Demanded of Labor}}{\%\Delta \text{ wage rate}}$$

where Δ = change in.

The three laws of derived demand are:

1. **The higher the price elasticity of demand for the product, the higher the wage elasticity of demand.** For example, in the 1960s and part of the 1970s, the Big Three of the automobile industry—Ford, Chrysler, and General Motors—produced over 90 percent of the automobiles purchased in the United States. Further, General Motors had the dominant share of the market and clearly was the price leader. Thus, the price inelasticity (few substitutes and similar prices) allowed General Motors to administer prices to allow generous profits. The only real constraint was a change in consumer income. Therefore, the auto industry could afford to pay the union its demands or the industry had an inelastic resource to demands for wage increases. The Big Three could "pass on" much of the increases of wages to consumers who are more affected by their rising incomes than the rising prices of the autos. However, with the increasing competition from automo-

bile companies of Japan, Germany, and other countries starting in the late 1970s and continuing into the twenty-first century, price elasticity of demand increased dramatically (the Big Three could no longer set prices since there were many lower-priced, fuel-efficient cars from overseas). Adding to the competitive intensity, many European and Japanese auto manufacturers began to produce their cars in the United States, hiring American workers and operating within the U.S. tariff area. An accompanying increase in the wage elasticity of demand also took place. The Big Three could no longer pass on union wage demands to the consumers in the form of price tag increases on their products. The history of the modern automobile industry affords us with many applications of the economics of product markets, resource markets, and elasticity.

2. **The higher the proportion of labor costs relative to total costs of production, the higher will be the wage elasticity of demand.** If we compare the higher education industry to the oil refinery industry, we can note the significance of the proportion of labor costs to total costs. In higher education, even with rising use of computer technology, usually 80 to 85 percent of the total budget of a college or university is in the form of salaries and wages, including fringe benefits (an ever-increasing proportion of total labor costs). Indeed, the increase in computer use has required additional labor costs for computer personnel. If we keep in mind the nature of derived demand, a relatively high labor cost would mean that firms would be resistant to a more than moderate pay increase. In the oil refining industry, labor costs are a relatively small proportion of total costs. Thus, even a more than modest pay increase is more likely to be tolerated as contrasted with the higher education industry.

3. **The greater the number of substitute resources available and the degree to which they are substitutable, the higher will be the wage elasticity of demand.** Related to this factor is the time period. We are subsuming the time period into the "greater availability of substitutes." That is, a longer time period typically allows the development of more substitutes, such as robotic or automated machinery. However, at least some resources are complements with other resources, as in the example of capital development of resources often requiring some additional labor to be hired. There is in this general discussion of derived demand the significance of more substitutes leading to more competition that, in turn, is reflected in greater elasticity. There is a symmetry on these linkages between product markets and resource markets; the more a firm can identify resources to substitute for labor, the more resistant (elastic, sensitive) the firm can be to suggestions for wage increases.

THE DEMAND FOR A RESOURCE (LABOR)

The demand for labor is derived from the demand for the product. However, this is not a *per se* demand; firms do not determine the wage rates they are willing to pay only on labor's physical contribution to the final product, such as the marginal physical product (MPP), but also on what this extra product will sell for in the marketplace. Thus, the worker could be very productive or actually increase her marginal products, but if the product price decreases, her effort might not be fully valued in any consideration of a wage increase. (Remember: Marginal Revenue Product, MRP, = Marginal Physical Product, MPP, times Marginal Revenue$_x$ or price$_x$ where x = product). To illustrate the demand for a resource (labor), see Figure 13.1.

Fig. 13.1 **Demand for Labor (Resource)**

The demand curve is downward sloping to the right, which demonstrates the inverse relationship between the wage rate and the quantity of labor demanded by the firm. If the wage rate is at $11, the firm is willing to hire X_1 units of labor. At a wage rate of $5, the firm is willing to hire a larger quantity, X_2 units of labor.

The firm's demand schedule is equal to the marginal revenue productivity (MRP) of labor as defined above. Think of this schedule as an indication to the firm of the addition to the firm's revenue with each additional unit of labor employed. Think of the wage rate at the point of deciding to hire one more unit of labor as the marginal factor cost (MFC). Thus, the firm that wants to maximize its profits in the hire of labor will continue to hire labor as long as the marginal revenue product (MRP_L) is greater than the marginal factor cost MFC_L up to the level of hiring at which the $MRP_L = MFC_L$. First, we will look at a perfectly competitive labor market.

Perfectly Competitive Labor Market

In a perfectly competitive labor market, the wage rate is determined in the market where all buyers and sellers of a particular type of labor, such as economists, meet. Each year, the Applied Social Services Association has a placement service in the city where its convention is held. Buyers (universities and other institutions) hold interviews with sellers (economists interested in securing research and teaching positions).

While this is not an example of a perfectly competitive market, it does suggest a market or a place where buyers and sellers of a labor service meet. A firm that hires labor in a perfectly competitive labor (resource) market must pay its hired workers the going or market-determined wage rate. The firm is a price-taker as in the symmetrical case of the firm in a perfectly competitive product market. In other words, the firm cannot afford to pay a higher wage rate than the market-determined wage and if the firm wants to pay less, any potential workers would simply move to another employer who pays the market wage rate. This is illustrated below in Figure 13.2.

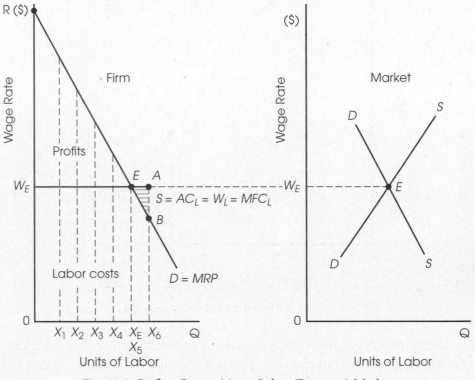

Fig. 13.2 Perfect Competition—Labor (Resource) Market

The hiring employer (firm) must pay the going wage of W_E, that is, the firm is a price (wage)-taker. Therefore, $W_E = AC_L = \text{Supply} = MFC_L$, where L = labor. Since the wage rate is dictated by the market, it becomes a perfectly horizontal supply (S) function, which means that the average cost of labor (AC_L) or the wage rate equals the marginal factor cost of labor (MFC_L). Regardless of the number of units of labor the firm wants to hire, the wage rate of labor stays the same—at X, $X_2, X_3 \ldots X_6$, the wage rate remains at the market given rate of W_E. Thus, the firm will continue to hire workers as long as the marginal revenue product (MRP) for each additional unit is greater than the associated marginal factor cost (MFC). For *each* of X_1, X_2, X_3, X_4, the $MRP_L > MFC_L$. That means with a wage rate of W_E, the firm adds more revenue at the margin of an additional unit of labor than it adds to its cost. This addition of smaller and smaller units of profits continues as long as $MRP_L > MFC_L$. At the level of hiring for which $MRP_L > MFC_L$, (level of X_5, or five units of labor), profits will be maximized in the hire of labor. You will note on Figure 13.2, the total profit triangle of REW_E and the total labor cost rectangle of W_EEX_E0. The total profit is the difference between MRP_L and MFC_L (or wage rate in this perfectly competitive market) for each unit of labor up to the five units hired at equilibrium ($MRP_L = MFC_L$). The cost rectangle is the result of the wage rate (W_E) times the number of units of labor hired (X_E or X_5). Also, observe what happens if the employer wants to hire one additional unit (the X_6 unit) of labor. This would reduce the total profits by the area of EAB. On Advanced Placement exams, there are often questions based on the above. For example, a bookstore observes that for each additional security guard hired, there is some reduction in the number of books stolen. Using an average retail price of books, the store devised the following schedule. The security guards are paid $120 per day (eight-hour shift times $15 an hour).

TABLE 13.1

Security Guards

No. of Guards Added	Total Value of Books Saved	MRP_L
1	$800	800
2	1,100	300
3	1,300	200
4	1,400	100
5	1,450	50

A table like the one above may not even use the term MRP or marginal revenue product; instead, the table heading might be "Total Value Produced or Saved." You need to think of total value saved as total revenue or total revenue product, and also, you need to devise or construct another column such as the one on this table (Table 13.1) headed marginal revenue product. For example, you would take the difference between zero guards added and one guard added as MRP and the result would be $800 in row 1 as MRP. In the second row, MRP would be $300 (difference between total value saved with one guard added, and total value saved with a second guard added or $800 and $100 or $300 as MRP). Thus, the bookstore would continue adding guards as long as the $MRP_L > MFC_L$ for each additional guard hired. At the third guard added, the MRP of $200 is still greater than the $120 paid for the guard's work; thus, the bookstore should add a third guard. What would happen if the store decided to hire a fourth guard? The marginal value of $100 saved is *less than* the marginal cost of the fourth guard ($120). Thus, the firm should hire three additional guards, but not a

TIP

The firm wants to hire additional guards as long as their marginal value in preventing books from being stolen is greater than the guard's per diem pay. Look at the MRP column. As long as the MRP column has a higher value than the $120 per day pay, the hiring will continue until MRP = $120 or any additional hiring would mean that the $120 is > than MRP.

fourth. You will note that there is no level of hiring at $MRP_L = MFC_L$. *This is an important note!* Some of the questions you will get will not have a level of resource (labor) use at which $MRP_L = MFC_L$. Therefore, choose the highest level of labor units at which $MRP_L > MFC_L$. In this particular example, the answer is three guards, which is the highest level of hiring additional guards for which MRP_L ($200) = MFC_L ($120). At the hiring level of a fourth guard, $MRP_L > MFC_L$ or $120 > $100. The firm saves less than it costs to hire another guard. At the end of this chapter, there is an exercise on MRP_L to complete. Remember, whenever the wage rate or resource price (cost) is constant, there is a perfectly competitive resource (labor) market.

Imperfectly Competitive Labor (Resource) Market (Monopsony)

We may find that some product markets are intensely competitive such as textiles, especially with competition from China. However, the resource or labor market may not be very competitive. Take the example of a U.S. textile company located in a small town with little or no sources of jobs outside the textile mill. The owner of this textile company is a monopsonist or a single buyer of a particular supply of labor, in this case textile workers. Given their skills as experienced textile workers and given no other viable employment opportunities, these workers can "sell" their labor to only one buyer, the textile mill. So, in this case the marginal factor cost (MFC_L) curve will vary from the average cost (AC_L) or supply (S) curve. Each time the firm wants to hire an additional unit of labor and is forced to pay a higher wage rate to attract labor, $MFC > AC_L$ or wage rate (W_E). The firm would then have to pay the higher wage to all of the existing workers at the same skill level in order to maintain their services. To illustrate this, see Figure 13.3 below.

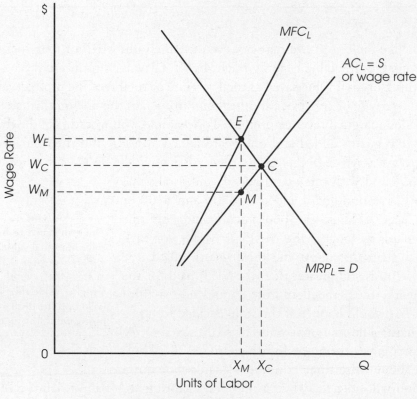

Fig. 13.3 Monopsony

In Figure 13.3, $MFC_L = MRP_L$ at E on the graph. However, we need to drop a line perpendicular to the horizontal axis to find the units of labor (X_M) that would maximize profits. At M this line intersects the supply curve (S) or average cost of labor (AC_L) at M from which we read the wage rate (W_M) that the monopsonist pays. Note that this wage rate, W_M is less than the value of the marginal revenue product at E (only wage rate, W_E, would be equal to MRP at X_M level of employees). Also note that the monopsonist pays a lower wage, W_M, than the competitive labor market. The competitive firm would pay W_C. Also, the monopsonist hires only X_M workers compared to the X_C level of a competitive labor market firm.

Cost Minimization (Least Cost Combination) and Profit Maximization in the Hire of More Than One Resource

1. Cost minimization or least cost combination of resources for a given level of output. The basic concept here is that the firm will find the least cost combination of two resources when the marginal physical product (MPP_L) of one resource, labor, per its marginal factor (MFC_L) is equal to the marginal physical product (MPP_K) of another resource, capital (K) per its marginal factor cost (MFC_K)

$$\frac{MPP_L}{MFC_L} = \frac{MPP_K}{MFC_K}$$

or where P_L and P_K are constant factor costs in perfectly competitive resource markets.

$$\frac{MPP_L}{P_L} = \frac{MPP_K}{P_K}$$

You may find a few questions on this cost minimization on the exam. The important thing to note is that the *ratios* are equal, not necessarily the marginal physical products. In other words, cost minimization is achieved for a given output when the extra product produced by labor per its cost is equal to the extra product produced by capital per its cost. No other combination of inputs, labor and capital, will produce any improvement in resource efficiency.

2. Profit maximization in the hire of two resources requires that

$$\frac{MRP_L}{MFC_L} = \frac{MRP_K}{MFC_K} = 1$$

$$\frac{MRP_L}{P_L} = \frac{MRP_K}{P_K} = 1$$

(when there is a perfectly competitive resource market), where P_L, P_K are constant prices or costs of the resources.

Note here that the ratios have to be equal but also equal to one. The rationale is that to maximize profits for one resource (such as labor), $MRP_L = MFC_L$. The same holds for capital, $MRP_K = MFC_K$. Hence, the reason for the ratios being equal to one.

SHIFTS IN DEMAND FOR A RESOURCE (LABOR)

The demand curve for a resource (labor) is equal to the marginal revenue product (MRP_L) of the resource of labor. The fundamental knowledge needed here, especially for test questions, is that marginal revenue product (MRP_L) = $MPP_L \times MR_X$ or P_X where X = product. So any condition that causes MPP_L or P_X to *increase* will cause an increase in demand for labor or a shift to the *right* in the demand curve. Conversely, any condition that causes MPP_L or P_X to *decrease* will cause a decrease in demand for labor or a shift to the *left* in the demand curve. For example, workers begin to produce more per hour because of a training program for workers. Even if the price of the product that they produce stays constant, the fact that the workers produce more per hour should increase their attractiveness to employers. If the price of the product the workers produce falls, then we expect, *ceteris paribus*, that the demand for labor will shift to the left or a decrease in demand for labor.

Other factors related to shifts in demand for labor include the number of buyers of the resource; for example, many firms in addition to high-tech firms are now hiring computer-trained personnel for the many computer-assisted tasks of industry. Such an increase in the number of firms demanding computer people would cause the demand curve for labor to shift to the right or an increase in demand for labor. Also the prices and availability of substitutes for labor will be a factor. Will distance learning eventually replace faculties of schools and universities? Some suggest that increases in the minimum wage caused more automated gasoline sales, and movie theaters without ushers. The availability and the technology of substituting capital goods for labor services may be more extensive in the long run than in the short run.

SUPPLY OF RESOURCES

We might need to take a look at supply of resources such as labor. Then we will look at factors causing supply curves to shift. The normal upward sloping supply curve is contrasted with the backward bending supply curve in the following illustration.

In the normal supply curve Figure 13.4(a), the amount of labor willing to be supplied varies directly with the wage rate, in other words, as the wage rate increases from $6 an hour to $8 an hour, the labor supplied increases from X_6 to X_8 on the horizontal axis. The higher the wage rate, the higher the amount of labor supplied on the horizontal axis representing the minimum wage that will be acceptable for each of the amounts of labor indicated on the horizontal axis. **Caution:** "Minimum wage" used in this context has nothing to do with a federal- or state-mandated minimum wage.

In the backward bending supply curve, Figure 13.4(b), the amount of labor willing to be supplied as the wage rate rises varies differently at different wage rate levels. At first, as the wage rate increases from $6 an hour to $8 an hour, the amount of labor supplied increases from X_6 to X_8 on the horizontal axis. However, once the wage rate reaches $12 an hour, there is *no increase* in the labor supplied when the wage rate then rises to $14 an hour; the horizontal axis marking of X_{12} and X_{14} at the same point indicates this constant level of amounts supplied (the curve is relatively vertical between $12 and $14). Further, when the wage rate increases from $14 to $16 and from $16 to $18, the amounts of labor willing to be supplied *decrease!* This is the "backward bending" portion of the labor supply curve S_{LB}.

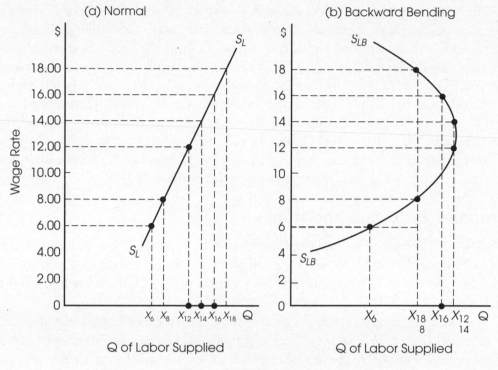

Fig. 13.4 Supply of Labor

Labor-Leisure Tradeoff

All of this suggests that labor supplied curve "a" (normal) might better apply to some labor force participants, and labor supplied curve "b" would better apply to others. This is a *labor-leisure trade-off*. Think of income from supplying labor enabling workers to increase their ability to buy goods and services. However, these workers might also like to have some leisure. Given a finite number of hours in a week (say 60 or 70 hours) in which to exercise an option to forego more consumption of goods and services, any additional hour of leisure (as a commodity) consumed will mean one less hour of work. So, if my wage rate increases from $6 an hour to $8 an hour, it costs me *more* now (at $8) to have an additional hour of leisure than when I was paid $6 an hour.

Substitution Effect

Intuitively, one would expect me to work the hour since I am now able to buy more goods and services at $8 than when the wage rate was $6. This is the substitution effect (when the "price" of the alternate commodity—leisure increases (opportunity cost), I would be expected to supply more labor). We might think of the normal supply curve as applicable to low-income, discriminated (age, race, gender) workers with low amounts of labor force experience. They cannot "afford" more leisure. This scenario would also seem more likely to apply to young, large families with home mortgages, home equity loans, debts, and even with children in college.

The "backward bending" curve would most likely apply to workers who are older, more experienced, and who have amassed some wealth including a mortgage-free house, perhaps a second home, and maybe, a bumper sticker on a mobile home reading "We are spending our kids' inheritance." These folks are more likely to look differently at the labor-leisure trade-off than the group we described as being applicable to the normal supply curve. These workers can now "afford" more leisure and if they consider leisure (over goods and services) as a superior good, we have the perfect recipe for a changed mix of leisure and work to favor relatively more leisure. This is the income effect that suggests the backward bend of the supply function; this income effect suggests leisure as the superior good.

Transfer Earnings and Rents

Now, we can explain a few additional aspects of the supply of labor including transfer earnings and rents. Also, we will examine an axiom of economics about supply and then discuss shifts in supply. The final section will be on the bases of wage differentials.

The axiom alluded to above fits nicely into a discussion of transfer earnings and rents. The axiom is that we must pay the supplier his or her costs in order to expect the supplier to continue the supply of goods or services and/or to expect continuing or new competition for price discipline. If we pay these costs including the value of what could be earned elsewhere with the same resources, we would be paying a transfer earning (the value of alternative use of the resources of suppliers). We discussed this definition of economic costs/profits in Chapter 8 on costs, production, and supply. The transfer earning is the minimum price we must pay, as consumers, in order to assure a continuing supply of goods and services. Rents are those payments that suppliers receive that are in excess of transfer earnings or are in excess of what those suppliers could earn elsewhere. These rents cause a reallocation of resources away from more productive uses of resources. We pay more for our goods and services than we would value in terms of transfer earnings.

SHIFTS IN SUPPLY

The following factors are determinants of shifts in the supply curve of resources. An increase in supply would be a shift to the right of an upward sloping supply curve. A decrease in supply would be a shift to the left of the supply curve. The factors:

1. **Attractiveness of an occupation.** It appears that we get more people interested in business careers, particularly in finance, as we have a boom in the economy and in the stock market. Also, entrepreneurs are encouraged to enter the business world through e-commerce and with venture capitalists opening their coffers. This would be represented by a shift to the right of a resource supply curve.

2. **The number of suppliers.** Computer scientists have a bright future, not only because of the rise in number of high-tech companies but also because of the extended use of computer technology in virtually every small and large-sized companies. Thus, we would expect an increased supply of computer scientists.

3. **The relative prices of competing uses of a resource such as labor.** If electrical engineers discover that their services are more valuable as computer scientists than in more conventional electrical uses, the supply of computer scientists will increase (shift to the right) and the supply of electrical engineers will shift to the left (a decrease in supply).

THE BASES OF WAGE DIFFERENTIALS

This is a particularly interesting topic since it relates well to the overall increases in wages in the United States over time, but also it is helpful in any discussion of the widening inequality in income distribution. The treatment in this chapter is a sketch but will outline the important bases of wage differentials. The bases:

1. **Not all jobs/occupations are equally attractive.** Being averse to the sight of blood, I am not about to consider a career in surgery. On the other hand, many would find the occupation of college professor to be uninspiring. Therefore, we may need to pay people in certain professions more than would be ordinarily necessary since there may be an insufficient supply of people into a particular occupation based on its sometimes unattractive nature.

2. **Innate differences.** All of us do not possess the necessary combination of skills, aptitude, and experience for all jobs. Thus, the fact that certain combinations of these traits are necessary for some high-paying jobs leads to wage differentials.

3. **Human capital.** Some workers have higher stocks of human capital (investment in education, job training and experience, health, etc.). Higher investment in human capital for some workers leads to higher returns in income over time.

4. **Compensating wage differentials.** Some workers are paid more than others because of special characteristics of the jobs such as risk. Take the example of two outside window washers. Both of these workers possess the same skills, aptitude, and experience. One worker washes the outside windows of very tall (skyscraper) windows, and the other worker washes the outside windows of one-story buildings. Besides the obvious inability of the skyscraper washer to "step back and admire" his or her work, there is a considerable difference in risk between the two workers. We would expect this difference to be reflected in a wage differential, with the higher-risk job receiving higher pay.

5. **Psychic income.** A college professor with both a Ph.D. and an M.B.A. might choose to be an academic (teaching) economist utilizing the Ph.D. but would receive a lower monetary income than if he or she entered the finance world with an M.B.A. The choice to teach may be based on the higher psychic compensation (attractive lifestyle) of the teaching career. We might qualify or measure that psychic income by that monetary income difference between the two occupations, for example, the opportunity cost. On balance, one might say that the monetary income and the higher psychic compensation of the college professor would equal the monetary income of the finance career.

6. **Discrimination.** It is accurate to say that many wage differentials are due to discrimination based on age, gender, sexual orientation, and race. It is beyond the scope of this book to have an extensive discussion of this extremely important topic.

7. **Immobility.** Because of sociological ties to an area, tenure/union seniority, lack of knowledge of job opportunities, and/or financial inability to seek opportunities, wage differentials exist. We do not all move to the best jobs.

8. **Labor market imperfections.** Monopsonists (single buyers of labor) pay lower wages than do more competitive labor market employers. Some unions, during certain periods of time, are able to extract rents for their union members.

9. **Government interference.** The imposition of minimum wage laws, licensing requirements, and government wage subsidies can create differentials.

INCOME INEQUALITY

The basis for wage differentials is a subject of the more general issue of income inequality. In order to be able to analyze income inequality, we need to develop ways to measure: The most referenced and quoted measure is the *Lorenz Curve*. This curve is contrasted with a line of proportionality or income equality. This line, as illustrated in Figure 13.5, has coordinate points that are equidistant from the two axes. Thus, ten percent of the population has ten percent of total income, 20 percent of the population has 20 percent of total income, 30 percent of the population has 30 percent of total income, etc. Points on the Lorenz Curve for any given population represent unequal shares of income per the deciles of the population. The greater the difference between the line of proportionality and the Lorenz Curve, the greater the degree of income inequality.

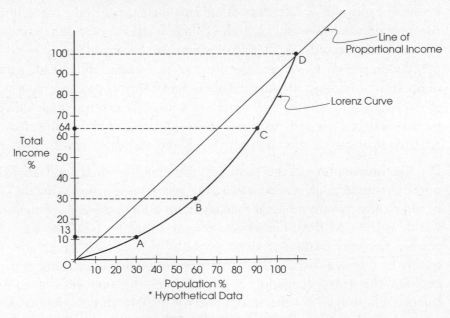

Fig. 13.5 Lorenz Curve

Curve OD represents the degree of inequality of income. We find that 30 percent of the population has 13 percent of total income, 60 percent of the population has 30 percent of total income, 90 percent has 64 percent of total income. These figures are cumulative. Thus, while 30 percent of the population has 13 percent of income, the next 30 percent of population adds another 17 percent of income share, resulting in the 30 percent (13% + 17% = 30%) of income. When we reach the final 10 percent of population, we add 34 percent of income share to reach 100 percent. The AD segment of the Lorenz Curve represents the idea that 100 percent of the population "owns" 100 percent of total income. We can use the Lorenz Curve to measure income inequality within a country or across several countries.

The Gini coefficient measures the dispersion of family income over time. This coefficient varies between 0 and 1. A value of 1 would represent all income going to one family (no dispersion), while a value of 0 would represent all families receiving the same amount of income. On Figure 13.5, the line of proportional income and the Lorenz curve would be identical with a Gini Coefficient of zero.

SUMMARY

- Marginal Revenue Product (MRP) of a resource represents the demand for labor and *marginal factor cost* (MFC) of a resource represents the cost of labor.
- The firm maximizes its profits by hiring the number of units of employees at which MRP = MFC.
- The demand for a resource is derived from the demand for a product to which the resource has contributed.
- The three laws of derived demand are: (a) The higher the price elasticity of demand for a product, the higher the wage elasticity of demand; (b) the higher the proportion of labor costs relative to total costs of production, the higher will be the wage elasticity of demand; and (c) the greater the number of substitute resources available and the degree to which they are substitutable, the higher will be the wage elasticity of demand.
- The firm in the perfectly competitive labor (resource) market is a price-taker in terms of the wage rate paid by the firm for its workers. The supply (of workers) curve is perfectly horizontal at the competitive market wage rate.
- The supplier of goods or services must be paid his or her costs including the opportunity costs or transfer earnings that could have been earned in alternative use of the supplier's resources.
- The factors that determine the shifts in the supply of labor as a resource include the attractiveness of an occupation, the number of suppliers and the relative prices of competing uses of labor.
- The bases of wage differentials include innate differences of workers, the unequal attractiveness to varying occupations, the amount of invested human capital, compensation for risk, psychic income, discrimination, immobility, labor market imperfections, and government interference.
- The "backward bending" supply curve for labor reflects changing ratios of labor/leisure. As workers reach certain goals of income, wealth, and goods, they begin to value leisure as a superior good and to substitute leisure for work.

TERMS

Derived Demand the demand for a resource such as labor is derived from the product that the resource helps to produce

Wage Elasticity of Demand the percentage change in quantity demanded of labor in response to a percentage change in a wage rate

Marginal Revenue Product (MRP) the addition to the firm's revenue as the result of an additional output for an additional unit of labor

Marginal Factor Cost (MFC) the additional cost for each additional unit of labor hired

Marginal Physical Product (MPP) the additional output produced as one more unit of labor (resource) is added

Monopsony a market in which there is a single buyer of labor

Human Capital the investment in people that increases their future monetary and psychic income

Compensating Wage Differentials the differences in wages due to higher pay for workers who have higher risks inherent in their work or for other work conditions such as a highly structured job

Lorenz Curve a curve that measures the degree of income inequality as contrasted with income equality

FORMULAS

$$\frac{MRP_L}{MFC_L} = \frac{MRP_K}{MFC_K} \cdots \frac{MRP_N}{MFC_N} = 1$$

Profit maximization in the hire of more than one resource.

$$\frac{MRP_L}{MFC_L} = \frac{MRP_K}{MFC_K} \cdots \frac{MRP_N}{MFC_N} = 1$$

Criterion for cost minimization (least-cost) for more than one resource.

$$\frac{\%\Delta \text{ Quantity Demanded of Labor}}{\%\Delta \text{ wage rate}}$$

Formula for wage elasticity of demand when Δ = change in.

MULTIPLE-CHOICE REVIEW QUESTIONS

Labor Units	Total Output	MPP	Output* Price	TR	Labor** Price	MRP
1	5	5	10	50	60	
2	20	15	10	200	60	
3	30	10	10	300	60	
4	35	5	10	350	60	
5	35	0	10	350	60	

*Output price constant at $10 indicates a perfectly competitive product market, $P_X = MR_X$ where X = output product.
**Labor price constant at $60 indicates a perfectly competitive labor market, $P_L = W_L = MFC_L$ where L = labor, P = price of labor, W_L = wage rate of labor, and MFC_L = marginal factor cost of labor.

1. With the data in the table above, how many units of labor would the employer hire?

   (A) 1
   (B) 2
   (C) 3
   (D) 4
   (E) 5

2. The basis for the answer in number 1 is

   (A) P or wage rate of labor > MRP of labor and with one additional unit of labor, wage rate < MRP.
   (B) P or wage rate of labor < MRP of labor and with one additional unit of labor W_L > MRP.
   (C) total revenue is at a maximum.
   (D) total output is at a maximum.
   (E) marginal physical product is at a maximum.

3. Which of the following is *not* the basis for a wage differential?

   (A) Higher risk job.
   (B) Investment in human capital.
   (C) Increase in production of SUVs.
   (D) Racial discrimination.
   (E) Psychic income.

4. A monopsonist is identified by one of the following:

   (A) A wage payment lower than the marginal revenue product of labor.
   (B) Employment level greater than that of a competitive labor market.
   (C) A wage payment higher than that of a competitive labor market.
   (D) A single seller of labor services.
   (E) A marginal factor cost curve lower than the supply curve.

5. If for two resources, Labor (L) and Capital (K), the ratios of their marginal physical products are

$$\frac{MPP_K}{P_K} > \frac{MPP_L}{P_L}$$

the firm should:
   (A) hire more capital (K) until the ratios are equal.
   (B) hire more labor (L) until the ratios are equal.
   (C) lower the price of capital (P_K).
   (D) lower the price of labor (P_L).
   (E) seek union membership for labor (L).

6. The backward bending supply curve is characterized by which of the following?

 (A) As wage rates rise, the quantity of labor supplied continues to rise at every wage rate increase.
 (B) The labor-leisure trade-off continues to favor the supply of more jobs, or the substitution effect.
 (C) The labor-leisure trade-off favors the income effect or more leisure at higher wage rates.
 (D) inexperienced, low-income, younger workers at the backward bending portion.
 (E) discriminated workers.

Multiple-Choice Review Answers

MRP in table going down the column starting with labor unit 2: 150, 100, 50, 0.

1. **(C)** 3, MRP (100) > labor price (60); at 4 labor units, MRP (50) < labor price (60).
2. **(B)** (see explanation in 1)
3. **(C)**
4. **(A)**
5. **(A)**
6. **(C)**

FREE-RESPONSE REVIEW QUESTION

1. A. Draw a monopsony graph.

 B. Use this graph to contrast wage rates and units of labor employed under a perfectly competitive labor market and under a monopsony market.

 C. Under what kind of market structure would the marginal factor cost of labor equal the wage rate (average cost of labor)?

Free-Response Review Answer

1. A.

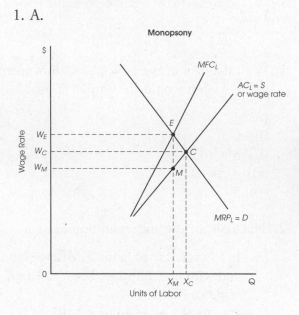

Monopsony

B. X_M units of labor and W_M wage rate for monopsony; X_C units of labor and W_C wage rate for a perfectly competitive labor market.

C. perfectly competitive labor market

MODEL AP EXAM IN MICROECONOMICS

Answer Sheet
MICROECONOMICS

Multiple-Choice Questions

1 Ⓐ Ⓑ Ⓒ Ⓓ Ⓔ	21 Ⓐ Ⓑ Ⓒ Ⓓ Ⓔ	41 Ⓐ Ⓑ Ⓒ Ⓓ Ⓔ
2 Ⓐ Ⓑ Ⓒ Ⓓ Ⓔ	22 Ⓐ Ⓑ Ⓒ Ⓓ Ⓔ	42 Ⓐ Ⓑ Ⓒ Ⓓ Ⓔ
3 Ⓐ Ⓑ Ⓒ Ⓓ Ⓔ	23 Ⓐ Ⓑ Ⓒ Ⓓ Ⓔ	43 Ⓐ Ⓑ Ⓒ Ⓓ Ⓔ
4 Ⓐ Ⓑ Ⓒ Ⓓ Ⓔ	24 Ⓐ Ⓑ Ⓒ Ⓓ Ⓔ	44 Ⓐ Ⓑ Ⓒ Ⓓ Ⓔ
5 Ⓐ Ⓑ Ⓒ Ⓓ Ⓔ	25 Ⓐ Ⓑ Ⓒ Ⓓ Ⓔ	45 Ⓐ Ⓑ Ⓒ Ⓓ Ⓔ
6 Ⓐ Ⓑ Ⓒ Ⓓ Ⓔ	26 Ⓐ Ⓑ Ⓒ Ⓓ Ⓔ	46 Ⓐ Ⓑ Ⓒ Ⓓ Ⓔ
7 Ⓐ Ⓑ Ⓒ Ⓓ Ⓔ	27 Ⓐ Ⓑ Ⓒ Ⓓ Ⓔ	47 Ⓐ Ⓑ Ⓒ Ⓓ Ⓔ
8 Ⓐ Ⓑ Ⓒ Ⓓ Ⓔ	28 Ⓐ Ⓑ Ⓒ Ⓓ Ⓔ	48 Ⓐ Ⓑ Ⓒ Ⓓ Ⓔ
9 Ⓐ Ⓑ Ⓒ Ⓓ Ⓔ	29 Ⓐ Ⓑ Ⓒ Ⓓ Ⓔ	49 Ⓐ Ⓑ Ⓒ Ⓓ Ⓔ
10 Ⓐ Ⓑ Ⓒ Ⓓ Ⓔ	30 Ⓐ Ⓑ Ⓒ Ⓓ Ⓔ	50 Ⓐ Ⓑ Ⓒ Ⓓ Ⓔ
11 Ⓐ Ⓑ Ⓒ Ⓓ Ⓔ	31 Ⓐ Ⓑ Ⓒ Ⓓ Ⓔ	51 Ⓐ Ⓑ Ⓒ Ⓓ Ⓔ
12 Ⓐ Ⓑ Ⓒ Ⓓ Ⓔ	32 Ⓐ Ⓑ Ⓒ Ⓓ Ⓔ	52 Ⓐ Ⓑ Ⓒ Ⓓ Ⓔ
13 Ⓐ Ⓑ Ⓒ Ⓓ Ⓔ	33 Ⓐ Ⓑ Ⓒ Ⓓ Ⓔ	53 Ⓐ Ⓑ Ⓒ Ⓓ Ⓔ
14 Ⓐ Ⓑ Ⓒ Ⓓ Ⓔ	34 Ⓐ Ⓑ Ⓒ Ⓓ Ⓔ	54 Ⓐ Ⓑ Ⓒ Ⓓ Ⓔ
15 Ⓐ Ⓑ Ⓒ Ⓓ Ⓔ	35 Ⓐ Ⓑ Ⓒ Ⓓ Ⓔ	55 Ⓐ Ⓑ Ⓒ Ⓓ Ⓔ
16 Ⓐ Ⓑ Ⓒ Ⓓ Ⓔ	36 Ⓐ Ⓑ Ⓒ Ⓓ Ⓔ	56 Ⓐ Ⓑ Ⓒ Ⓓ Ⓔ
17 Ⓐ Ⓑ Ⓒ Ⓓ Ⓔ	37 Ⓐ Ⓑ Ⓒ Ⓓ Ⓔ	57 Ⓐ Ⓑ Ⓒ Ⓓ Ⓔ
18 Ⓐ Ⓑ Ⓒ Ⓓ Ⓔ	38 Ⓐ Ⓑ Ⓒ Ⓓ Ⓔ	58 Ⓐ Ⓑ Ⓒ Ⓓ Ⓔ
19 Ⓐ Ⓑ Ⓒ Ⓓ Ⓔ	39 Ⓐ Ⓑ Ⓒ Ⓓ Ⓔ	59 Ⓐ Ⓑ Ⓒ Ⓓ Ⓔ
20 Ⓐ Ⓑ Ⓒ Ⓓ Ⓔ	40 Ⓐ Ⓑ Ⓒ Ⓓ Ⓔ	60 Ⓐ Ⓑ Ⓒ Ⓓ Ⓔ

Model AP Exam in Microeconomics

Two hours are allotted for this exam: 1 hour and 10 minutes for Section I, which consists of multiple-choice questions; and 50 minutes for Section II, which consists of three mandatory essay questions.

SECTION I—MULTIPLE-CHOICE QUESTIONS

Time—1 hour and 10 minutes
Number of Questions—60
Percent of Total Grade—$66^2/_3$

Directions

Each of the questions or incomplete statements beginning on page 180 is followed by five suggested answers or completions. Select the one that is best in each case and then fill in the corresponding oval on the answer sheet.

1. Which of the following is NOT a character-istic of perfectly competitive industry?

   (A) Free entry into the industry.
   (B) Product differentiation.
   (C) Perfectly elastic demand curve.
   (D) Homogeneous products.
   (E) Many sellers and many buyers.

2. Which of the following is a characteristic of monopolistic competition in the long run?

   (A) Strong barriers to entry.
   (B) Homogeneous products.
   (C) Zero economic profits.
   (D) Minimum average total cost equals price.
   (E) Efficiency.

3. Which of the following is characteristic of oligopoly?

   I. Formidable barriers to entry.
   II. Price (P) = Marginal Revenue (MR).
   III. Relatively few sellers.

   (A) I only.
   (B) II only.
   (C) III only.
   (D) I and III only.
   (E) II and III only.

4. Which of the following is a characteristic of monopoly?

   (A) A single firm in the industry.
   (B) Price equal to marginal revenue.
   (C) Perfectly elastic demand curve.
   (D) Weak barriers to entry.
   (E) Zero economic profits.

5. Compared to perfect competition in the long run, monopoly has

   (A) more choices of products for consumers.
   (B) more efficiency.
   (C) lower prices.
   (D) higher output.
   (E) price greater than marginal revenue.

6. With the presence of a negative externality, which of the following would internalize (or correct) the externality?

   (A) A government subsidy.
   (B) A government tax.
   (C) A lower price.
   (D) A higher level of output.
   (E) A government-created task force.

7. With the presence of a positive externality, which of the following would correct the externality?

   (A) A government subsidy.
   (B) A government tax.
   (C) A higher price.
   (D) A lower level of output.
   (E) A government-created task force.

8. Which of the following is true?

   (A) A marginal social cost = marginal pri-vate cost + marginal social benefits.
   (B) Value of externality = marginal social costs.
   (C) Value of externality = marginal private costs.
   (D) Marginal social cost = marginal private cost + negative externality.
   (E) Marginal social cost = marginal private cost + positive externality.

9. Which of the following is true?

   (A) Average total cost = total fixed costs divided by the number of units produced.
   (B) Average total cost = average variable costs divided by the total number of units produced.
   (C) Average total cost = average variable cost plus marginal cost.
   (D) Average total cost = average variable cost plus average fixed cost.
   (E) All of the above.

10. Which of the following is true about the relationship of the average total cost (ATC) curve and the marginal cost (MC) curve?

    (A) ATC and MC are always equal.
    (B) ATC and MC are never equal.
    (C) The ATC curve intersects the MC curve at the minimum point of the MC curve.
    (D) The MC curve intersects the ATC curve at the minimum point of the ATC curve.
    (E) The MC curve intersects the ATC curve at the maximum point of the ATC curve.

Question 11 is based on the figure below:

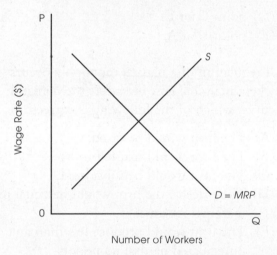

11. Which of the following will happen when a new computerized system for a firm increases the marginal productivity of its workers?

    (A) The marginal revenue product curve will shift to the left, which will cause the wage rate to decrease.
    (B) The supply curve will shift to the right, causing the wage rate to decrease.
    (C) The marginal revenue product curve will shift to the right, causing the wage rate to increase.
    (D) The supply curve will shift to the left, causing the wage rate to increase.
    (E) The marginal revenue product curve will shift to the right and the supply curve will shift to the left, leaving the wage rate unchanged.

12. Which of the following is true about a price floor?

    (A) It is used to correct government policy.
    (B) It is used when the equilibrium price is too high.
    (C) It will be located above the equilibrium price.
    (D) It will be located below the equilibrium price.
    (E) It is when the stock market has closed at a new low.

13. Which of the following is true about a price ceiling?

    (A) It is used to correct government policy.
    (B) It is used when equilibrium prices are too low.
    (C) It will be located above the equilibrium price.
    (D) It will be located below the equilibrium price.
    (E) It is when the stock market has closed at a new high.

14. Which of the following situations best exemplifies the concept of consumer surplus?

    (A) It refers to a consumer who no longer has any outstanding debts.
    (B) The federal government has taken in more revenue than it has paid out in expenditures.
    (C) A consumer pays *more* for a pizza than she thought it was worth at the margin of the purchase.
    (D) A consumer pays *less* for a pizza than she thought it was worth at the margin of the purchase.
    (E) A consumer pays exactly what she thinks the pizza is worth at the margin of the purchase.

TABLE 1

Number of Workers	Pair Sets Produced per Two Weeks
1	40
2	70
3	95
4	115
5	130
6	130

15. Given the data in the table above, and knowing that workers are paid $1,250 every two weeks and that the pair sets are sold to retailers at $50, how many workers would be hired?

(A) Two
(B) Three
(C) Four
(D) Five
(E) Six

Questions 16–19 are based on the figure below:

16. An unregulated monopoly would

(A) sell at price, P_A and produce output at X_A.
(B) sell at price, P_G and produce output at X_G.
(C) sell at price, P_E and produce output at X_E.
(D) sell at price, P_B and produce output at X_A.
(E) sell at price, P_B and produce output at X_A.

17. A regulated monopoly could occur at

(A) point A, G, or E.
(B) point A or G.
(C) point A or F.
(D) point G or E.
(E) point B or A.

18. If regulation of a natural monopoly occurs where marginal cost intersects the demand curve, which of the following is correct?

(A) The firm would be taxed.
(B) The firm would realize profits.
(C) The firm would be subsidized.
(D) The price of the firm would be equal to marginal revenue.
(E) The firm would produce less than an unregulated natural monopoly.

19. Which of the following is correct about the profits of an unregulated monopolist?

(A) The profits are the rectangle $P_A AHP_H$.
(B) The profits are the rectangle $P_H ABP_B$.
(C) The profits are less than those of a regulated monopoly.
(D) The profits are less than at a socially optimal output.
(E) None of the above.

Questions 20–23 are based on the figure below:

Perfectly Competitive Firm

Output (000)
Batteries

20. At a market price of $37, maximum profits are

(A) CBLM
(B) CBFD
(C) CBGE
(D) BAKL
(E) CAHE

21. At a market price of $19, how many batteries will the firm produce?

(A) 20,000
(B) 29,000
(C) 36,000
(D) 28,000
(E) Zero

22. At a market price of $22, how many batteries will the firm produce?

(A) 20,000
(B) 26,000
(C) 31,000
(D) Zero
(E) 10,000

23. At the market price of $22, the output will result in

(A) economic losses.
(B) economic profits.
(C) normal profits.
(D) business profits.
(F) shut-down.

24. If the government announces that the drinking of red grape juice reduces the risk of heart attacks, which of the following will be correct in terms of changes in quantity demanded, demand, and the price of red grape juice?

	Quantity demanded	Demand	Price of grape juice
(A)	Increases	Decreases	Increases
(B)	No change	No change	Decreases
(C)	No change	Increases	Increases
(D)	Decreases	Increases	Decreases
(E)	Decreases	Decreases	Decreases

Questions 25–28 are based on the figure below:

Market for Coffee

25. Using the figure above, which of the following is correct for the market for coffee?

   (A) If both the demand for and the supply of coffee increase, both the price of coffee and the quantity sold of coffee will increase.
   (B) If both the demand for and the supply of coffee increase, the quantity of coffee sold will increase.
   (C) If the demand for coffee decreases while the supply of coffee increases, the price of coffee will increase.
   (D) If both the demand for and the supply of coffee decrease, both the price of coffee and the quantity sold of coffee decrease.
   (E) If the demand for coffee increases, and the supply of coffee increases, the price of coffee will increase.

26. If the government provides a subsidy to the producers of coffee, which of the following will occur?

   (A) A shift to the left of the supply curve.
   (B) A shift to the left of the demand curve.
   (C) A move along the supply curve to the right.
   (D) A shift to the right of the demand curve.
   (E) A shift to the right of the supply curve.

27. If the producers of coffee have to pay an increase in wages and fringe benefits to their workers, which of the following is correct?

   (A) A shift to the left of the supply curve.
   (B) A shift to the left of the demand curve.
   (C) A move along the supply curve to the right.
   (D) A shift to the right of the demand curve.
   (E) A shift to the right of the supply curve.

28. If the price of coffee increases, which of the following is most likely to happen?

   (A) An increase in the amount of coffee consumers want to purchase.
   (B) No change in the amount of coffee consumers want to purchase.
   (C) A decrease in the amount of coffee consumers want to purchase.
   (D) An increase (shift) in the demand for coffee.
   (E) A decrease (shift) in the demand for coffee.

29. Which of the following is NOT a source of wage differentials?

   (A) Differences in human capital stock.
   (B) Racial or gender discrimination.
   (C) Immobility of workers.
   (D) Compensation for risk.
   (E) Decrease in the birth rate.

Questions 30–31 are based on the figure below:

Monopolistic Competition

30. For this firm operating under monopolistic competition, which of the following is the profit-maximizing output and price?

   (A) OX output and OA price.
   (B) OX output and OD price.
   (C) OX output and OB price.
   (D) OZ output and OC price.
   (E) OZ output and OA price.

31. At the profit-maximizing output, which of the following is correct?

   (A) Economic profits are zero and the firm is operating efficiently.
   (B) Economic profits are above normal and output is greater than under perfect competition.
   (C) Economic losses are present.
   (D) Price is less than marginal cost.
   (E) Economic profits are zero and the firm is operating inefficiently.

32. Which of the following best exemplifies economies of scale?

   (A) As a firm's output decreases, average costs for production decrease.
   (B) As a firm's output increases, average costs for production increase.
   (C) As a firm's inputs triple, its output quadruples.
   (D) As a firm's inputs triple, its output doubles.
   (E) As a firm's inputs triple, its output stays constant.

33. Which of the following is correct?

   (A) In the long run, all inputs are variable.
   (B) In the short run, all inputs are variable.
   (C) In the long run, supply is not able to adjust fully to changes in demand.
   (D) In the short run, supply is able to adjust fully to changes in demand.
   (E) A short run is any distance less than one mile.

34. If a firm decreases its prices by 15 percent and its total revenue increases by 30 percent, which of the following is correct?

   (A) The price elasticity of demand is unit elastic.
   (B) The price elasticity of demand is inelastic.
   (C) The price elasticity of demand is elastic.
   (D) The numerical coefficient of elasticity is equal to one.
   (E) The numerical coefficient of elasticity is less than one.

35. If one person has the only original signed copy of *The Wealth of Nations* by Adam Smith, which of the following would illustrate this situation?

   (A) A downward sloping demand curve.
   (B) An upward sloping supply curve.
   (C) An invisible hand.
   (D) A perfectly vertical supply curve.
   (E) A perfectly horizontal demand curve.

36. When marginal cost equals price in a perfectly competitive product market at long run equilibrium, which of the following is NOT correct?

    (A) There is a socially optimal or efficient output and price.
    (B) Other product markets are inefficient by contrast.
    (C) It is a sign of high concentration among sellers.
    (D) The value placed on the product by the buyer is equal to the cost of production of the seller at the margin of an additional sale.
    (E) Marginal cost equals minimum average total cost.

37. Which of the following is a correct statement?

    (A) Average total cost equals marginal cost plus average fixed costs.
    (B) Average total cost equals marginal costs plus average variable costs.
    (C) Average total cost equals average fixed costs plus average variable costs.
    (D) Total fixed costs vary with output.
    (E) Total fixed costs equal total variable costs at zero output.

38. Which of the following correctly identifies the condition that explains inefficiency for firms in a monopolistically competitive industry?

    (A) Higher output than competitive industries.
    (B) Lower price than competitive industries.
    (C) Price equals marginal cost.
    (D) Price equals marginal revenue.
    (E) Excess capacity compared to competitive industries.

Questions 39–41 are based on the figure below:

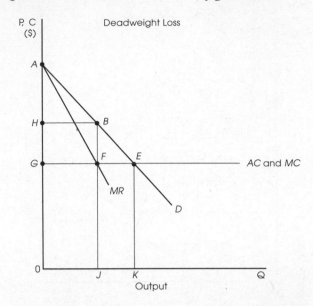

39. The original consumer surplus (before monopoly) is

    (A) AHB
    (B) BFE
    (C) AGE
    (D) HGFB
    (E) GOKE

40. The dead-weight loss as the result of monopoly is

    (A) AHB
    (B) BFE
    (C) AGE
    (D) HGFB
    (E) GOKE

41. The reduced consumer surplus as the result of monopoly is

    (A) AHB
    (B) BFE
    (C) AGE
    (D) HGFB
    (E) GOKE

42. If the price of Product X increases, which of the following will be true of the quantity demanded, total revenue, and the price elasticity of demand?

	Quantity demanded	Total revenue	Price elasticity of demand
(A)	Increases	Decreases	>1, Elastic
(B)	Increases	Increases	<1, Inelastic
(C)	Decreases	Increases	<1, Inelastic
(D)	Decreases	No change	>1, Elastic
(E)	Decreases	Decreases	=1, Unit elastic

43. If the price of one good (A) increases and the quantity demanded of another good (B) increases, the two goods are

   (A) substitute goods.
   (B) complement goods.
   (C) inferior goods.
   (D) normal goods.
   (E) independent goods.

44. If, as the price of a particular good increases, the added satisfaction of each additional unit of this good for the consumer decreases, which of the following correctly identifies the concept?

   (A) Diminishing marginal productivity.
   (B) Diminishing marginal utility.
   (C) Increasing marginal utility.
   (D) Increasing marginal productivity.
   (E) Constant costs.

45. If, for each additional unit of a variable input, the increases in output become smaller, which of the following correctly identifies the concept?

   (A) Diminishing marginal productivity.
   (B) Diminishing marginal utility.
   (C) Increasing marginal utility.
   (D) Increasing marginal productivity.
   (E) Constant costs.

46. Which of the following is correct about the demand for labor?

   (A) The demand for labor is independent of the demand for other inputs or resources.
   (B) The demand for labor is independent of the demand for the products produced by labor.
   (C) The demand for labor is independent of the availability of other inputs or resources.
   (D) The demand for labor is derived from the demand for the products produced by labor.
   (E) The demand for labor is derived from the demand for labor unions.

47. The greater (higher) the wage elasticity of demand, the

   (A) greater the proportion of capital costs to labor costs in the production of goods.
   (B) greater the price elasticity for the product produced by labor.
   (C) the smaller the number of substitutes for labor.
   (D) the smaller the time period.
   (E) the smaller the proportion of labor costs to total costs.

48. Which of the following is an example of a transfer earning?

    (A) A superstar basketball player's $40 million earnings.
    (B) A social security retirement income.
    (C) A welfare payment from social services.
    (D) A check to a college student from a parent or guardian.
    (E) A cashier at a restaurant receiving the same $8 an hour that other cashiers receive.

49. Which of the following is an example of an economic rent?

    (A) A superstar basketball player's $50 million earnings.
    (B) A social security retirement income.
    (C) A welfare payment from social services.
    (D) A check to a college student from a parent or guardian.
    (E) A cashier at a restaurant receiving the same $8 an hour that other cashiers receive.

50. The Lorenz Curve is used to measure which of the following:

    (A) The ratio of income to wealth in different countries.
    (B) The ratio of public goods to private goods in different countries.
    (C) The ratio of income inequality to income equality in different countries.
    (D) The ratio of the working poor to the non-working poor.
    (E) The ratio of shares of taxation to shares of total income.

TABLE 2 TRUMPED'S (T) PRICE			
		$40	$35
BUMPED'S (B) PRICE	$40	T 60 B 57	T 55 B 59
	$35	T 68 B 51	T 58 B 56

51. The matrix above represents profits for two oligopolists, Trumped (T) and Bumped (B), under different pricing strategies. Which of the following is correct?

    (A) Both Trumped and Bumped have a dominant strategy.
    (B) Neither Trumped nor Bumped has a dominant strategy.
    (C) Trumped has a dominant strategy. Bumped does not have a dominant strategy.
    (D) Bumped has a dominant strategy but Trumped does not have a dominant strategy.
    (E) The outcome of the game is not determinable.

52. Which of the following statements is correct?

    (A) Economic Profits = Accounting Profits.
    (B) Economic Costs = Explicit Costs plus Implicit Costs.
    (C) Economic Costs = Explicit Costs minus Implicit Costs.
    (D) Opportunity Costs = Economic Profits.
    (E) Accounting Costs = Implicit Costs.

53. Which of the following is true for a firm operating under perfect competition in the long run?

   (A) The firm will engage in non-price competition.
   (B) The firm will realize economic profits.
   (C) The firm will incur economic losses.
   (D) The firm will realize zero economic profits.
   (E) The firm will have a price greater than its marginal revenue.

54. Which of the following conditions is characteristic of oligopoly?

   (A) A rival firm matches price decreases of rivals, but fails to match any price increases of rivals.
   (B) A rival firm matches price increases of rivals, but fails to match any price decrease of rivals.
   (C) A rival firm fails to match both price increases or price decreases of rivals.
   (D) Rival firms act independently of each other.
   (E) There is such a large number of firms that firms cannot exercise any price strategy.

55. Which of the following is NOT a characteristic of monopolistic competition in the long run?

   (A) Non-price competition
   (B) Product differentiation
   (C) Pricing strategy
   (D) Underutilization of capacity
   (E) P = MC

56. Usually, the supply curve of firms operating under conditions of perfect competition in product market would be identified as

   (A) perfectly vertical in the long run.
   (B) perfectly horizontal in the short run.
   (C) more elastic in the long run.
   (D) more elastic in the short run.
   (E) discontinuous in the long run.

57. Relatively free or easy entry (low or nonexistent barriers to entry) is best matched by which of the following?

   (A) More consumer choices, greater price elasticity of demand, more competitors.
   (B) More consumer choices, lower price elasticity of demand, more competitors.
   (C) More consumer choices, greater price elasticity of demand, fewer competitors.
   (D) Fewer consumer choices, lower price elasticity of demand, fewer competitors.
   (E) Fewer consumer choices, greater price elasticity of demand, more competitors.

58. Which of the following represents a measure of a firm's monopoly pricing or market power, i.e., the larger the value of the index, the greater the firm's market pricing power?

   (A) (MC-P)/MC
   (B) (MC-P)/P
   (C) (P-MC)/P
   (D) (P-MC)/MC
   (E) (P-MR)/MC

59. Which of the following correctly illustrates why price (P) equals marginal revenue (MR) under perfect competition, and why price (P) is greater than marginal revenue under monopoly or imperfect competition?

   I.   MR = P = demand on horizontal function for perfect competition.
   II. P > MR as downward sloping functions for imperfect competition.
   III. Demand and Price are represented as a vertical function for imperfect competition.

   (A) I, II, and III.
   (B) I and II.
   (C) I only.
   (D) I and III.
   (E) II only.

60. In the design of a competitive market system, which of the following does NOT describe how resources are allocated?

   (A) Price signals that guide producers on what, when, how, and for whom to produce goods and services.
   (B) Active government ownership and direction of production.
   (C) Voluntary market exchange between buyers and sellers.
   (D) Distribution of income and goods on the basis of contribution or productivity.
   (E) Profit motivation.

SECTION II—FREE-RESPONSE QUESTIONS

Planning Time—10 minutes
Writing Time—50 minutes
Percent of Total Grade—$33^1/_3$

Directions

You have 50 minutes to answer all three of the following questions. It is suggested that you spend approximately half your time on the first question and divide the remaining time equally between the next two questions. In answering the questions, you should emphasize the line of reasoning that generated your results; it is not enough to list the results of your analysis. Include correctly labeled diagrams, if useful or required, in explaining your answers. A correctly labeled diagram must have all axes and curves clearly labeled and must show directional changes.

Students should consider doing a "sketch" (main points, quick graph, etc.) of the answer before actually answering the free-response questions. Good luck! When you use graphs on the free-response questions, label the axes and make direct references to any symbols, e.g., MR, P, output, on the graphs when you respond to questions.

> **NOTE**
>
> Recent Advanced Placement exams require *three* questions. Some of the questions may be based on material covered in the common chapters, such as production possibilities frontier or curve when applied to international trade. For these questions, please refer to those chapters.

1. With the use of graphs, clearly labeled, explain the following:

   A. How price (P) and marginal revenue (MR) are differently related under perfect competition than under monopoly (or imperfect competition).

   B. *Explain* why these relationships between MR and P differ between perfect competition and monopoly.

   C. Identify a significant effect for pricing strategy of this relationship of P and MR in the two markets.

2. A. For a perfectly competitive firm and for an imperfectly competitive market, explain how the index (P-MC)/P demonstrates the degree of pricing or market power.

   B. What would be the significant consequences of the differences between perfectly competitive markets and imperfectly competitive markets?

3. Drawing graphs for the firm and for the market under perfect competition, show the process of adjustment from the short run and the long run. Assume that the only form of adjustment is the entry and exit of firms and that adjustment process does not alter the cost curves of the firms.

4. Butter and margarine are substitutes and are sold in perfectly competitive product markets. The Lots of Cream creamery company, one of 300 butter producers, develops a new automated churner that reduces costs.

   A. What will be the effect of this change on price, short-run profits, and the quantity of butter for the Lots of Cream Company? Explain your answer.

   B. If the other perfectly competitive firms use this same churner, what will be the effect on the price and quantity of butter produced in the market?

   C. What will be the effect of these changes in the butter market on the price and quantity produced of margarine?

Answer Key
MICROECONOMICS

Multiple-Choice Questions

1.	**B**	21.	**E**	41.	**A**
2.	**C**	22.	**C**	42.	**C**
3.	**D**	23.	**A**	43.	**A**
4.	**A**	24.	**C**	44.	**B**
5.	**E**	25.	**B**	45.	**A**
6.	**B**	26.	**E**	46.	**D**
7.	**A**	27.	**A**	47.	**B**
8.	**D**	28.	**C**	48.	**E**
9.	**D**	29.	**E**	49.	**A**
10.	**D**	30.	**B**	50.	**C**
11.	**C**	31.	**E**	51.	**A**
12.	**C**	32.	**C**	52.	**B**
13.	**D**	33.	**A**	53.	**D**
14.	**D**	34.	**C**	54.	**A**
15.	**B**	35.	**D**	55.	**E**
16.	**A**	36.	**C**	56.	**C**
17.	**D**	37.	**C**	57.	**A**
18.	**C**	38.	**E**	58.	**C**
19.	**A**	39.	**C**	59.	**B**
20.	**C**	40.	**B**	60.	**B**

ANSWERS EXPLAINED

MICROECONOMICS

MULTIPLE-CHOICE QUESTIONS

1. **(B)** (Chapters 9,10) The other answers are all correct characteristics of a perfectly competitive industry. Products are homogeneous (the same, identical) under perfect competition.

2. **(C)** (Chapters 9,12) All of the other characteristics listed as choices are *not* appropriate for monopolistic competition. Choices **B**, **D**, and **E** are characteristics of perfect competition in the long run; choice **A** is characteristic of oligopoly and monopoly.

3. **(D)** (Chapters 9,12: Table 9.1) This table reveals the characteristics of oligopolies including "few sellers" and "formidable barriers to entry/exit" among others. Price (P) = Marginal Revenue (MR) is a characteristic of perfect competition. Price (P) > Marginal Revenue (MR) is a characteristic of oligopoly.

4. **(A)** (Chapters 9,11) This is the most telling characteristic of monopoly; it defines monopoly. To change the other choices to fit monopoly, you would have to rewrite choices **B**, **C**, **D**, and **E** as follows:

   B: P > MR (downward sloping demand curve)
   C: imperfectly elastic demand curve
   D: complete barriers to entry
   E: usual presence of profits

5. **(E)** (Chapters 9,10,11) The other choices represent the "opposite" answers. Choice **A** should read fewer choices; choice **B** should read inefficiency; choice **C** should read higher prices; choice **D** should read lower output.

6. **(B)** (Chapter 7) The rule to follow is a tax for a negative externality and a subsidy for a positive externality. Both would internalize or correct the externality.

7. **(A)** (Chapter 7) See number 6.

8. **(D)** (Chapter 7) A negative externality is an outcome of a market transaction that is not "captured" by the price mechanism by the buyer or the seller and thus, it is incurred by other parties and is added to private costs.

9. **(D)** (Chapter 8) This is simply definitional. See the chapter on costs for other definitions (Chapter 8).

10. **(D)** (Chapter 8) This is a mathematical characteristic of average and marginal cost curves. See Chapter 8 on costs for other explanations.

11. **(C)** (Chapter 13) If you look at the graph for this question, you will see the demand for workers curve (D) is equal to the marginal revenue productivity (MRP) of the workers. $MRP_L = MPP_L \times P/$or MR_X). Thus, if the price for the product (P_X) stays constant and if the computerized system increases MPP_L (marginal physical productivity), then MRP_L will increase illustrated as a shift of $D(MRP_L)$ to the right (shift to right, increase in demand for workers).

12. **(C)** (Chapter 4) The price floor is established since the market equilibrium price would be too low, e.g., when a $5 market wage (price) for labor is deemed insufficient. So, the government says no one can be paid less than $6 an hour (minimum wage).

13. **(D)** (Chapter 4) If interest rates for mortgage loans are 12 percent (market equilibrium) and the government says that this is too high, the government (state government under old usury laws) might establish a ceiling rate of 10 percent (below the equilibrium rate).

14. **(D)** (Chapter 6) A consumer surplus is established as the difference between the total utility (satisfaction) received and the price paid by the consumer. Because of diminishing marginal utility, consumers are able to buy a product at the price of the last unit sold (lower marginal utility) while the marginal utility of previous units would be higher.

15. **(B)** (Chapter 13) First, construct a third column headed marginal physical product (MPP) which would be the difference in pair sets for each additional worker hired (e.g., 30 MPP as the difference between 40 pair sets for one worker, and 70 pair sets for two workers) Second, construct a fourth column headed MRP_L (marginal revenue product) which is the function of $MPP_L \times P_X$. Then you will find the *number* of workers (first column) hired that will maximize the profits of the firm doing the hiring. This number will be the level of hiring at which $MRP_L \times P_L$ (or wage rate, which = $1,250). Thus,

(1) Number of Workers	(2) Pair Sets Produced for Two Weeks	(3) MPP_L	(4) MRP_L (#3 × $50, P_X)
1	40		—
2	70	30	$1,500
3	95	25	1,250
4	115	20	1,000
5	130	15	750
6	130	0	—

Since the pair sets are sold at $50, column 4 is $MPP_L \times P_L$ ($50). The profit-maximizing level is three workers whose MRP_L is $1,250, which is equal to the wage paid every two weeks of $1,250 per worker. If there is no level at which the wage rate = MRP_L, then the firm would hire the highest level of workers where MRP_L is greater than the wage rate paid.

16. **(A)** (Chapter 11) The reference is to the graph supplied for Questions 16–19. The profit-maximizing (best) output and the selling price are determined by the intersection of marginal cost and marginal revenue (MR = MC). The price, P_A, is read from the demand curve or by extending a vertical line from the intersection of MR and MC to the demand curve (point A); the related point on the price axis is P_A. Similarly, the best output is X_A, which is found by dropping a vertical line from the intersection of MC and MR to the output (horizontal) axis.

17. **(D)** (Chapter 11) Point A is the unregulated position as described above in the response to Question 16. At "G" is the typical point for regulation of public utilities (at least, this was the case before deregulation of the generating function of these utilities); it is supposed to approximate the "fair return" for investors in public utilities. In other words, price would be set at average total cost (ATC), which would include implicit costs or normal returns that would be equal to the returns in competitive, similar risk markets. The other form or regulation would require the government to subsidize firms to sell and produce at the socially optimal or efficient level of P = MC (point E).

18. **(C)** (Chapter 11) The firm would be subsidized at the point at which P = MC (socially efficient, see 17 above) or the point of intersection of MC with the demand curve.

19. **(A)** (Chapter 11) We start with point A and the related point P_A (see answer 16). Then to complete the rectangle, we extend a vertical line from point B (MC = MR) to its intersection with average total cost (ATC) to find the per unit cost at point H. We then extend a line horizontally from H to its intersection with the price (vertical) axis at point P_H; thus, the rectangle P_AAHP_H.

20. **(C)** (Chapter 10) The correct answer is CBGE in reference to the graph supplied for Questions 20–23. Profits for the perfectly competitive firm are at the level of MR = MC. Remember, with perfect competition P = MR for the firm. The demand function is horizontal (P = MR). Also, MC intersects ATC at the minimum point of ATC. Thus, profits are maximized (with a market price of $37) at output level of 39 batteries. Point E is where MR = MC and a line dropped perpendicular to the output axis indicates a level of output of 39.

21. **(E)** (Chapter 10) With a price of $19, price is less than AVC at all levels of output. The minimum price of AVC (average variable cost) is $20 (point K). If the price is less than the average variable cost, the firm should shut down in the short run. Its best output would then equal its total fixed costs (TFC). Thus, the firm's best output is zero.

22. **(C)** (Chapter 10) At $22 (P = MR), MC = MR (intersection of MR ($22) with MC) at output level of 31,000 batteries. See point J.

23. **(A)** (Chapter 10) At a price of $22, P is less than ATC (see graph for Questions 20–23). This would result in a loss.

24. **(C)** (Chapter 4) The government accounce-ment would result in an increase in demand for red grape juice. With supply constant, the price for red grape juice would increase. The change would **not** be a change along a demand curve or a change in quantity demanded. There are only two choices that include an increase in demand with only one of them (C) showing an increase in price as well as no change in quantity demanded.

25. **(B)** (Chapter 4) When there is an increase in demand for coffee, both the equilibrium quantity and equilibrium price increase with an increase in supply; the equilibrium quantity also increases while the price decreases. A

suggestion for answering Questions 25–28: Draw the appropriate changes (e.g., shift in D and shift in S) and compare the results with the original equilibrium position. Use the graph supplied to make these comparisons.

26. **(E)** (Chapter 4) In the chapter on the basics of supply and demand (Chapter 4), there is a list of factors that will cause shifts in supply and demand curves (those determinants that we hold constant, *ceteris paribus*, when analyzing changes along a supply or demand curve). When the government provides a subsidy to the producer, there is a decrease (in effect) in the cost of production that encourages more production (shift to the right of the supply curve).

27. **(A)** (Chapter 4) An increase in costs of production such as wage increases will lead to the opposite of answer 26, a decrease in supply.

28. **(C)** (Chapter 4) A change in the price of coffee, *ceteris paribus*, will be a change along a demand curve for coffee. A price increase would cause consumers to want to buy less coffee.

29. **(E)** (Chapter 13) All other factors could cause wages to differ among workers.

30. **(B)** (Chapter 12) This is a reference to the graph supplied for Questions 30–31. This is the typical tendency, in the long run, for monopolistic competitors—price equals average total cost (not at minimum ATC), allowing firms normal profits (zero economic profits). At MC = MR, price is at OD and output is at OX.

31. **(E)** (Chapter 12) See the answer for 30 above for zero economic profits. The firm operates inefficiently since ATC is above minimum level.

32. **(C)** (Chapter 8) With economies of scale, as production increases there are savings in average costs of production. When output increases more than proportionately to increases in input, the firm is getting more output per added input or, in effect, there is a decrease in cost of production.

33. **(A)** (Chapter 8) In other words (in contrast to the other answers or choices), supply is able to adjust fully to changes in demand in the long run. In the short run, all inputs are not variable; some are fixed in quantity. In the short run, supply is unable to adjust fully to the changes in demand.

34. **(C)** (Chapter 5) Elastic means a coefficient of elasticity greater than 1 or a more than proportional increase of quantity demanded to a decrease in price. Since P × Q = total revenue, if prices decrease by 15 percent and while total revenue increases by 30 percent, there is a factor of 2. That is, the response in quantity demanded was twice the percentage change in price, leading to an increase in total revenue. Price elasticity = 1 (unit elastic, proportional); Price elasticity > 1 (elastic, more than proportional); price elasticity < 1 (inelastic less than proportional).

35. **(D)** (Chapter 5) Only one copy available means the supply is fixed (vertical supply curve) and does not change with changes in price (perfectly inelastic).

36. **(C)** (Chapter 10) This is the only choice that is not a characteristic of perfectly competitive markets; instead, it is a characteristic of oligopolies or other forms of imperfect competition.

37. **(C)** (Chapter 8) This is purely definitional.

38. **(E)** (Chapter 12) None of the other choices is appropriate. Monopolistic competition is characterized by lower output, higher price than competitive industries. Price is greater than MR and greater than MC.

39. **(C)** (Chapter 11) Consumer surplus is that excess of utility over price paid for goods or services. If you measure total utility as the area under the demand curve up to the amount of output consumed (AEKO), and if you subtract the cost (GOKE), you are left with the consumer surplus, triangle AGE. This is in reference to the graph for Questions 39–41.

40. **(B)** (Chapter 11) This occurs after the monopolist extracts HGEB as profits from the consumer surplus.

41. **(A)** (Chapter 11) The original surplus is AGE. If the monopolist's profit is HGFB and if the dead-weight loss is BFE, then the reduced consumer surplus must be the remaining triangle, AHB.

42. **(C)** (Chapter 5) As a device, consider the following table:

P	Q	TR	Elasticity
increases	decreases	increases	inelastic, E <1
increases	decreases	decreases	elastic, E >1
increases	decreases	no change	unit elastic, E = 1
decreases	increases	no change	unit elastic, E = 1
decreases	increases	increases	elastic, E >1
decreases	increases	decreases	inelastic, E <1

43. **(A)** (Chapter 4) If the question had read "If the price of one good (A) increases and the quantity demanded of other good decreases," the answer would be **B**, complement goods. Review these definitions.

44. **(B)** (Chapter 6) This is definitional. You should review the other terms as well. One is in the next question.

45. **(A)** (Chapter 8) This is definitional. You can place "productivity" with inputs and outputs for firms or suppliers. You can place "utility" with satisfaction in purchases and consumers.

46. **(D)** (Chapter 13) This is a very important concept, derived demand.

47. **(B)** (Chapter 13) The key concept here is that the demand for labor is derived from the demand for the product that labor produces. Thus, the greater the price elasticity of demand for the product, the greater the wage elasticity of demand for labor. Also, each of the other choices for this question are the opposites of the correct answer, for example, for **E** the answer should read "the greater the portion of labor costs to total costs." See Chapter 13, Resource Markets, for the complete analysis.

48. **(E)** (Chapter 13) A transfer earning is a reflection of a competitive labor (resource) market. It is the earning that could have been received elsewhere. A payment in excess of a transfer earning is called an *economic rent* (as in the next question).

49. **(A)** (Chapter 13) This is above the earnings of other basketball players and qualifies as a *rent*. See the explanation above for number 48.

50. **(C)** (Chapter 13). This is definitional. You should review this along with bases for wage differentials.

51. **(A)** (Chapter 12). Both Trumped and Bumped have a dominant strategy. If Trumped charges $40, regardless of whether Bumped charges $40 or $35, Trumped profits of $60 (when both charge $40) and $58 (when Bumped charges $35) are higher than if Trumped dropped the price to $35. That is, $60 > $55 and $68 > $58. High price is the dominant strategy for Trumped. Similarly, the dominant strategy of high price ($40) is that of Bumped. With high price of $50, Bumped is better off no matter which pricing strategy is employed by Trumped. Thus, for Bumped $57 of profits > $51 and $59 of profits > $56 of profits.

52. **(B)** (Chapter 8) This is definitional. Review the various definitions of economic (accounting) costs/profits in Chapter 8, Costs, Production, Supply.

53. **(D)** (Chapter 10) This refers to a firm operating under perfect competition in the long run. For each firm in the long run, P = minimum average cost (zero economic profits). Also, P = MR; P = MC and all the competition is based on price.

54. **(A)** (Chapter 12) This refers to the interdependence characteristic of oligopoly. Price decreases are matched in the hope of maintaining or increasing market share. Price increases are *not* matched for fear of losing market share or having the possibility of gaining market share over the price-increasing rival.

55. **(E)** Review Table 12.1 in Chapter 12 for a comparison of pure competition and monopolistic competition. P = MC is a long run characteristic of pure competition.

56. **(C)** (Chapter 8) This refers to the supply curve of perfectly competitive firms in product markets. Elasticity tends to be greater in the long run since the firm will be able to adjust to changes in demand. The firm will have more options in availability of resources in order to substitute less expensive resources (inputs) for more expensive resources in the long run.

57. **(A)** (Chapter 9) This refers to "relatively free or easy entry." That is, if competitors are allowed easy entry, there will be more consumer choices. The increased choice for consumers means that they will be more sensitive (elastic) to price increases. Review the table of characteristics of product markets in Chapter 9, Introduction to Product Markets.

58. **(C)** (Chapter 11) $(P - MC)/P$ is the Lerner index of monopoly pricing power. The higher the value of this ratio, the higher the pricing power of a firm. In effect, the index measures the firm's ability to price its goods over marginal cost. If the socially optimal price for efficiency is $P = MC$, this ability to price greater than marginal cost suggests inefficiency.

59. **(B)** (Chapters 10,11,12) This fundamental difference between perfect competition and imperfect competition is crucial to success on the exam. It is often asked on free-response questions.

60. **(B)** (Chapter 4) This is in reference to "Which of the following does NOT describe how resources are allocated (competitive market)?" All of the other choices are related to allocation in a competitive market system. Active government ownership and direction of production is more akin to non-market systems such as socialism.

FREE-RESPONSE QUESTIONS

For each of the free-response questions, we have provided answers that contain the significant concepts and their relationship to the question. We have also supplied the necessary graphs (labeled) with their relationship to the answer. For each of these suggested answers, you should refer to the question as asked in the free-response section of this model examination.

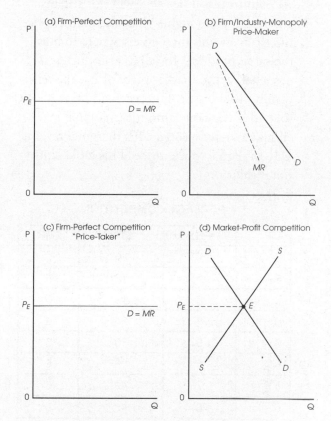

1. A. Price (P) and Marginal Revenue (MR) are differently related under perfect competition and monopoly. Graph 1(a) shows the demand function as the marginal revenue curve, for perfect competition. That indicates that *P = MR under perfect competition*, e.g., Price at P_E in graph 1(a). For monopoly, P > MR (graph 1(b)). MR is derived from the downward sloping demand curve. As illustrated in graph 1(b), the marginal revenue function becomes more distant from the demand function as price decreases.

B. These relationships between P and MR differ for the two markets basically on the basis of a firm being a price-taker (perfect competition) or a price-maker (monopoly). The perfectly competitive firm is a price-taker, for example, the market where all buyers and sellers meet determines the price. Graph 1, parts (c) and (d) illustrate this point. In 1(d), the market determines the price, P_E, that each seller must use. The seller will not sell any goods at a price higher than the market price since buyers will then go elsewhere to buy the same product. To sell the product at a price below the market price of P_E, the seller would incur losses. Thus each additional unit sold adds the same amount (marginal revenue) to total revenue. This marginal revenue (MR) is equal to the price. This table illustrates this point:

PERFECT COMPETITION

$P	Q	$TR	$MR
6	1	6	
6	2	12	6
6	3	18	6
6	4	24	6
6	5	30	6
6	6	36	6
6	7	42	6
6	8	48	6

For monopoly or other forms of imperfect competition, there is a downward sloping demand curve that indicates that the seller can induce more sales of a product by lowering the price. Since marginal revenue is derived from the demand function or price, we find that P > MR. As illustrated below:

MONOPOLY

$P	Q	$TR	$MR
10	1	10	
9	2	18	8
8	3	24	6
7	4	28	4
6	5	30	2
5	6	30	0
4	7	28	-2
3	8	24	-4

This indicates that the monopolist can be a price-maker.

C. All of the above suggests a significant effect on price strategy that will be different for the monopolist as contrasted with the perfect competitor. Essentially, the perfect competitor has no price strategy. As explained and illustrated above, the perfect competitive firm is a price-taker—accepts the price as determined by the market and does not vary price as more units are sold. P = MR is reflective of this. The price competitor's only market decision is how many units to sell. To attempt sales at a higher than market price would result in loss of sales to competitors; to attempt sales at lower than market price would result in losses in the long run.

For the monopolist, there is a pricing strategy. As explained and illustrated above, the monopolist faces a downward sloping demand function (P > MR) and can induce more sales by lowering the price. Thus the monopolist can be a price-maker. This power is enhanced by the monopolist having no competitors (within the industry) that have close substitutes. Of course, the price elasticities of demand can place limits on both the lowering of prices and the increasing of prices. The relationship among price, elasticity of demand, and marginal revenue is $MR = P[1 - (1/\eta]$ where η = numerical coefficient of elasticity.

2. A. The ratio of $(P - MR)/P$ demonstrates the degree of marketing power for firms, that is, the larger the value of the index, the larger the mark-up pricing power of the firm. The smaller the firm's demand elasticity at the profit-maximizing output, the greater the Price minus MC market-up and the greater the monopoly power. We start with the criterion for profit maximization being that level of output where $MR = MC$. As explained in essay number 1, $P > MR$ for the imperfectly competitive firm and $P = MR$ for the perfectly competitive firm. Therefore, for the monopolist $P > MC$. Thus, the numerator for the monopolist will be positive or greater than zero. However, for the perfectly competitive firm the index value of the ratio will equal zero. This follows from $P = MR$ and $MR = MC$ for perfect competition. All of this can be put to symbols and values of the ratio as follows:

For imperfectly competitive firms:

$$\frac{(P - MC)}{P} \rightarrow P > MC \rightarrow \text{positive value}$$
$\rightarrow$ positive since all prices are above zero. Thus, ratio is positive (follows from $P > MC$ and $MR = MC$)

For perfectly competitive firms:
since $P = MC$ and $P = MR$ and $MR = MC$

$$\frac{(P - MC)}{P} = \frac{0}{>0} = 0$$

Therefore, since $P > MC$ in imperfectly competitive markets and $P = MC$ in perfectly competitive markets, the pricing power is clearly that of monopolists or other imperfectly competitive firms. They can charge a price higher than their marginal costs.

B. The consequences of A are that the perfectly competitive firm must charge a price that is equal to marginal cost. This is a socially optimal or efficient price. In other words, the consumer is able to coax out an additional unit of a product at a price exactly equal to the added cost (MC) of the producer. Society pays what is minimally necessary to induce or maintain production of goods. Conversely, if consumers pay a price greater than marginal cost, consumers are paying a rent to the producer, a price *higher* than would be minimally necessary to induce additional production. The monopolist has pricing power, a price-maker, subject to constraints. The perfect competitor has no pricing power, or $P = MC$, $P = MR$.

3. For this question, we advise that you draw two graphs, side by side, as illustrated in graph 2(a) and (b).

Perfect Competition Adjustment to LR

We begin at equilibrium with the market at price, P_E, and with each firm selling and producing at P_E. At P_E and associated output, X_E, each firm sells and produces its output where $P = MC$, $P = MR$, $P = $ minimum average cost. Next, demand increases from DD to D'D'. Each firm now sees its demand increasing to D'. Since $MR = P$, price (P_E) is now in excess of average cost and short run profits are realized. The profits induce new firms to enter in such a way that supply SS increases to S'S'. This excess supply suppresses prices to P''_E and firms incur losses (D''D'' lower than AC). Some (less efficient) firms exit and the consequent new equilibrium point (E''') is at the same level of price (P_E) as the original equilibrium.

Consequently, the old equilibrium of P_E and X_E are restored. Thus, in long run equilibrium under perfect competition, $P = MC$; $P = MR$; $P =$ minimum average cost and profits are zero economic profits. The economy is operating efficiently and the socially optimal price, $P = MC$, obtains.

4. For the butter and margarine markets, the following graphs are provided.

A. The new churner allows the Lots of Cream company to lower its average costs so that, given a market price of P_E, it will increase its short-term profits. The firm's price will stay the same since the price is set in the market (price-taker), but its profits will rise from zero to positive profits. The decrease in costs is illustrated as average cost moves from AC to AC'. Thus, economic profits exist as P stays the same and AC decreases. Before the cost decrease, P = minimum AC resulting in zero profits.

B. The effect of the other competitive firms adopting the same cost-saving technology is that the supply curve in graph 3(a) for the butter market would increase (shift in supply to the right), which is illustrated as a shift from SS to S'S'. The effect of this would be a decrease in the equilibrium price from P_E to P'_E and an increase in equilibrium quantity from X_E to X'_E. If costs of production decrease, the market would increase its supply of butter, *ceteris paribus*. This means that the price-cost ratio increases with price staying constant (competitive market) and costs decreasing so that suppliers are motivated to provide more products.

C. The effects of the above changes on the price and quantity of margarine would be that since margarine and butter are substitutes, and since the price of butter has decreased, the demand for margarine would decrease (from DD to D'D') resulting in a decrease in the equilibrium price from P_E to P'_E and a decrease in equilibrium quantity from X_E to X'_E as illustrated in Graph 3(b).

MACROECONOMICS

As you work toward achieving that 5 on your AP Macroeconomics exam, here are five essentials that you **MUST** know above everything else:

1

Understand the aggregate supply/aggregate demand model. This concept is critical for doing well on the exam. It is likely to appear on a free-response question and will be used to answer multiple-choice questions.
- As with any diagram, be able to label all axes and curves.
- You should know what can shift the aggregate supply and aggregate demand curves.
- You should be able to use the model to conclude what will happen in the long run and in the short run when one or both of the curves shifts.

2

Vocabulary is important. Very few, if any, of the questions on the AP exam will ask you to define a specific term but you need to know the definition of technical ones.
- For instance, a multiple-choice question may ask about closing an inflationary gap. You will be at a total loss if the term "inflationary gap" is not in your vocabulary.
- Be sure you know the terms listed at the end of each chapter.

3

Monetary and fiscal policy are critical concepts. One of the most important things a student learns in introductory macroeconomics is that monetary and fiscal policy can be used to help fight unemployment and inflation.
- Be able to demonstrate how monetary and fiscal policy work on an aggregate supply/aggregate demand diagram.
- There are several reasons why monetary and fiscal policy may not work. You should be able to list and explain these reasons.
- Monetary and fiscal policy are not as effective in economies that rely heavily on international trade and have flexible exchange rates. You should be able to explain why.

4

Diagrams are more important than formulas. Important formulas are listed at the end of each chapter. However, calculators are not allowed on the exam, so complex calculations will not be required.
- Easy formulas such as Fisher's hypothesis or the formula for the unemployment rate are more likely to come into play on the exam.
- Specific diagrams, such as the supply and demand for loanable funds, are often required. Be sure to label all axes and curves. If you forget a label, use something general like "Q" for quantity or "D" for demand.

5

Be definite in your conclusions to free-response questions. Some questions are complex and have different conclusions in different circumstances. Nevertheless, be definite in your response.
- If you use the wrong approach on a free-response question but your conclusion is correct, you will still earn points. State your conclusion clearly.
- You can earn points on a free-response question just for having the appropriate graph correctly labeled. To obtain full credit, explain what is happening on the graph and reach the correct conclusion.

CHAPTER 14

The National Economic Accounts

- Gross domestic product (GDP)
- Real GDP
- The underground economy
- Gross national product (GNP)
- National income
- Personal income

THE ACCOUNTS

The National Economic Accounts (NEA) make up a comprehensive group of statistics that measure various aspects of the economy's performance. For instance, if everyone's income in the United States was summed together, how much would that be? The figure for personal income in 2010 was $12,546.7 billion. What were corporate profits in 2010? $1,624.8 billion. Personal income and corporate profits are two examples of the hundreds of statistics included in NEA.

NEA includes a variety of measures of income and production. The most recent updates on these figures are published by the Department of Commerce in a periodical titled the "Survey of Current Business." On the Internet, updates are available at *www.bea.gov*, the home page of the Bureau of Economic Analysis (BEA), an agency within the Department of Commerce.

GROSS DOMESTIC PRODUCT

The premier statistic for measuring the overall performance of the economy is gross domestic product (GDP). GDP measures the dollar value of production within the nation's borders. Generally speaking, the more that is produced, the healthier the economy.

The BEA provides "flash" estimates of GDP for each quarter about 30 days after the quarter ends, but these rough estimates are subject to large revisions. The annual estimates of GDP are more reliable, but they, too, are subject to revision.

An amazing feature of these estimates is that they are available on such a timely basis. Consider all of the goods and services produced in the United States in a year, from toothpicks and cellular phones to haircuts and surgery. How does the BEA keep track of all this production? For 2010, GDP was estimated to be $14,660.4 billion.

How did the BEA arrive at this figure? A small army of statisticians and analysts keeps track of production and sales of a wide variety of goods and services. For instance, one person is responsible for Popsicle sticks, toothpicks, and tongue depressors. This person gets in touch with the major suppliers and retailers of these products. From this survey an estimate of the number of toothpicks sold is obtained. There is a difference between the number of toothpicks sold and the number produced, but this difference will be allowed for later. The survey of manufacturers and retailers also yields an average price of toothpicks. Then the number of toothpicks sold is multiplied by their price to get the dollar value of toothpick sales.

The dollar values of all other products sold are added to the figure for toothpicks to obtain an estimate of total sales of goods and services. The resulting figure is known as "final sales" and is part of NEA. But it is not GDP. GDP measures *production* not sales. There may be goods that are produced but not sold. They will show up in inventories at the manufacturers or at the retailers. Therefore, the change in business inventories is added to final sales to arrive at GDP.

Table 14.1 shows the calculation of GDP for a hypothetical economy that produces only two products—pizza and soda. In the year 2010, four pizzas are produced at an average retail price of $10; 12 sodas are produced at a price of $2. GDP is $64. In the year 2011, pizza production is up to five pizzas and the price has increased to $11. Soda production is up to 15 units, but the price has fallen to $1. GDP is $70.

TABLE 14.1

Calculating GDP

Year 2010

Production	Price	Value
4 Pizzas	$10	$40
12 Sodas	$2	$24
		GDP = $64

Year 2011

Production	Price	Value
5 Pizzas	$11	$55
15 Sodas	$1	$15
		GDP = $70

This is a general overview of how GDP is estimated. In practice, many more complications arise. Some of these complications will come to light as we examine the expenditure and the income approaches to calculating GDP.

THE EXPENDITURES APPROACH

Consumption Expenditures

If you look up the estimates of GDP in the "Survey of Current Business," don't expect to see the dollar value of toothpicks sold or produced. That level of detail would require a publication much thicker than the *Oxford English Dictionary*. Instead, the BEA lumps together all the goods and services sold to households and calls this consumption expenditures.

Government Expenditures

However, state, local, and federal governments also make expenditures. The things that are produced and sold to governments are summed together and referred to as government expenditures. Some of the products that governments buy are unique to this category. For instance, fighter jets are sold to our federal government but not to individual households. On the other hand, our government purchases many of the same items bought by households, such as personal computers; but the value of personal computers purchased by the government will be different than that of households.

$$C + G + I + NX$$

Investment Expenditures

Expenditures by businesses on plant and equipment are called investment expenditures; thus, the term "investment" means something very different in its economic sense. It does not refer to households buying stocks or bonds. The complete definition of investment is business expenditures on plant and equipment plus the change in business inventories. The change in business inventories was mentioned in the previous section. It changes the figure for final sales into GDP. The BEA lumps the change in inventories in with business spending on plant and equipment to get what it calls investment.

Exports and Imports

Many goods and services are produced here and sold abroad. These are called exports. Some of the expenditures made by households, government, and businesses will be on goods and services from abroad. These imports should not be included in our GDP since they represent production outside our nation's borders. That is why imports are subtracted from exports to get "net exports."

GDP represents production. Some of the goods and services produced go to households, some to government, some to businesses, and some are sold abroad. Imports are subtracted out because these products were not made domestically, yet they are counted in consumption expenditures by households, purchases by government, and investment by firms.

The expenditure approach to calculating GDP is often summarized with the formula:

$$GDP = C + I + G + X$$

where C is consumption expenditures by households
I is investment by firms
G is government purchases
X is net exports = exports − imports

The formula appears deceptively simple. Remember that to obtain the figure for C, consumption expenditures, quite a bit of effort is required. The average price and quantity sold of millions of products must be gathered. The same must be done for I, G, and X.

Table 14.2 shows the components of the expenditures approach to calculating GDP with their values for 2010. Notice that about 70 percent of all the goods and services produced go to households.

TABLE 14.2

The Expenditure Approach to GDP—2010

(Billion of Dollars)	
Consumption expenditures	10,349.1
Government expenditures	3,000.2
Investment	1,827.5
Net exports	−516.4
GDP	14,660.4

Source: U.S. Department of Commerce, Bureau of Economic Analysis

THE INCOME APPROACH

The BEA takes the trouble to calculate GDP in a manner completely different from the expenditures approach outlined above. This second way of calculating GDP is known as the income approach. The income approach yields several statistics that are incorporated into NEA and provides a check on the expenditures approach.

Theoretically, both techniques for calculating GDP will result in exactly the same figure because when anything is produced, whether it is a stick of gum or a sky-scraper, just enough income is generated in the production process to equal the value of what is produced.

Consider a toaster that retails for $15. Suppose it costs $10 to manufacture:

Labor	$6
Materials	$3
Overhead	$1

Since the toaster retails for $15, then $5 in profits were made when it was sold. So, if everyone who had anything to do with the manufacture of the toaster chipped in the income they made, it would equal $15 exactly. Workers made $6; raw material owners made $3; the utility company (overhead) made $1; and the owner of the toaster company made $5. Altogether, this comes to $15.

Notice that if the toaster sold for $15.01, then $5.01 in profits would have been earned and the principle would still hold true: whenever anything is produced, just enough is earned to buy it back. Therefore, an alternate way to measure GDP, which measures production, would be to add up all the income that was earned in the economy. That is the income approach to calculating GDP.

Table 14.3 outlines the income approach for calculating GDP. Wages and salaries are the predominant type of income. But there is also proprietors' income, rental income, and interest income. Corporate profits must also be included because this represents corporate income and corporations are owned by their shareholders. There are some adjustments that must be made once all the types of income are summed together. Specifically, indirect business taxes (such as business licenses) and depreciation must be added in.

TABLE 14.3

The Income Approach to GDP—2010

(Billion of Dollars)	
Compensation of employees	7,991.1
Proprietors' income	1,055.0
Rental income	300.9
Interest income	738.1
Corporate profits	1,624.8
Taxes on production and imports	1,081.6
Depreciation	+1,868.9
GDP	14,660.4

Source: U.S. Department of Commerce, Bureau of Economic Analysis

ADJUSTING FOR PRICE CHANGES

GDP measures production, but one cannot conclude that more was produced simply because this year's GDP was greater than last because prices may have risen. The rise in prices could offset a decline in production volume, resulting in a higher figure for GDP. Clearly, if the prices of the goods and services produced changes, so will GDP, regardless of production.

There is, however, a simple way to correct for price changes: When calculating GDP for different years, use prices from just one of those years. This way the prices are constant from one year to the next and any change in GDP must be due to a change in production.

TIP

Any economic statistic with the term "real" inserted in front of it means that statistic has been adjusted for inflation, i.e., real interest rate, real consumer spending.

The BEA routinely makes this correction and the resulting figure is known as "real GDP," or "constant-dollar GDP." In order to make the distinction, regular GDP is sometimes referred to as "nominal" or "current-dollar GDP." The year from which prices are taken to calculate real GDP is called the base year. It does not matter which year is chosen as the base year. The important feature is that prices are held constant, so that any changes in real GDP are the result of changes in the amount of production.

Table 14.4 shows nominal and real GDP over the years. An astute reader could deduce that 2005 is the base year since real and nominal GDP are equivalent in that year. Once nominal and real GDP have been calculated, it is a simple matter to obtain a measure of price changes. But this statistic will be discussed in the next chapter when inflation and price indexes are taken up.

TABLE 14.4

Nominal and Real GDP

	Nominal GDP (billions of $)	Real GDP (billions of chained 2005 $)
2000	9,951.5	11,226.0
2001	10,286.2	11,347.2
2002	10,642.3	11,553.0
2003	11,142.1	11,840.7
2004	11,867.8	12,263.8
2005	12,638.4	12,638.4
2006	13,398.9	12,976.2
2007	14,601.8	13,228.8
2008	14,369.1	13,228.8
2009	14,119.0	12,880.6
2010	14,660.4	13,248.2

THE UNDERGROUND ECONOMY

Each year there are trillions of dollars of goods and services that are produced and never counted in GDP. All of this production falls into what is called the underground economy. The first thing that comes to mind with regard to the underground economy is illegal items and activities, but illegal production and ill-gotten income are the smaller part of the underground economy.

Marry your auto mechanic, the saying goes, and you will lower GDP. This is true because when you took your car to the shop to be repaired, the BEA was able to estimate the transaction and include it in GDP under household consumption. Now that the mechanic is your spouse, the auto repairs are done out back under the shade tree. The BEA does not attempt to measure this sort of production.

Anything households do for themselves and that does not pass through a market goes unmeasured. This amounts to quite a bit of production. The backyard gardens, the lawn maintenance, the cleaning, the babysitting, etc. One estimate of underground household production puts it at 30 percent of official GDP.

Illegal gambling services, prostitution, and drugs are not counted in official GDP estimates. The housepainter who insists on being paid in cash to avoid taxes is part of the underground economy.

Adding together the legal and illegal sides of the underground economy, some analysts get a figure that is 150 percent of the official figure. That implies that production in the United States in 2010 was closer to $22,000.0 billion than the official figure of $14,660.4 billion.

OTHER THINGS NOT COUNTED IN GDP

The underground economy is a subset of total production that is not counted in GDP but, technically speaking, should be. The illegal nature of the goods and services involved often prohibits estimation. However, there is a list of things that are not counted in GDP and rightly so.

1. For instance, it would be incorrect to count **secondhand sales** in GDP. When you sell your 1997 Ford truck, this does not represent production in the current year. The truck was counted in the GDP of 1997 and there is no reason to count it, or any portion of it, again simply because it is being resold.

2. **Transactions that are purely financial** are not, and should not be, counted in GDP. If you buy 100 shares of IBM stock, this does not directly represent any new production. Someone got your money and you got their shares of IBM. This swap does not affect GDP.

3. **Intermediate sales** are not included in GDP. These are sales to firms that will incorporate the item into their final product. An example will help here. When a corporation that makes Popsicles buys Popsicle sticks, this is an intermediate sale. When a person buys a Popsicle, he cannot avoid buying the stick as well. This latter transaction is counted in GDP and valued at the price of the Popsicle and the stick. So the stick would be counted twice if the purchase of sticks by the manufacturer was included in GDP and the final sale to the consumer was also counted.

   As another example of an intermediate transaction, the purchase of flour by a baker is not counted in GDP because the flour will get counted when the bread is purchased by a household. However, when a baker buys a delivery truck, this is not an intermediate transaction and the purchase gets counted in GDP under investment expenditures.

OTHER MEASURES IN THE NATIONAL ECONOMIC ACCOUNTS

Table 14.5 highlights several other important measures in NEA aside from GDP. Again, GDP measures overall production, and therefore income as well, in the economy. Gross national product is similar to GDP except GNP includes production by American workers abroad and excludes production by foreign workers in America.

TABLE 14.5

GDP and Other Measures in NEA—2010

(Billions of Dollars)	
Gross Domestic Product (GDP)	14,660.4
Gross National Product (GNP)	14,848.7
National Income (NI)	12,828.2
Personal Income (PI)	12,546.7
Disposable Personal Income (DPI)	11,379.9

Source: U.S. Department of Commerce, Bureau of Economic Analysis

Another figure, national income (NI), measures the income earned by households and profits earned by firms after adjusting for depreciation and indirect business taxes. NI is often defined as the income earned by all the factors of production. The factors of production are land, labor, and capital.

NI represents the income earned by households and firms, but personal income (PI) represents the income received by households only.

Finally, disposable personal income (DPI) is the income of households after taxes have been paid. It is easily derived by subtracting personal taxes from PI. Disposable income represents the discretionary income of households. It can be spent or saved.

SUMMARY

- NEA are a bank of internally consistent statistics that measure various aspects of the economy's performance. Basically, NEA measure production and income in their various forms. An implicit assumption behind the statistics is that more production and more income means a better economy.

- Some economists have questioned this assumption. Are we really better off when we produce more gadgets and gizmos, and pollute the environment in the process? Is it possible for more to be produced and more income to be earned while the quality of life deteriorates? Another criticism of NEA concerns leisure time. Don't rising production levels sometimes result in less leisure time? If so, this is not reflected in the statistics where the negative side effects of increased production levels are not taken into account.

- Despite these criticisms, NEA are the best measures available for gauging the economy's health. One final note: Other nations have similar statistics, but they may not be defined or collected in the same way. There are, however, some organizations that generate and publish international data that are comparable across countries. Putting the statistics on a per capita basis also facilitates international comparisons.

TABLE 14.6

GDP and GDP Per Capita for Selected Countries, 2006

Country	GDP (billions of $)	GDP per Capita ($ per person)
Canada	1,251	38,400
China	2,668	2,000
Japan	4,340	34,000
Switzerland	380	51,000
United Kingdom	2,345	38,800
United States	13,399	44,200

Source: Central Intelligence Agency, World Fact Book

TERMS

Consumption Expenditures the dollar value of all the goods and services sold to households

Disposable Personal Income (DPI) the income of households after taxes have been paid

Government Expenditures the dollar value of goods and services sold to governments

Gross Domestic Product (GDP) dollar value of production within a nation's borders

Gross National Product (GNP) dollar value of production by a country's citizens

Intermediate Sales sales to firms that will incorporate the item into their final product

Investment Expenditures expenditures by businesses on plant and equipment and the change in business inventories

National Income (NI) the income earned by households and profits earned by firms after subtracting depreciation and indirect business taxes

National Economic Accounts (NEA) a comprehensive group of statistics that measures various aspects of the economy's performance

Net Exports exports minus imports

Personal Income (PI) income received by households

Real GDP GDP adjusted for price changes

Underground Economy all the illegal production of goods and services and legal production that does not pass through markets

FORMULAS

$$GDP = C + I + G + X$$

$$GDP \text{ per Capita} = \frac{GDP}{Population}$$

MULTIPLE-CHOICE REVIEW QUESTIONS

1. GDP is calculated for each _____ by _____.

   (A) quarter; The Bureau of Economic Analysis
   (B) week; The Bureau of Economic Analysis
   (C) month; The Bureau of Economic Analysis
   (D) month; The Bureau of Labor Statistics
   (E) quarter; The Bureau of Labor Statistics

2. "Flash" estimates of GDP

   (A) are subject to revision.
   (B) do not require revision.
   (C) are available after a thirty-day lag.
   (D) both (A) and (C)
   (E) both (B) and (C)

3. According to the way in which economists use the word, the bulk of "investment" is done by

   (A) households.
   (B) businesses.
   (C) government.
   (D) foreigners.
   (E) all of the above.

4. In the equation GDP = C + I + G + X, X stands for

   (A) exports.
   (B) expenditures.
   (C) exports minus imports.
   (D) imports minus exports.
   (E) export taxes.

5. GDP measures

   (A) production within a nation's borders.
   (B) production by a nation's citizens wherever they may be.
   (C) income earned by the factors of production plus depreciation and indirect business taxes.
   (D) (B) and (C)
   (E) (A) and (C)

6. National income measures

   (A) household income in the nation.
   (B) income earned by the factors of production.
   (C) GDP minus depreciation and indirect business taxes.
   (D) the income earned by households and profits earned by firms after adjusting for depreciation and indirect business taxes.
   (E) (B), (C), and (D).

7. Imagine an economy that produces only two goods, cheese and crackers. Calculate GDP for this economy if cheese retails for $3 a pound and 10 pounds are produced while crackers sell for $2 a pound and 20 pounds are produced.

   (A) $35
   (B) $1,200
   (C) $70
   (D) $150
   (E) Not enough information is given to calculate GDP.

8. Assume Country Z only produces hot dogs and buns. Given the table below, what is the value of GDP in Country Z?

Production	Price
4 hot dogs	$1.00
4 buns	$0.50

(A) $1.50
(B) $12.00
(C) $6.00
(D) $8.00
(E) $4.50

9. If XYZ Corporation buys an original Matisse painting to hang in its board room, then

(A) GDP decreases by the amount of the purchase because C decreases.
(B) GDP increases by the amount of the purchase because I increases.
(C) GDP is unaffected because it is a second hand sale.
(D) GDP decreases because I decreases.
(E) I increases, but C decreases.

10. The cabbages you grow in your summer garden are

(A) counted in GDP under C.
(B) counted in GDP under I.
(C) counted in GDP but not NDP.
(D) not counted in GDP.
(E) counted in final sales but not GDP.

11. Suppose transfer payments are greater than Social Security contributions, corporate taxes, and retained earnings combined. In that case,

(A) NDP will be greater than GDP.
(B) NI will be greater than GDP.
(C) PI will be greater than NI.
(D) DPI will be greater than PI.
(E) PI will be greater than GDP.

12. GDP measures

 I. production
 II. income earned during the production process
 III. spending by consumers, businesses, governments, and foreigners

(A) Only I is correct.
(B) Only II is correct.
(C) Only III is correct.
(D) Only I and II are correct.
(E) I, II, and III are correct.

13. Real GDP

(A) is actual GDP as opposed to the estimate made by the BEA.
(B) is also called current-dollar GDP.
(C) is GDP adjusted for price changes.
(D) is not calculated for the United States.
(E) (B) and (C) are both correct.

14. Which of the following events has no effect on GDP?

(A) You buy a 1957 Chevy from a friend.
(B) The Department of Transportation repaves a road.
(C) Your friends make a music CD that doesn't sell any copies.
(D) A college buys computers.
(E) You buy a bottle of French wine.

15. Which of the following will have an effect on GDP?

(A) You lose $50 betting with a friend.
(B) You fix your brother's car without buying any new parts.
(C) Your father's firm makes computers and exports them to China.
(D) You buy 1,000 shares of stock in a corporation.
(E) Your wealthy uncle buys a painting by Picasso.

Multiple-Choice Review Answers

1. **(A)**   4. **(C)**   7. **(C)**   10. **(D)**   13. **(C)**
2. **(D)**   5. **(E)**   8. **(C)**   11. **(C)**   14. **(A)**
3. **(B)**   6. **(E)**   9. **(C)**   12. **(E)**   15. **(C)**

FREE-RESPONSE REVIEW QUESTIONS

I. Explain the difference between nominal GDP, real GDP, and GDP per capita.

II. Suppose that production and prices rise from one year to the next, but population stays constant. Will each of the three statistics above rise, fall, or remain unchanged? Explain your reasoning.

III. In what type of situation is GDP per capita more appropriate than nominal or real GDP?

IV. Is GDP an under- or overestimate? Explain.

Free-Response Review Answers

I. Nominal GDP measures the production of goods and services within a nation's borders. Nominal GDP could increase because of an increase in output or an increase in the prices of the goods and services produced. Real GDP measures production, but adjusts for any price changes. Real GDP does not change if prices change because it values current output in terms of prices of the given base period. Only one thing can cause real GDP to change and that is a change in output. GDP per capita is production per person.

II. If production and prices rise while population stays constant then all three statistics, GDP, real GDP, and GDP per capita will rise.

III. GDP per capita is most appropriate for making international comparisons of GDP. The GDP of the United States is much greater than that of Switzerland, but production per person, and therefore living standards, are not all that different between the two nations.

IV. GDP is a vast underestimate of output because of all the production that is not counted. Items that do not go through standard markets are not counted. This includes illegal drugs and gambling, but also home car repair and household vegetable gardens. All of this uncounted production is known as the underground economy. Estimates are that the underground economy could be half the size of the official economy.

Inflation and Unemployment

CHAPTER

- Consumer price index (CPI)
- GDP deflator
- Costs of inflation
- Nominal vs. real interest rate
- Types of unemployment

THE TWIN EVILS

Both *inflation* and *unemployment* exert an enormous toll on the economy and, therefore, on our standard of living. The cost of unemployment is obvious: an important resource, labor, is being underutilized. This implies that we are not producing as much as if we were using our resources fully. In economic terms, we are producing inside the production possibilities frontier. Moreover, the households that are experiencing unemployment face real hardships.

The costs associated with inflation are less obvious. Many people understand that rising prices can hurt families on fixed incomes, but this is only a minor issue because most incomes keep pace with rising prices. When prices rise, someone benefits—the owners of the firms that produce the goods and services whose prices are rising. In general, rising prices imply rising incomes, so falling real incomes are not a major cost of inflation.

We will see that a more significant cost associated with inflation is the inefficiencies that ensue when people respond to rising prices. Again, we will be producing at a point inside the production possibilities frontier if we do not use our resources efficiently.

In addition, inflation arbitrarily takes purchasing power from some households and puts it in the hands of others. A massive redistribution of wealth is yet another cost of inflation.

The costs to society of rising prices are much more subtle than the blunt and obvious damages caused by unemployment. Nevertheless, it is unclear which economic evil is more pernicious. Only normative conclusions are possible on this question.

INFLATION

How Inflation Is Measured

Inflation is a sustained rise in most prices in the economy. The inflation rate is the rate at which prices are rising. It is much easier to define inflation than to measure it.

Each month the Bureau of Labor Statistics (BLS) checks prices on 90,000 items at more than 23,000 retail and service outlets. The BLS checks prices in urban, suburban, and rural areas. Because prices are liable to be different in different regions, the BLS must check prices on the same items in every part of the country.

The result of all this effort is the predominant measure of the cost of living in the United States—the consumer price index (CPI). The CPI measures the average change over time in the prices paid by urban consumers for a market basket of consumer goods and services. The BLS computes the CPI for each month.

Consider a simple example where the typical household in the economy consumes 5 packages of cheese and 8 boxes of crackers in a month. If the price of cheese rises to $2.25 from $2.00 and the price of crackers climbs to $1.50 from $1.25, then the CPI rises to 116.25 from 100. The calculations are shown in Table 15.1. The assumption is that period 1 is the base period, the period to which all other periods are compared.

TABLE 15.1

Calculating the Consumer Price Index

Period 1

Item	Price	Amount	Cost
Cheese	$2.00	5	$10.00
Crackers	$1.25	8	$10.00

Total cost = $20.00

$$CPI = \frac{\text{Total Cost this Period}}{\text{Total Cost Base Period}} \times 100 = \frac{20.00}{20.00} \times 100 = 100$$

Period 2

Item	Price	Amount	Cost
Cheese	$2.25	5	$11.25
Crackers	$1.50	8	$12.00

Total cost = $23.25

$$CPI = \frac{\text{Total Cost this Period}}{\text{Total Cost Base Period}} \times 100 = \frac{23.25}{20.00} \times 100 = 116.25$$

Period 3

Item	Price	Amount	Cost
Cheese	$2.35	5	$11.75
Crackers	$1.60	8	$12.80

Total cost = $24.55

$$CPI = \frac{\text{Total Cost this Period}}{\text{Total Cost Base Period}} \times 100 = \frac{24.55}{20.00} \times 100 = 122.75$$

In period 3, the CPI rises to 122.75. To calculate the inflation rate between any two periods, take the percentage change in the CPI. For example, the inflation rate between periods 2 and 3 is:

$$\text{Inflation Rate} = (122.75 - 116.25)/116.25 = .0559 = 5.59\%$$

The inflation rate between periods 1 and 3 is:

$$\text{Inflation Rate} = (122.75 - 100.00)/100.00 = .2275 = 22.75\%$$

These calculations indicate that the cost of living for a typical family in this economy increased 5.59 percent between periods 1 and 2 and 22.75 percent between periods 1 and 3.

In the real world, many complications arise when calculating the CPI that are not apparent in this simple example. For instance, what should be done when the quality of a product changes? The price of automobiles has risen dramatically since the 1950s, but so has the quality of the product. A new car these days comes with seat belts and air bags—safety devices that were not available in earlier versions of the product. Quality improvements such as this account for some portion of the price increase. The CPI overstates the amount of inflation since it does not account for all quality improvements.

This is just one example of how the CPI can overstate cost of living increases. A 1996 study from a bipartisan commission concluded that the CPI overstates inflation by more than one percentage point a year. The discrepancy is important because most income maintenance programs, such as Social Security, adjust their benefit payments with the CPI.

The GDP Deflator

Inflation can be measured with another statistic—the GDP deflator. In the previous chapter we discussed how GDP and real GDP are calculated. Both of these statistics can be used to obtain the GDP deflator through a simple formula:

$$\text{GDP Deflator} = (\text{GDP}/\text{Real GDP}) \times 100$$

In 2010 GDP was \$14,660.4 billion, while real GDP equaled \$13,248.2 billion. Therefore the GDP deflator for 2010 was 110.7 (= (14,660.4 / 13,248.2) × 100). Table 15.2 shows GDP, real GDP, and the GDP deflator over the years.

To calculate the inflation rate between any two years simply take the percentage change in the GDP deflator. By what percent did prices rise from 2000 to 2010? 24.9 percent (= (110.7 − 88.6)/88.6)). In other words, there was 24.9 percent inflation between 2000 and 2010.

The GDP deflator, like the CPI, measures the level of prices in the economy. The inflation rates derived from the GDP deflator, however, do not match the inflation rates obtained from the CPI. Both inflation gauges suggest the same general pattern of inflation over the years.

The GDP deflator ignores import prices. If the price of imported beer increased, the CPI would rise in response, but not the GDP deflator. Still, for most years the CPI and the GDP deflator do not differ markedly.

TABLE 15.2

GDP, Real GDP, and the GDP Deflator

$$GDP\ Deflator = \frac{Nominal\ GDP}{Real\ GDP} \times 100$$

$$Real\ GDP = \frac{Nominal\ GDP}{Real\ GDP} \times 100$$

Year	Nominal GDP	Real GDP	GDP Deflator
2000	9,951.5	11,226.0	88.6
2001	10,286.2	11,347.2	90.7
2002	10,642.3	11,553.0	92.1
2003	11,142.1	11,840.7	94.1
2004	11,867.8	12,263.8	96.8
2005	12,638.4	12,638.4	100.0
2006	13,398.9	12,976.2	103.3
2007	14,061.8	13,228.8	106.3
2008	14,369.1	13,228.8	108.6
2009	14,119.0	12,880.6	109.6
2010	14,660.4	13,248.2	110.7

Source: U.S. Department of Commerce, Bureau of Economic Analysis

TIP

Inflation can be measured with a variety of statistics. The most common measures of inflation are the percentage change in the consumer price index and the percentage change in the GDP deflator.

In some instances we may have data on the GDP deflator and GDP; then we can calculate real GDP with the following formula:

Real GDP = (GDP/GDP Deflator) × 100

In 2010 GDP was $14,660.4 billion and the GDP deflator equaled 110.7. Therefore, real GDP was $13,248.2 billion (= (14,660.4/110.7) × 100). (**Note:** Due to rounding, this calculation is not exact.)

The Costs of Inflation

Many people think that the most damaging aspect of inflation is that it erodes purchasing power. It is true that any household whose income does not keep pace with inflation will be hurt. But for the vast majority of households, incomes keep pace with, if not exceed, price increases.

1. To understand why, consider the circular flow diagram presented earlier in the text (page 39). If the prices paid for goods and services produced by firms increases, firms take in more revenue. If this revenue is not passed back to households in the form of higher wages or rent, the firms make more profits.

But someone owns the firms and the profits become their income. More specifically, the profits are returned to households in the form of dividends. So higher prices always translate into higher levels of income.

2. Inflation can be detrimental even if a household's income rises as fast as prices. This is because the value of savings accounts, trust funds, brokerage accounts, and other forms of financial wealth will be worth less than before the inflation. In other words, inflation erodes the purchasing power of savings. Savings play an important role in the economy. Households, businesses, and governments often need to borrow funds. Inflation discourages savings.

3. Another problem with inflation is the resources that are wasted dealing with higher prices. Firms have to print new brochures, restaurants need to produce new menus, and price lists in all the media will have to be revised. This takes time and effort. Resources that could have been used more productively are deployed to cope with rising prices. The misallocation of resources because of inflation is sometimes called "menu costs."

4. A final issue associated with inflation has to do with borrowing and lending in inflationary conditions. Lenders can be hurt by inflation because the dollars they loaned out are repaid at a later date with dollars that are not worth as much because of inflation. Imagine lending a friend $100 for a year at 10 percent interest. A year later the friend repays you $110. But suppose prices had risen 12 percent over the course of the loan. Your $110 could not even buy what your $100 could a year ago.

   By the same token, borrowers could benefit from inflation because they get to repay their borrowings with inflated dollars. Why don't banks get hurt by inflation? Aren't they big lenders? They are, but they are also smart enough to add an inflation surcharge onto the interest rate that they charge. When a bank lends $100 dollars to your friend it might charge 22 percent—10 percent for their real return and 12 percent to cover the cost of inflation that they expect over the course of the loan.

   The idea that some lenders would protect themselves from inflation by charging higher interest on loans was codified into a formula by Irving Fisher in the early 1900s; the formula is known as "Fisher's Hypothesis":

   Nominal Interest Rate = Real Interest Rate + Expected Inflation

   The nominal interest rate is the rate actually paid. The real interest rate is the actual return the lender receives net of inflation.

   The end result is that lenders who do not anticipate inflation will be hurt, but the borrower would benefit in this case. The biggest lender in the economy is households if you consider putting money in a bank account a loan to the bank. Notice that the nominal interest rate paid by banks is not adjusted upward for expected inflation. Households are big lenders who do not anticipate inflation; therefore, they will be hurt by rising prices.

   The federal government is the biggest borrower in the United States' economy. It stands to benefit from inflation because it can repay its borrowings with inflated dollars.

If you think about it, inflation works just like a tax, because households are major lenders and the government is a major borrower. It is as if Uncle Sam reaches into your wallet every night while you sleep and slips out just a little cash so that you don't even notice. The inflation tax is the result of the federal government benefiting from inflation while households are harmed. This redistribution of wealth from lenders to borrowers is yet another cost of inflation.

The costs of inflation are summarized in Table 15.3.

TABLE 15.3

The Costs of Inflation

- Financial wealth is eroded
- Savings are discouraged
- Menu costs—resources are misallocated with rising prices
- Inflation tax—wealth is redistributed from lenders to borrowers

UNEMPLOYMENT

The costs associated with unemployment are obvious. Households will encounter hardships, maybe even hunger. Unemployment means that a resource, labor, is not being used to its fullest potential. We are producing inside the production possibilities frontier. We could be producing more and enjoying more goods and services.

Unemployment is a problem during recessions—periods when real GDP is declining. During a recession fewer goods and services are being produced. The amount of labor and other resources required for production is reduced and people find themselves out of work.

The unemployment rate is defined as the number of unemployed persons divided by the labor force. The labor force does not include retired persons, those too young to work, and anyone who has not been actively seeking employment. In order to be counted as unemployed you have to be out of work and looking for a job.

The Bureau of Labor Statistics (BLS) reports the unemployment statistics based on two broad surveys taken each month. One survey contacts employers and asks about employment levels at various business establishments, while the other survey interviews households.

Economists classify the unemployed into five general categories:

1. Those who are able to work, but not actively seeking employment because they are discouraged about their prospects for finding employment, are referred to as *discouraged workers* or the *hidden unemployed*. This situation is unfortunate because these people lack basic skills or suffer from other problems and have a difficult time finding work. Discouraged by their prospects, they no longer bother to pursue employment. These people do not show up

in the unemployment statistics because they are not considered to be part of the labor force; thus the name "hidden" unemployment.

2. A form of unemployment that does show up in the official statistics is *structural unemployment.* The structurally unemployed are out of work because the economy is structured, or set up, to their disadvantage. For instance, there may be welders looking for work in Cleveland, but the welding jobs are in Dallas. Or welders may be out of work in Boston, but their are plenty of secretarial jobs open in that same area. Since it is often difficult for a person to relocate or retrain, structural unemployment is not easily remedied.

3. Some persons are able to find work for only a portion of the year due to the seasonal nature of their jobs. These individuals are considered to be *seasonally unemployed* as long as they actively look for work in the off-season. Farmers and construction workers may fall into this category.

4. As mentioned previously, unemployment rises during the contractionary phase of the business cycle. Individuals who lose their jobs during a recession and the corresponding slowdown in production are said to be *cyclically unemployed.* They are out of work specifically because of the business cycle. Hopefully, these people will be back to work when production picks up during the next expansion.

5. Finally, a number of persons are not working because they are in between jobs. Someone who is scheduled to begin a new job next month and does not presently hold a job is considered to be *frictionally unemployed.* It is unlikely that people will be able to switch jobs without some time off. Indeed, some people take advantage of this time to relax or move their households and get their affairs in order. Also, someone who quits one job to look for another is considered to be frictionally unemployed.

In 2010 the labor force was estimated to be 153.9 million persons, while the unemployed numbered 14.8 million. This implies an unemployment rate of 9.6 percent (= 14.8/153.9). Some analysts contend that the unemployment picture is actually much worse than this figure indicates. For one, the 9.6 percent does not count hidden unemployment. Remember, those too discouraged to look for work are not counted as being unemployed or even in the labor force. They are simply not counted.

TIP 🖉

People who are not actively looking for work are not in the labor force and therefore are not counted as unemployed.

Another factor to consider is that persons who are working part time are counted as if they are fully employed, even if they would like to have a full-time job. Again, the reported statistic of 9.6 percent understates the unemployment problem.

A related point to keep in mind is that 9.6 percent is the average unemployment rate across the nation. There are sections of the country where the rate is much higher and sections where it is lower. Moreover, it is well known that the unemployment rate is worse for certain groups within the population, such as teenagers.

Many of the people counted as being unemployed are merely frictionally unemployed. In fact, it is estimated that of the 14.8 million persons unemployed in 2010, anywhere from 4 to 8 million are frictionally unemployed. Indeed, economists consider the economy to be at full employment when the unemployment rate reaches the 4 to 6 percent range since the frictionally unemployed account for about that much of the unemployment rate. If the unemployment rate were to fall further, inflation would most likely be a problem. The full employment rate of unemployment is sometimes called NAIRU for the nonaccelerating inflation rate of unemployment.

Despite the criticisms of the unemployment statistic, the fact remains that it is tabulated in the same manner each time, so that a drop in the rate means more people are working or the labor force has shrunk. The unemployment rate is a useful statistic, but care should be taken with its interpretation.

SUMMARY

- Inflation and unemployment are serious economic problems. Inflation causes the misallocation of resources and an arbitrary redistribution of income. Inflation is typically a problem when the economy is overheated—growing faster than normal. But inflation can also occur during recessions. Later we shall see why.
- Unemployment occurs when the economy is operating below its potential. Our most important resource is labor, and unemployment exists when this resource is not being fully utilized. We could have produced more and enjoyed more goods and services if not for the unemployment.
- We have reviewed the major statistics that measure unemployment and inflation and found that they are not perfectly accurate. It is important to understand how the numbers are generated so that their potential deficiencies can be anticipated. For instance, if the price of imported oil is rising rapidly, it is critical to know that the GDP deflator will not reflect this increase. The GDP deflator does not include the prices of imported products. The CPI does.

The most important question concerning inflation and unemployment has been ignored in this chapter: What causes inflation and unemployment? A complete answer is provided in the chapters ahead.

TERMS

Consumer Price Index (CPI) measure of the average change over time in the prices paid by urban consumers for a market basket of consumer goods and services

Cyclical Unemployment loss of jobs by individuals during a recession and the corresponding slowdown in production

Fisher's Hypothesis Nominal Interest Rate = Real Interest Rate + Expected Inflation

Frictional Unemployment state of being out of work because the person is in between jobs

GDP Deflator measure of the level of prices in the economy

Hidden Unemployment describing those who are able to work but who are not actively seeking employment because they are discouraged about their prospects for finding employment

Inflation a sustained rise in most prices in the economy

Menu Costs the misallocation of resources because of inflation

Nonaccelerating Inflation Rate of Unemployment the full employment rate of unemployment; when employment falls below this rate, inflation accelerates

Seasonal Unemployment state of being out of work because of the time of year

Structural Unemployment state of being out of work because the economy is structured, or set up, to a person's disadvantage

Unemployment Rate the number of unemployed persons divided by the labor force

FORMULAS

$$CPI = \frac{\text{Total Cost this Period}}{\text{Total Cost Base Period}} \times 100$$

$$\text{Inflation Rate} = \frac{CPI\,(\text{this period}) - CPI\,(\text{previous period})}{CPI\,(\text{previous period})} \times 100$$

$$\text{GDP Deflator} = (\text{GDP/Real GDP}) \times 100$$

$$\text{Real GDP} = (\text{GDP/GDP Deflator}) \times 100$$

$$\text{Nominal Interest Rate} = \text{Real Interest Rate} + \text{Expected Inflation}$$

$$\text{Unemployment Rate} = \text{Number of Unemployed/Civilian Labor Force}$$

MULTIPLE-CHOICE
REVIEW QUESTIONS

1. The CPI is calculated for each _____ by
_____.

   (A) week; The Bureau of Economic
   Analysis

   (B) month; The Bureau of Economic
   Analysis

   (C) month; The Bureau of Labor Statistics

   (D) quarter; The Bureau of Economic
   Analysis

   (E) quarter; The Bureau of Labor Statistics

2. If the CPI goes to 150 from 120, then
prices have

   (A) risen 20 percent.
   (B) risen 25 percent.
   (C) fallen 30 percent.
   (D) risen 30 percent.
   (E) risen 150 percent.

3. According to experts, the CPI

   (A) overstates increases in the cost of
   living.
   (B) understates increases in the cost of
   living.
   (C) accurately estimates changes in the cost
   of living.
   (D) could over- or underestimate changes
   depending on the season.
   (E) should be abandoned in favor of the
   GDP Deflator.

4. When products improve in quality the
CPI will

   (A) automatically increase.
   (B) automatically decrease.
   (C) become negative.
   (D) overestimate the inflation rate.
   (E) underestimate the inflation rate.

5. The GDP Deflator

   I.   is used to calculate inflation rates.
   II. is an alternative to the CPI.
   III. is more accurate than the CPI.

   (A) Only I is true.
   (B) I and II are true.
   (C) I and III are true.
   (D) II and III are true.
   (E) I, II, and III are true.

6. If nominal GDP equals $5,000 and real
GDP equals $4,000, then the GDP
Deflator equals

   (A) 125
   (B) 1.25
   (C) 800
   (D) .8
   (E) 300

7. If nominal GDP equals $6,000 and the
GDP deflator equals 200, then real
GDP equals

   (A) $30
   (B) $3,000
   (C) $12,000
   (D) $1,200
   (E) $1,200,000

8. Which of the following is NOT a major
cost of inflation?

   (A) Resources will be misallocated.
   (B) Wealth will be redistributed.
   (C) Savings will be discouraged.
   (D) Real incomes will fall.
   (E) Financial wealth will be eroded.

9. The term "menu costs" refers to

   (A) less choices due to inflation.
   (B) financial assets being worth less due to inflation.
   (C) "à la carte" savings falling.
   (D) food prices rising due to inflation.
   (E) resource misallocation due to inflation.

10. Inflation

    (A) encourages households to save more.
    (B) does not affect savings in the economy.
    (C) forces households to save more.
    (D) forces households to save less.
    (E) discourages savings.

11. Rising prices are a problem because

    (A) money in household savings accounts can now buy fewer goods and services.
    (B) household incomes generally do not rise with prices.
    (C) the economy could run out of money.
    (D) borrowers have to repay loans with more dollars.
    (E) households are encouraged to save more.

12. Fisher's Hypothesis states that

    (A) the real interest equals the nominal interest rate plus the inflation rate.
    (B) the nominal interest rate equals the real interest rate minus the inflation rate.
    (C) the nominal interest rate equals the unemployment rate plus the real interest rate.
    (D) the nominal interest rate equals the unemployment rate minus the real interest rate.
    (E) the nominal interest rate equals the real interest rate plus the inflation rate.

13. Sue loses her job at a shoe factory when the economy falls into a recession. Sue is

    (A) frictionally unemployed.
    (B) cyclically unemployed.
    (C) seasonally unemployed.
    (D) structurally unemployed.
    (E) a discouraged worker.

14. There is a strong demand for welders in California but Bill, an unemployed welder, lives in New York. Bill is

    (A) frictionally unemployed.
    (B) cyclically unemployed.
    (C) structurally unemployed.
    (D) considered to be a hidden worker.
    (E) not counted in the ranks of the unemployed.

15. It is unlikely that the unemployment rate will ever fall to zero because of

    (A) frictional unemployment.
    (B) cyclical unemployment.
    (C) government policies.
    (D) corporate policies.
    (E) the aged and infirm in our population.

Multiple-Choice Review Answers

1. **(C)**	4. **(D)**	7. **(B)**	10. **(E)**	13. **(B)**
2. **(B)**	5. **(B)**	8. **(D)**	11. **(A)**	14. **(C)**
3. **(A)**	6. **(A)**	9. **(E)**	12. **(E)**	15. **(A)**

FREE-RESPONSE REVIEW QUESTIONS

Inflation exerts significant costs on the economy. Specifically, explain how inflation

I. causes a misallocation of resources.

II. discourages savings.

III. redistributes wealth from lenders to borrowers.

Free-Response Review Answers

I. Inflation causes a misallocation of resources. Resources are spent dealing with rising prices and the repercussions of rising prices. Instead, these resources could have been spent producing more goods and services for the constituents of the economy to enjoy. For example, some firms will have to print new catalogs and revise their web sites when the prices of their products change. This time and effort would not have been expended if prices had not risen. Some households will take the trouble to stock up on goods whose prices are expected to rise. The effort and storage costs are another misallocation of resources.

II. Inflation erodes the value of financial assets. Bank and brokerage accounts, trust funds, and other accounts cannot buy as many products when the prices of those products rise. Why save if inflation will simply eat away at the value of savings?

III. Inflation allows borrowers to repay their loans with dollars that are not worth as much as the ones they borrowed. Lenders, on the other hand, are being repaid with dollars that have lost some of their value. Shrewd lenders understand this and charge higher rates of interest to cover the inflation that may occur over the course of a loan. However, lenders who do not anticipate inflation will be hurt while those who borrow from them will benefit.

Aggregate Supply and Aggregate Demand

- Business cycles
- Aggregate supply

- Aggregate demand
- Equilibrium

WHY THE ECONOMY MOVES IN CYCLES

1. The average growth rate of the United States economy, as measured by the percentage change in real GDP, is just over three percent per year for the postwar period, yet only in a very few instances has the economy grown at its average rate. It typically grows faster than average and then in some years real GDP falls or shows negative growth. We call these negative growth periods *recessions.*

2. All economies experience fluctuations in economic activity—contractions and expansions. The ups and downs in economic activity are recurrent but do not conform to a uniform schedule. The longest recession lasted 16 months, the shortest just 6 months. The longest expansion was more than 10 years, while the shortest lasted only 12 months.

3. One business cycle is comprised of an expansion and a recession. The fact that business cycles do not conform to a time schedule and differ in other respects, such as their severity, makes them extremely difficult to predict. Economic forecasters get lower grades for accuracy than the weatherman.

Our task in this chapter, however, is not to predict when the next recession will occur, but to explain *why* the economy moves in cycles. We will build a replica, or model, of the economy and see if that model moves in fits and starts like the real economy. Our model should also display other well-known characteristics of capitalist economies. For instance, large increases in income tend to result in inflation. Does our model confirm this? Technological advances tend to increase output while putting downward pressure on prices. Does our model explain this? Inflation and unemployment tend to be inversely related—when one is up, the other is down—but not always. Does our model explain this tendency and is it flexible enough to allow for exceptions to the relationship?

The name of the model that addresses all of these questions is the *aggregate supply/aggregate demand (AS/AD) model.* The AS/AD model highlights the factors that determine output, income, employment, and prices in the economy. Before we begin to build the model, we must consider what Classical economic theory indicates are the important factors determining output, income, employment, and prices in the economy.

CLASSICAL ECONOMIC THEORY

Classical economic theory was the predominant paradigm in economic analysis from about 1800 until 1930. The basis of Classical thought is Say's Law—supply creates its own demand. As we pointed out earlier, whenever anything is produced, it generates an amount of income equal to its value. Say's Law indicates that it would be impossible to produce too much because of this fact. When something is produced (supplied), it generates enough income to purchase (demand) the item.

However, there is no rule that says the income generated in the production process must be used to purchase the item produced. Workers and managers may decide to save a portion of their earnings. Say had a response to this: The unpurchased items would collect in inventories. Swelling inventories would induce producers to lower prices, the items in inventory would now sell. In other words, even if wage earners do not use their incomes to purchase all that was produced, prices would adjust to ensure there was no excess production.

Therefore, demand for products was never a concern for Classical thinkers. There would always be enough demand. The most important factor determining output was supply. And the most important factors determining supply were the amount of resources in the economy and the state of technology. Classical analysis has a very simple response to the question, "What determines the amount of output in the economy?" Resources and technology.

Given this analysis it is easy to understand why Classical theory fell out of favor in 1930 during the Great Depression. Here, output in the economy had fallen sharply, yet there was no decrease in the amount of land, labor, and capital available. What's more, the productivity of those resources had not diminished either. That is to say, the state of technology was not deteriorating. The Classical economists could not explain why output fell so precipitously during the Great Depression.

KEYNESIAN THEORY

In 1936 John Maynard Keynes (pronounced KANES), a British economist, published a book entitled *The General Theory of Employment, Interest, and Money*. The book pointed out flaws in Classical theory and went on to suggest another, more general, theory. Basically, Keynes suggested that the price adjustment the Classical economists relied upon to ensure that supply would always equal demand did not work under certain circumstances. Essentially, Keynes pointed out that Say's Law, the basis for Classical analysis, did not hold true in all cases.

Keynes' model of the way the economy works is handed down to us in the form of the AS/AD model. The model indicates that the Great Depression was caused by a lack of demand for goods and services. Based on this assessment of the situation, Keynes developed a brilliant remedy for the Great Depression. Unfortunately, the remedy Keynes suggested was considered too radical and the Great Depression lingered on until World War II when both Great Britain and the United States were forced to apply Keynes' remedy.

To truly appreciate Keynes' solution to the Great Depression (and to do well on the Advanced Placement exam) we have to build an AS/AD from scratch.

Aggregate Supply

Aggregate means "sum total"; aggregate supply is the supply of all goods and services by all suppliers in the economy. In other words, aggregate supply is the supply of everything by all producers.

We are specifically interested in how the supply of everything by all suppliers is affected by the level of prices in the economy. We already know from our look into the production possibilities frontier that output depends on the amount of resources available and the state of technology, not prices. So if we drew an aggregate supply curve in line with that reasoning, it would be perfectly vertical, indicating that the price level in the economy can be high or low, it doesn't matter, because output or supply is going to be the amount indicated by where the vertical aggregate supply curve touches the horizontal axis. In Figure 16.1 the horizontal axis is labeled *Real GDP*. In many textbooks it is labeled *Quantity of Output* since real GDP is a measure of the quantity of output.

 TIP

Questions concerning the economy in the long run should be addressed using the vertical aggregate supply curve. For questions concerning the short run, use the upward sloping aggregate supply curve.

Fig. 16.1 A Long-Run Aggregate Supply Curve

The long-run aggregate supply curve touches the horizontal axis at the economy's protential GDP. This is the amount that can be produced using the economy's resources fully and efficiently. It corresponds to an economy operating on its production possibilities frontier.

There may be situations, however, where the price level in the economy does indeed affect the amount supplied by all producers. For instance, in recessionary or depressionary conditions an increase in prices may result in an increase in supply. This is because it is easy to increase supply during a recession when there are plenty of unused resources. The increase in prices induces suppliers to provide more output. This idea is reflected in an aggregate supply curve that slopes upward from left to right.

If the aggregate supply curve is drawn as an upward sloping line then it reflects the fact that supply can be increased or decreased in the short run in response to changes in the price level.

Fig. 16.2 A Short-Run Aggregate Supply Curve

Shifts in Aggregate Supply

Both long-run and short-run aggregate supply will shift if there is a change in resources or productivity in the economy. However, some of these changes may affect only the short-run aggregate supply curve. For example, Hurricane Katrina destroyed many resources in a vast region of our macroeconomy. Fewer resources means aggregate supply shifted left. However, the long-run aggregate supply curve would not shift in this instance since the loss in resources was temporary. (Some would argue that Katrina resulted in a long-run loss of resources.)

A technological advance in production techniques would shift both short- and long-run aggregate supply to the right. However, if the technological advance was dependent on a licensing agreement with a foreign company and therefore only temporary, then only short-run aggregate supply would shift right.

There is one critical factor that will shift short run, but not long-run, aggregate supply: a change in the expected price level. If suppliers think that they can get better prices for their products in a month, then they are often able to withhold supply until prices do indeed rise. However, changing expectations about future price levels does not shift long-run aggregate supply.

> ## FACTORS SHIFTING AGGREGATE SUPPLY
>
> **Changes in resouce availability**
> - Relaxing immigration laws to allow more labor into the country shifts aggregate supply right.
> - Discovering new oil fields shifts aggregate supply right.
>
> **Changes in productivity**
> - New technologies that benefit producers shift aggregate supply right.
> - Relaxing government regulations can increase productivity and shift aggregate supply right.
>
> **Changes in the expected price level (shifts only short-run aggregate supply)**
> - If suppliers expect prices to be lower in the future, they will supply more right now, shifting aggregate supply right.

Aggregate Demand

The aggregate demand curve represents the total demand for goods and services in the economy by households, businesses, governments, and foreigners. In other words, aggregate demand is the demand for everything by everyone.

If the prices of goods and services rise, aggregate demand will fall, as shown in Figure 16.3.

Fig. 16.3 An Increase in the Price Level Reduces Aggregate Demand

The question is why? Most people would say because high prices turn consumers off. But this answer is totally incorrect in this context. When the price level rises, incomes rise by the exact same proportion. Remember, whenever something is produced, it generates an equivalent amount of income. As prices rise in the economy, someone is benefiting. For example, the owners of businesses that manufacture the products that are rising in price are making more profits that eventually translate into more income for the owners. If incomes rise in proportion with prices, then why would aggregate demand fall?

There are three reasons why aggregate demand would fall when the price level rises: the wealth effect, the interest rate effect, and the foreign purchases effect. Each of these explanations takes into account that rising prices means rising incomes. They suggest aggregate demand would fall even though incomes are keeping pace with rising prices.

> The aggregate demand curve slopes downward due to the
>
> - Wealth effect
> - Interest rate effect
> - Foreign purchases effect

The Wealth Effect

The wealth effect points to the fact that rising prices erode financial wealth. Suppose you had $200,000 saved up for your retirement. As the price level rises, that $200,000 can buy less and less. You may decide to begin saving at a greater rate. Therefore, as prices rise in the economy, the value of financial wealth declines and people respond to this by saving more and demanding fewer goods and services.

The Interest Rate Effect

As the price level rises, so does the nominal interest rate. That is because lenders charge higher interest rates when they expect to be paid back with dollars that have lost some of their value due to inflation. Irving Fisher pointed this out long ago. The Fisher Hypothesis states that the nominal interest rate is equal to the real return lenders desire plus expected inflation.

> ### FISHER'S HYPOTHESIS
>
> Nominal Interest Rate = Real Interest Rate + Expected Inflation

Suppose you loan a friend $100 and would like a 5 percent return. You would ask for $105 to be repaid after a year. However, if inflation was 3 percent over the course of the loan, your real return would have been only 2 percent. If you expected inflation to be 3 percent over the course of the loan, then you would have charged 8 percent interest in order to have a real return of 5 percent.

A rising price level causes inflationary expectations to rachet upward. This, in turn, causes lenders to charge higher interest rates. The higher interest rates lead to lower aggregate demand because spenders often borrow the funds to make purchases. This is the interest rate effect.

> ### THE INTEREST RATE EFFECT
>
> Price level ↑ → Interest rate ↑ → Interest-sensitive spending ↓ →
> Aggregate demand ↓

The Foreign Purchases Effect

If the price level in the United States rises, then its goods will be more expensive to foreigners. The nation will export less. Moreover, foreign goods will be more competitively priced, so U.S. imports will rise. Net exports will decline, the result being a direct decrease in aggregate demand.

> - **The wealth effect**—if the price level rises, consumers feel less wealthy even if their income keeps pace with inflation because their financial assets are worth less. They therefore save more and spend less.
>
> - **The interest rate effect**—if the price level rises, so will the nominal interest rate. This reduces interest-sensitive spending.
>
> - **The foreign purchases effect**—if the U.S. price level rises, U.S. goods look more expensive to foreigners, and U.S. exports fall. Foreign goods are relatively less expensive, and U.S. imports rise. Thus, total demand for U.S. goods falls.

It should be pointed out that all three effects work in reverse to ensure that a decrease in the price level causes an increase in aggregate demand.

Notice that a change in the price level will move the economy up or down the aggregate demand curve. We have not mentioned anything that will shift the aggregate demand curve. That is the subject of the next section.

Shifts in Aggregate Demand (AD)

It is important to know what can shift the aggregate demand curve left and right. A change in the price level will cause the economy to move from one point to another along the same aggregate demand curve. It will not cause a shift.

Many things can shift aggregate demand. Remember, aggregate demand is demand from households, businesses, governments, and foreigners. An increase in consumer confidence can shift aggregate demand. An increase in income taxes causes consumers to spend less and shift aggregate demand left. If foreigners suddenly decided that they did not want American products, aggregate demand would decrease and therefore shift left. An increase in federal spending would shift aggregate demand to the right. If it was paid for with a tax increase, that would lessen the effect because taxes reduce spending.

Anything that effects total spending in the economy, except a change in the price level, will shift aggregate demand. The box below delineates some aggregate demand shifters.

FACTORS SHIFTING AGGREGATE DEMAND

Changes in consumer spending:
- A rise in consumer confidence would shift AD right.
- A tax hike would shift AD left.

Changes in investment spending:
- An increase in expected future sales would shift AD right.
- A rise in interest rates shifts AD left.

Changes in government spending:
- An increase in military spending shifts AD right.
- A decrease in welfare spending shifts AD left.

Changes in net exports:
- A decrease in the value of the dollar shifts AD right.
- The French begin to loathe American products, AD shifts left.

Anything that affects C or I or G or NX (except the price level) shifts AD. Also, changes in the money supply shift AD. That's because an increase in the money supply would reduce interest rates and cause an increase in interest-sensitive spending.

Aggregate Supply and Aggregate Demand Together

The aggregate supply curves and the aggregate demand curve have the price level on the vertical axis and the quantity of output on the horizontal axis. We can, therefore, draw the curves on the same diagram.

You may recall that we discussed two different aggregate supply curves. Let's ignore the long-run aggregate supply curve for now and examine how the macroeconomy behaves in the short run.

The economy will have a tendency to operate at point E in Figure 16.4 with a quantity of output of Qe and price level of Pe. Say the price level was not Pe but P′. At P′ aggregate supply is greater than aggregate demand. This will cause inventories of products to bulge. Producers would respond by lowering prices.

A similar analysis suggests that if the price level was P″ aggregate demand would exceed aggregate supply. Inventories would fall. Producers would realize that they could raise their prices. In short, surpluses and shortages will drive the price level to Pe and the quantity of output Qe. Only then will there be no surplus or shortage of output.

The economy will produce Qe and experience price level Pe until something changes. Specifically, the equilibrium point will change when the aggregate supply curve or the aggregate demand curve shifts.

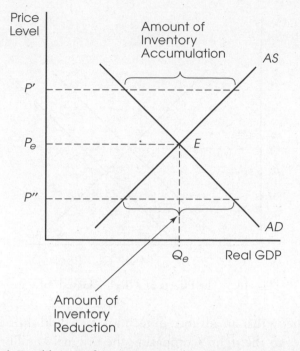

Fig. 16.4 Equilibrium of Aggregate Supply and Aggregate Demand

USING THE AS/AD MODEL

We are now in a position to put the AS/AD model through its paces. We can use the model to help us analyze what will happen under various conditions. For instance, suppose there is a technological advance that makes workers more productive. An example might be the development of the personal computer so that just about everyone can have one at his or her desk. In the 1970s computers were not developed to the point where one would fit on a desk and the cost of owning a personal computer was prohibitive. Now that productivity-enhancing computers are just about everywhere, how would this affect the economy?

Remember that a technological advance shifts the aggregate supply curve to the right. This is shown in Figure 16.5.

The original equilibrium is E1. After the technological advance, the new equilibrium is E2. Four specific conclusions can be made by comparing E1 to E2. First, prices are lower at E2. Second, real GDP is higher. We are at Q2 compared to Q1. Because real GDP is higher we can draw two further conclusions: Unemployment will fall and income will rise.

Our AS/AD model tells us that we can expect lower prices, more output, less unemployment, and more income after a technological advance. Would a Classical economist respond differently? Let's redo the analysis using a long-run aggregate supply curve.

Fig. 16.5 The Effects of a Technological Advance

Figure 16.6 shows that an advance in technology would shift the long-run aggregate supply curve to the right. Comparing the original equilibrium, E1, with the new equilibrium, E2, gives the same results as when the aggregate supply curve was upward sloping: Prices are lower at E2 and real GDP is higher. Higher output means unemployment will be lower and income will be higher. The results are the same using either aggregate supply curve.

**Fig. 16.6 The Effects of a Technological Advance
with a Long-Run Aggregate Supply Curve**

Let's try another example where the results will differ depending on what type of aggregate supply curve is used. This time let's consider the effects of a drop in consumer confidence on the economy. When consumers feel less confident about their future job prospects and income levels, they are not willing to spend as much of their current incomes. This causes the aggregate demand curve to shift to the left.

Comparing the initial equilibrium, E1, with new equilibrium, E2, in Figure 16.7 indicates that prices and real GDP will fall because of the decline in consumer confidence. Once real GDP falls we can conclude that unemployment will rise and income will fall. It seems that we have a self-fulfilling prophesy here. Consumers begin to think that the economic future will be bleak; so they reduce spending right now because they are not as certain of their job prospects in the future. Our AS/AD analysis indicates that this would cause a recession, where output falls along with income and employment. Prices should also fall.

Fig. 16.7 The Effects of a Drop in Consumer Confidence

Would the same results hold if we used a long-run aggregate supply curve? Figure 16.8 indicates that they would not. The drop in consumer confidence again shifts the aggregate demand curve to the left, but the results of this are a steeper decline in prices than with a short-run aggregate supply curve and no change in real GDP. In the long run, prices fall even farther, and this pushes equilibrium real GDP to its original postion at Q_1.

**Fig. 16.8 The Effects of a Drop in Consumer Confidence
with a Long-Run Aggregate Supply Curve**

According to long-run analysis, when aggregate demand falls, prices fall, and this drop in prices should help maintain spending levels. Therefore, real GDP does not fall with the decline in aggregate demand.

The Short Run versus the Long Run

We can consider the short- and long-run effects of any change in the economy with our aggregate supply and aggregate demand model. Figure 16.9 shows the effects of a tax cut on an economy that is already operating at its potential.

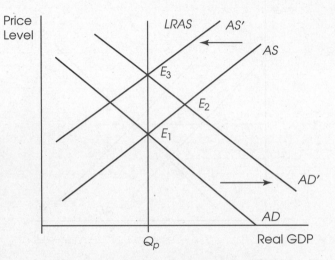

Fig. 16.9 The Effects of a Tax Cut on an Economy Operating at Potential GDP

Begin at E_1, where all three curves cross. This economy is operating at its potential because output is at Q_p, which represents potential GDP. The tax cut shifts the AD curve to the right, and the economy is now operating at E_2. This is the short-run effect of the tax cut. Output is up, which means that income and employment have increased as well. The price level is higher at E_2 than at E_1 as well.

Since E_2 is to the right of potential GDP, we know this economy is operating above potential. Resources are strained, and the price level is up. This leads to the expectation that prices will be higher in the future. If suppliers expect higher prices for their products in the future, many of them can reduce the supply right now. This shifts the AS curve to the left, and the economy winds up at E_3.

In the short run the tax cut stimulated the economy to produce beyond its potential. In the long run the economy was back at its potential. The price level is higher in the long run, but wages and incomes will be proportionally higher as well. The tax cut had no effect on living standards in the long run. This makes sense. Living standards in the long run depend on resources and technology, not tax cuts.

Let's use our model to understand the Great Depression. It is well known that the Great Depression was caused by a a severe drop in aggregate demand. Several causes for the decline in aggregate demand have been highlighted by economic historians. First, the financial panic caused a 33 percent decline in the money supply. That would shift aggregate demand left. The stock market crash caused businesses and households to cut spending. Some say new tariffs on international trade added to the reduction in aggregate demand.

Figure 16.10 shows the short- and long-run effects of a reduction in aggregate demand. In the short run the economy moves to E_2. Production, income, and employment are down. The price level has fallen as well. The Great Depression evinced all these effects. In the long run, the expectation is that a depression will lead to a further drop in prices. This is because resources are idle and there is plenty of labor to be employed at low nominal wages. When suppliers expect prices to be lower in the future, they attempt to supply more right now. This causes the aggregate supply curve to shift right. The economy ends up at E_3, producing at its potential.

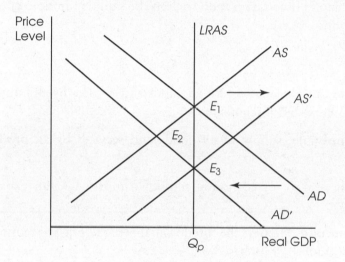

Fig. 16.10 The Effects of a Reduction in Aggregate Demand

There was just one problem with this analysis during the 1930s. Ten years went by, and the economy still had not returned to potential. Prices were falling, but some said they had not fallen enough. Government policies were put in place to prevent prices from falling because the lower prices were driving businesses into bankruptcy.

Keynesian economists like to point out that sticky prices do not allow the economy to return to its long-run potential as our analysis suggests. These economists say the government should take action during recessions because the long run may never come. Exactly what the government can do to move the economy toward its potential is the subject of the next two chapters.

SUMMARY

At this point some readers may be thinking, which analysis is correct, long run or short run? It turns out that the two analyses can be reconciled. We will do so in the coming chapters.

- The AS/AD model is a very powerful tool for thinking about how an economy will respond to given events, such as a technological advance or a dip in consumer confidence. If you are interested in the long-run effects, then it is best to use a vertical aggregate supply curve. Use a short-run aggregate supply curve in the opposite circumstances.

- The question we asked at the beginning of this chapter got lost in all the details: What causes business cycles? The AS/AD model suggests that shifts in the aggregate supply and demand cause fluctuations in economic activity. We listed the factors that could shift these curves. The resulting changes in equilibrium output and prices are the business cycles that we observe in the real world.

Finally, keep in mind that the AP exam in Macroeconomics emphasizes the material in this chapter. It will pay for you to become familiar with the graphs and understand what can cause the curves in each graph to shift. You may think about repeating the chapter if you do not do well on the sample multiple-choice and free-response questions.

TERMS

Aggregate Demand the demand for all goods and services by all households, businesses, governments, and foreigners

Aggregate Supply the supply of all goods and services by all producers in the economy

Business Cycle a wave of economic activity comprised of an expansion and a recession

Classical Economic Theory the predominant paradigm in economic analysis from about 1800 until 1930, based on Say's Law

Equilibrium Price Level the price level that equates aggregate supply and aggregate demand, the average level of prices in the economy

Equilibrium Quantity the amount of output that results in no shortage or surplus, the amount of goods and service bought and sold in the economy

Expansion a sustained improvement in economic activity

Potential GDP the amount that can be produced when all of the economy's resources are used fully and efficiently

Recession a sustained decline in economic activity

Say's Law theory that supply creates its own demand

FORMULAS

$$\text{Marginal Propensity to Consume} = \frac{\text{Change in Spending}}{\text{Change in Income}}$$

$$\text{Multiplier} = 1/(1 - \text{MPC})$$

$$\text{Total Change in Income} = \text{Initial Change in Spending} \times \text{Multiplier}$$

MULTIPLE-CHOICE REVIEW QUESTIONS

1. Business cycles

   (A) occur infrequently in capitalist economies.
   (B) refer to reusing resources in production.
   (C) are predictable ups and downs in economic activity.
   (D) are each comprised of a recession and an expansion.
   (E) are the same as depressions.

2. Recessions

   (A) are a thing of the past.
   (B) are very severe depressions.
   (C) are marked by a sustained decline in output.
   (D) are regular occurrences in capitalist economies.
   (E) are typically accompanied by falling unemployment.

3. Say's Law

   (A) is the basis of Keynesian economic analysis.
   (B) is the basis of Classical economic analysis.
   (C) states that demand creates its own supply.
   (D) indicates that prices will be stable in capitalist economies.
   (E) was verified by the Great Depression.

4. Keynes

   (A) advanced Classical economic theory by making several refinements.
   (B) showed how Say's Law operated in capitalist economies.
   (C) was a great American economist.
   (D) explained the cause of and cure for the Great Depression.
   (E) advanced Classical economic theory by building on Say's Law.

5. Which of the following would NOT shift the aggregate supply curve?

   (A) An increase in the price level.
   (B) A decrease in the amount of resources in the economy.
   (C) An increase in the amount of resources in the economy.
   (D) An increase in technology.
   (E) A decrease in productivity.

6. Which of the following would shift the aggregate demand curve to the left?

   (A) An increase in consumer confidence.
   (B) Business firms expect lower sales in the future.
   (C) Foreigners develop a preference for our products.
   (D) Government increases its level of spending.
   (E) An increase in the money supply.

7. Which of the following would NOT shift the aggregate demand curve?

   (A) A change in consumer confidence.
   (B) A change in technology.
   (C) A change in the money supply.
   (D) A change in spending by state governments.
   (E) A change in foreign tastes for our products.

8. What will happen to the equilibrium price level and the equilibrium quantity of output if the aggregate demand curve shifts to the right? Assume an upward-sloping aggregate supply curve.

(A) The equilibrium price level increases while the equilibrium quantity of output decreases.
(B) The equilibrium price level decreases while the equilibrium quantity of output increases.
(C) The equilibrium price level and quantity of output increase.
(D) The equilibrium price level and quantity of output decrease.
(E) The equilibrium price level increases while the equilibrium quantity of output remains unchanged.

9. What will happen to the equilibrium price level and the equilibrium quantity of output if consumer confidence increases? Assume an upward-sloping aggregate supply curve.

(A) The equilibrium price level increases while the equilibrium quantity of output decreases.
(B) The equilibrium price level decreases while the equilibrium quantity of output increases.
(C) The equilibrium price level and quantity of output increase.
(D) The equilibrium price level and quantity of output decrease.
(E) The equilibrium price level increases while the equilibrium quantity of output remains unchanged.

10. What will happen to the equilibrium price level and the equilibrium quantity of output if the aggregate demand curve shifts to the right? Assume a long-run aggregate supply curve.

(A) The equilibrium price level increases while the equilibrium quantity of output decreases.
(B) The equilibrium price level decreases while the equilibrium quantity of output increases.
(C) The equilibrium price level and quantity of output increase.
(D) The equilibrium price level remains unchanged while the equilibrium quantity of output increases.
(E) The equilibrium price level increases while the equilibrium quantity of output remains unchanged.

11. What will happen to the equilibrium price level and the equilibrium quantity of output if the aggregate supply curve shifts to the left? Assume an upward-sloping aggregate supply curve.

(A) The equilibrium price level increases while the equilibrium quantity of output decreases.
(B) The equilibrium price level decreases while the equilibrium quantity of output increases.
(C) The equilibrium price level and quantity of output increase.
(D) The equilibrium price level and quantity of output decrease.
(E) The equilibrium price level increases while the equilibrium quantity of output remains unchanged.

12. What will happen to the equilibrium price level and the equilibrium quantity of output if a major earthquake destroys much of the plant and equipment on the West Coast? Assume an upward-sloping aggregate supply curve.

    (A) The equilibrium price level increases while the equilibrium quantity of output decreases.
    (B) The equilibrium price level decreases while the equilibrium quantity of output increases.
    (C) The equilibrium price level and quantity of output increase.
    (D) The equilibrium price level and quantity of output decrease.
    (E) The equilibrium price level increases while the equilibrium quantity of output remains unchanged.

13. What will happen to the equilibrium price level and the equilibrium quantity of output if the aggregate supply curve shifts to the left? Assume a long-run aggregate supply curve.

    (A) The equilibrium price level increases while the equilibrium quantity of output decreases.
    (B) The equilibrium price level decreases while the equilibrium quantity of output increases.
    (C) The equilibrium price level and quantity of output increase.
    (D) The equilibrium price level remains unchanged while the equilibrium quantity of output increases.
    (E) The equilibrium price level increases while the equilibrium quantity of output remains unchanged.

14. An increase in the price level

    (A) shifts aggregate demand left.
    (B) increases real financial wealth and therefore decreases consumer demand.
    (C) reduces real financial wealth and therefore increases consumer demand.
    (D) increases real financial wealth and therefore increases consumer demand.
    (E) reduces real financial wealth and therefore decreases consumer demand.

15. According to the interest rate effect, aggregate demand slopes downward because lower prices

    (A) reduce interest rates and therefore decrease aggregate demand.
    (B) increase interest rates and therefore decrease aggregate demand.
    (C) reduce interest rates and therefore increase aggregate demand.
    (D) increase interest rates and therefore increase aggregate demand.
    (E) None of the above are correct.

Multiple-Choice Review Answers

1. **(D)**	4. **(D)**	7. **(B)**	10. **(E)**	13. **(A)**
2. **(C)**	5. **(A)**	8. **(C)**	11. **(A)**	14. **(E)**
3. **(B)**	6. **(B)**	9. **(C)**	12. **(A)**	15. **(C)**

FREE-RESPONSE REVIEW QUESTIONS

I. Draw an aggregate supply/aggregate demand diagram. Label the axes of your diagram. Make the aggregate supply curve upward sloping. Show which curve shifts when foreigners suddenly develop a distaste for our products. What will happen to equilibrium output and the equilibrium price level in the short run?

II. Would you expect the same thing to happen to equilibrium output and the equilibrium price level in the long run? Redraw the aggregate supply/aggregate demand diagram using a vertical aggregate supply curve. Now what happens when foreigners develop a distaste for our products?

III. Explain why the long-run aggregate supply curve is drawn as a vertical line and the short-run aggregate supply curve is drawn upward sloping. Explain why the long-run effects of a change in foreign tastes are different from the short-run effects.

Free-Response Review Answers

I. AS/AD Model when foreigners develop a distaste for our products

When foreigners develop a distaste for our products the aggregate demand curve shifts to the left. This causes the equilibrium price level and the equilibrium quantity of output to fall.

II. AS/AD Model when foreigners develop a distaste for our products (with long-run aggregate supply curve)

The long-run, or Classical, economic analysis indicates that the equilibrium price level will fall when foreigners develop a distaste for our products, but the equilibrium quantity of output will remain unchanged.

III. The long-run aggregate supply curve is drawn as a vertical line because aggregate supply is not affected by the price level in the long run. Only the amount of resources and the state of technology affect aggregate supply in the long run. In the short run, however, an increase in the price level induces suppliers in the economy to bring more product to market. Therefore, when foreigners develop a distaste for our products, prices fall and this reduces the amount of product that suppliers are willing to bring to market. But in the long run, the change in foreign tastes has not affected the amount of resources we have or our state of technology, so the quantity of output remains unchanged.

Fiscal Policy

- Recessionary gap
- Crowding out
- Loanable funds market
- Inflationary gap
- Phillips curve

- Stagflation
- Rational expectations
- Automatic stabilizers
- Marginal propensity to consume
- Multiplier for fiscal policy

KEYNES' REMEDY FOR THE GREAT DEPRESSION

Imagine an economy that is suffering from low levels of output and income. Unemployment is high and prices are falling. The AS/AD model (see Chapter 16) tells us that this is exactly what would occur in an economy where the aggregate demand curve has shifted to the left. Keynes concluded that the Great Depression was caused by a deficiency of spending, or aggregate demand, in our terms. His remedy was to get a boost in spending. But how? Consumers were tapped out and barely had enough to put food on the table. The unemployment rate was 25 percent in the United States. Why should businesses spend more on plant and equipment? Many of them were on the verge of bankruptcy. Maybe foreigners could be called upon to spend more? No, our major trading partners were experiencing depressions of their own.

Keynes recommended that the federal government boost its level of spending. That would shift the aggregate demand curve to the right where it belonged. The only catch was that the government couldn't tax more to pay for the increased spending. Increasing taxes would only shift the aggregate demand curve back to the left; the government would have to spend money it didn't have. It would have to run a deficit and borrow the money to increase spending. This was unheard of at the time. Prudent governments did not spend more than they took in by way of tax revenues.

In fact, during the Great Depression tax collections were down because so many businesses were not making any profits to tax and so many households were making no income to tax. There was talk of raising the tax rate. Our aggregate supply and demand model tells us that this is exactly the wrong thing to do—increasing taxes would only shift the aggregate demand curve further to the left.

No government was willing to try Keynes' radical new idea to remedy the Great Depression and the economic bad times persisted. It wasn't until the early 1940s that World War II forced many governments to spend more money than they had and borrow to make up the difference. That was how the Great Depression was finally put behind us.

Today, governments have gotten over their qualms about deficit spending. Governments have been known to deficit spend even when there was no recession. Keynes would be appalled. During expansions governments should spend less than they take in through taxes. Run a surplus. These surpluses could be used to pay off the borrowings from the deficits.

FISCAL POLICY

Fiscal policy is changes in government spending and taxes to fight recessions or inflations. To remedy recessions the government should increase its level of spending and/or reduce taxes. In other words, the government should run a deficit.

The aggregate supply/aggregate demand (AS/AD) model can be used to show how deficit spending would work to cure a recession. Consider Figure 17.1, which shows an economy experiencing a recession. The aggregate demand curve and the short run aggregate supply curve cross to the left of the long run aggregate supply curve. Remember that the long run aggregate supply curve is vertical at the quantity of output the economy could produce if it used its resources fully and efficiently. Since the short run equilibrium is to the left of the vertical long run aggregate supply curve, the economy must not be using its resources fully and/or efficiently.

Fig. 17.1 A Recessionary Gap

The horizontal distance between the quantity of output the economy is producing, Q1, and its potential, Qf, is called the recessionary gap. The economy depicted in Figure 17.1 is experiencing a recession. Output is below potential and if output is low, so is income. And unemployment must be a problem if production is low. These are recessionary conditions.

Fiscal policy could be used to close the recessionary gap. An increase in government spending would shift the aggregate demand curve to the right. So would a decrease in taxes. Either of these policies would mean deficit spending on the part of the government. But when the aggregate demand curve shifts to the right, the recession is over. This is shown in Figure 17.2.

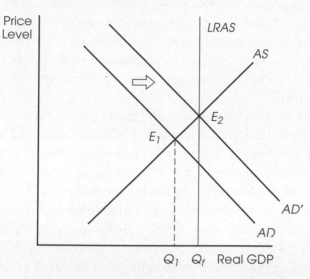

Fig. 17.2 Fiscal Policy to Close a Recessionary Gap

After the aggregate demand curve shifts to the right, the new equilibrium occurs where all three curves cross. The new quantity of output is Qf (f for full employment) and the recession is ended. Unfortunately, the price level is higher at the new equilibrium. This means the economy experienced some inflation as a result of the fiscal policy that cured the recession. Hopefully, the costs of this inflation were worth the benefits of ending the recession.

An economy can experience the opposite sort of trouble from a recessionary gap. An inflationary gap occurs when an economy is producing above its potential. Figure 17.3 illustrates this situation.

Fig. 17.3 An Inflationary Gap

The short-run aggregate supply curve crosses the aggregate demand curve to the right of the long-run aggregate supply curve. The quantity of output is Q1, which is more than the economy's potential, Qf. You may well ask how an economy can produce above its potential. One response is overtime. Resources are being worked more than full time. Another response is that unemployment is below 5 percent. Remember that full employment does not mean zero unemployment. We are at full employment when the unemployment rate reaches 5 percent or so. If the unemployment rate falls lower still, we can wind up producing more than our full employment potential.

The situation is not good when the economy is producing more than its potential. Inflation is typical during these times. Resources are being strained and the economy may be overheating. Prices are usually driven higher in these situations. That is why the distance between Qf and Q2 in Figure 17.3 is called the *inflationary gap*. Fiscal policy can be applied to resolve the problem.

The appropriate fiscal policy to close an inflationary gap is to decrease government spending and/or increase taxes. These policies would result in a surplus where government tax collections exceed government spending. This would slow the economy by curtailing the amount of spending that occurs. The aggregate demand curve shifts to the left when the government decreases its level of spending or raises taxes. This is shown in Figure 17.4.

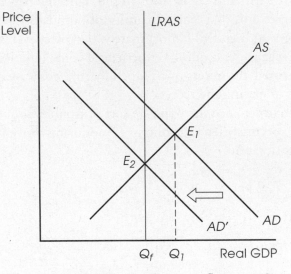

Fig. 17.4 Fiscal Policy to Close an Inflationary Gap

TIP

No matter what kind of trouble the economy finds itself in, recession or inflation, fiscal policy is a potential remedy.

After the aggregate demand curve shifts to the left, the new equilibrium is where all three curves cross. The new level of output is Qf and there is no longer an inflationary gap; in fact, the price level is lower at the new equilibrium. This fall in prices is the inflation being cured.

To sum up, fiscal policy can be used to reposition the aggregate demand curve. Expansionary fiscal policy (tax cuts and/or increases in government spending) shifts the aggregate demand curve to the right. Contractionary fiscal policy shifts aggregate demand to the left.

MULTIPLIERS FOR FISCAL POLICY

Imagine an economy in the midst of a recession. The appropriate fiscal policy is to increase government spending or reduce taxes. Either of these changes in the government's budget will have a magnified effect on the overall economy. This is because an increase in government spending will engender further spending.

The marginal propensity to consume (MPC) is how much is spent out of an extra dollar of income. Young people are well known to have an MPC =1. Give them an extra dollar, and it is spent. But middle-aged people thinking about their retirement or their children's education may save 15 cents out of any extra dollars they may earn, giving them an MPC = .85.

Suppose the MPC = .8 and government spending increases by $20 billion. If the government spends the $20 billion on new roads, then the company and crews that build these roads earn $20 billion in income. They will spend $16 billion of that since the MPC = .8. That $16 billion will become an increase in income for the people and businesses that sold products and services to the road builders. And the story goes on and on because the .8 of the $16 billion will be spent in the next round.

TIP

Be careful not to say that an increase in government spending increases the money supply. It does not. An increase in government spending increases aggregate demand which, in turn, increases real GDP, income, and prices in the short run. But the money supply is unchanged.

Round	Spending	MPC = 0.8
1	$20	
2	$16	
3	$12.8	
4	$10.24	
Total	$100	

We know that the total increase in spending after all the ensuing rounds amounts to $100 billion. This figure was obtained from the formula:

Change in Real GDP = Initial Change in Spending × Multiplier
$100 billion = $20 billion × 5.0

The marginal propensity to save (MPS) is simply 1 − MPC. If the MPC is .85, then the MPS = .15. That is, given an extra dollar of income, 15 cents will be saved.

The multiplier is equal to $1/(1 - MPC) = 5.0 (= 1/(1 - .8) = 1/.2)$. This means any change in government spending will be magnified 5 times.

However, real GDP will not rise by $100 billion if the government lowers taxes by $20 billion. This is because when consumers get their tax breaks totaling $20 billion they will initially increase spending by $16 billion, assuming once again that the MPC equals 0.8. Households save $4 billion of the tax cut.

Change in Real GDP = Initial Change in Spending × Multiplier
$80 billion = $16 billion × 5.0

In this case, real GDP increases by $80 billion.

The fact that a $20 billion dollar change in government spending has a slightly more powerful impact on real GDP than a $20 billion change in taxes has an interesting implication. What would happen if the government were to increase spending by $20 billion while simultaneously *increasing* taxes by $20 billion? The increase in government spending of $20 billion would cause a $100 billion increase in real GDP, while the $20 billion increase in taxes would reduce real GDP by $80 billion. The net effect is a $20 billion increase in real GDP.

If the government has a balanced budget so that spending equals tax revenues, it can maintain the balanced budget and still stimulate real GDP. This is because if spending and tax revenues were both raised by some amount, say $20 billion, then real GDP would increase by $20 billion.

TABLE 17.1

Frequently Used Multipliers

MPC	Multiplier
.5	2
.75	4
.8	5
.9	10

Balanced-budget Move

Whenever the government changes spending and taxes so that the effects on the budget are neutral, this is known as a "balanced-budget" move. So an increase in government spending of $5 million and an increase in taxes of $5 million is a balanced-budget move. Similarly, a decrease in government spending of $4 billion and a decrease in taxes of $4 billion is a balanced-budget move.

In each of these cases, the change in government spending has a stronger impact than the change in taxes. Real GDP will be affected by the amount of the spending and tax change. For instance, when government increases spending by $5 million and taxes by the same amount, real GDP will increase by $5 million.

If government decreases spending by $4 billion and lowers taxes by the same amount, real GDP will decrease by $4 billion. You can arrive at this conclusion the long way: calculate the impact of the government spending change and the impact of the tax change. Then figure the net effect. Or you can take the shortcut: the balanced-budget multiplier is equal to 1. This means an increase in government spending of x dollars that is matched by an increase in tax revenues of x dollars results in an increase in real GDP of x dollars. Based on the same reasoning, a decrease in government spending of x dollars that is matched by a decrease in tax revenues of x dollars results in a decrease in real GDP of x dollars.

The Phillips Tradeoff

Fiscal policy, however, has its drawbacks. We have already seen that a fiscal policy designed to remedy a recession will result in inflation. Similarly, a fiscal policy designed to combat inflation will result in declines in output and possibly a recession. It seems that fiscal policy cannot remedy both unemployment and inflation at the same time.

The idea that inflation and unemployment move in opposite directions was first noticed by a British economist, A. W. Phillips. Looking back over 100 years of British economic history he discovered that when inflation was high, unemployment was low. When inflation was low, unemployment tended to be high. The inverse relationship between inflation and unemployment became known as the Phillips tradeoff.

Phillips graphed the relationship between inflation and unemployment. The results were similar to Figure 17.5. A high inflation rate, such as point A, is associated with a low unemployment rate. A low inflation rate, such as point B, is associated with a high unemployment rate.

Phillips published his findings in 1958 and his relationship has been looked for in many economies over various time periods. For instance, it is well known that unemployment and inflation behaved according to this relationship in the United States in the 1960s, but the 1970s defied the Phillips tradeoff—both inflation and unemployment were high in the mid-1970s.

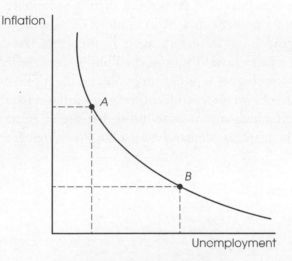

Fig. 17.5 The Phillips Curve

Economists are now able to explain why the Phillips relationship holds in some periods and not in others. Notice that when the aggregate demand curve shifts to the left, it results in the price level falling (lower inflation) and the quantity of output falling (higher unemployment). When the aggregate demand shifts to the right, just the opposite occurs—inflation rises and unemployment falls. All of this is in line with what Phillips discovered. This indicates that the aggregate demand curve must have been shifting about in the United States in the 1960s, while the aggregate supply curve remained stable.

Now consider what happens when the aggregate supply shifts left. Figure 17.6 depicts this event for the short run. The initial equilibrium is E1. Then the aggregate supply curve shifts left and the new equilibrium is E2. Prices are higher at E2 (inflation is up) and output is lower (unemployment is up). This goes against the Phillips relationship. Indeed, it is the worst of all situations, with both inflation and unemployment rising. Economists call this *stagflation*.

Fig. 17.6 Stagflation

If the aggregate demand curve shifts right, then the economy will slide down the Phillips curve from a point such as A in Figure 17.5 toward point B. However, if the aggregate supply curve shifts left, as in Figure 17.6, then the whole Phillips curve shifts right. The rightward shift of the Phillips curve reflects the fact that the economy has to suffer higher levels of inflation and unemployment.

The Phillips curve protrays the tradeoff between inflation and unemployment in the short run. In the long run, it is doubtful that such a relationship exists. Consider an increase in aggregate demand with a long-run aggregate supply curve:

Fig. 17.7 An Increase in Aggregate Demand in the Long Run

The result is an increase in the price level from p1 to p2, but output does not change from Qp. Therefore, unemployment will not change. We have an increase in the price level but no change in unemployment. In other words, the Phillips relationship is a vertical line in the long run.

Stagflation

Stagflation occurs whenever the aggregate supply curve shifts to the left. Since both inflation and unemployment are rising, this defies the Phillips relationship, which concludes that unemployment and inflation move in opposite directions.

Stagflation occurred in the 1970s in the United States when the supply of a very important resource, oil, was curtailed by the formation of an oil cartel. Notice that stagflation poses a special problem for fiscal policy. If both inflation and unemployment are high, should fiscal policy be used to fight the high unemployment or the high inflation? It cannot remedy both at the same time.

Figure 17.8 shows what would happen if fiscal policy were used to fight inflation during stagflation. The initial equilibrium is E1. Then the aggregate supply curve shifts to the left because resources are not as available. This results in stagflation and takes us to E2. Then the government runs a surplus by raising taxes and/or lowering spending. This shifts the aggregate demand curve to the left and we end up at E3. The price level is brought back down to its original level, but the quantity of output has fallen to new lows. The inflation has been cured but the recession has been made worse.

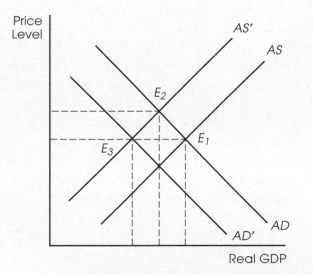

Fig. 17.8 Using Fiscal Policy to Fight Inflation During Stagflation

If fiscal policy is used to combat the recession during stagflation, then inflation will be taken to even higher levels. This is a major drawback of fiscal policy. It cannot cope with stagflation because it can remedy only one problem at the expense of another.

The true solution to stagflation is to get the aggregate supply curve to shift back to the right. This can be accomplished by making resources more available or a technological advance. There are no standard government policies that can accomplish this quickly and effectively. *Supply-side economics* is an attempt to shift the aggregate supply curve to the right to cure stagflation. Supply-side economists recommend special tax policies and less government regulation to accomplish the task. So far, however, these policies have not been effective.

In any event, the Phillips relationship poses a problem for advocates of fiscal policy. The relationship indicates that fiscal policy can remedy only one of the two economic evils at a time. When both inflation and unemployment rear their heads simultaneously, fiscal policy is not appropriate.

Crowding Out

Crowding out can render fiscal policy ineffective. Crowding out is the increase in interest rates and subsequent decline in spending that occurs when the government borrows money to finance a deficit.

To see how crowding out works, imagine an economy mired in a recessionary gap. Suppose the government implements the appropriate fiscal policy and runs a deficit. This means the government will need to borrow money. However, we have been ignoring the fact that if the government borrows a large portion of the funds available for lending, then interest rates would rise.

To understand this consider what would happen if you walked into a bank for a car loan just after the government had borrowed a good portion of the bank's loanable funds. They could give you the car loan, but probably at a higher rate of interest than before.

Now, you may decide that the monthly payments on the car and loan would be too high. You do not buy the car and hundreds of people make decisions similar to yours. The demand for cars drops and autoworkers are laid off.

Crowding out can be shown in a diagram of the market for loanable funds such as Figure 17.9, panel A. The supply of loanable funds is upward sloping to reflect the idea that more people, banks, and institutions are willing to loan funds when interest rates are higher. The demand for funds is downward sloping to indicate that more loans are desired when the real interest rate is lower.

Do not confuse the supply and demand for loanable funds with the supply and demand for money. The supply of money is vertical because the Federal Reserve controls it. The supply of loanable funds is upward sloping because loans can come from many sources. Households are the biggest lenders in the economy if you consider depositing money in a bank a loan to the bank. Foreign central banks have become a welcome source of loanable funds in the U.S. economy.

One of the largest demanders of loanable funds in the U.S. is the federal government. When the federal government deficit-spends in order to stimulate the economy, the demand for loanable funds shifts right in Figure 17.9, panel A. This results in a higher equilibrium real interest rate. The higher interest rate discourages borrowing and spending, especially for investment. The decrease in investment spending by businesses can offset the government's expansionary fiscal policy.

Diagrammatically, crowding out is reflected in an aggregate demand curve that shifts back to the left after a fiscal policy has just shifted it to the right. This is shown

TIP

Recent AP exams have tested students' understanding of crowding out by asking questions concerning the market for loanable funds.

in Figure 17.9, Panel B. Originally the economy is in a recession at E1. An expansionary fiscal policy is used to shift the aggregate demand curve to the right. The new equilibrium is E2 and the recessionary gap is closed. However, interest rates rise because of the government borrowing associated with the fiscal policy. This is shown in the loanable funds market in Panel A. The higher rates of interest induce consumers and businesses to borrow and spend less than before. This drop in consumer and business spending shifts the aggregate demand curve back to its original position and the economy ends up back at E1 and in recession.

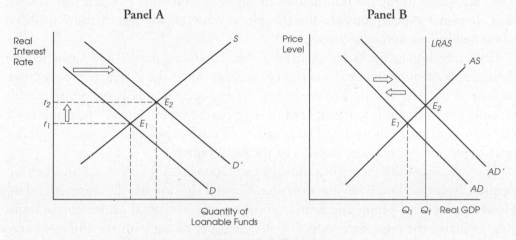

Fig. 17.9 Crowding Out

This is how crowding out can nullify the beneficial effects of fiscal policy. Crowding out is not always an issue. Sometimes there are plenty of loanable funds available and the government can borrow and deficit spend without an adverse effect on fiscal policy. Other times, the government borrowing raises interest rates, which chokes off consumer and business spending. The declines in consumer and business spending offset the increase in government spending and fiscal policy is ineffective.

Rational Expectations

In 1995 Robert Lucas of the University of Chicago won the Nobel Prize in economics "for having developed and applied the hypothesis of rational expectations, and thereby having transformed macroeconomic analysis and deepened our understanding of economic policy." This hypothesis is based on the idea that households and businesses will use all the information available to them when making economic decisions. This seems like a logical and harmless assumption, but carried to its logical conclusion, rational expectations implies that fiscal policy will be ineffective at changing the quantity of output.

Suppose the government tries to stimulate the economy through expansionary fiscal policy. The government deficit-spends. People understand that such a policy results in higher prices. Even if they don't have the economic education to make this conclusion, others will, and they will read about it in the press: prices are expected to rise with expansionary fiscal policy. When households and firms expect prices to be higher in the future, they supply less labor and products right now. Why supply labor and products now when you can supply them next month at a higher price?

This reduction in supply nullifies the expansionary effect of the fiscal policy. Only prices rise because of the deficit spending by the government. The situation is illustrated in Figure 17.10.

Initially the economy is in equilibrium at E1. The government then deficit spends in order to increase the quantity of output. This shifts the aggregate demand curve to the right. Normally we would end up at E2 and that would be the end of the story. However, under rational expectations we never get to E2 because households and firms realize that the expansionary fiscal policy will result in higher prices. They are simply using the information in any economics text to reach this conclusion. Rational expectations are that people will use all the information available when making economic decisions.

Expecting higher prices for their labor and products, people and firms reduce their supply of labor and products right now. This causes the aggregate supply curve to shift to the left. The shift to the left of the aggregate supply curve occurs simultaneously with the shift to the right of the aggregate demand curve. The result is we move from E1 directly to E3. The quantity of output never increases; it remains unchanged. Only prices rise because of the fiscal policy.

The validity of the theory of rational expectations is still very much in question despite Professor Lucas having won the Nobel Prize for his development of it. However, the more people and firms in the economy who use the information available to them, the less effective fiscal policy will be. Along with the Phillips curve and crowding out, rational expectations are one more reason to suspect that fiscal policy will not work to cure all recessions or inflations.

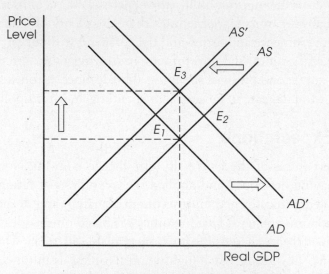

Fig. 17.10 Rational Expectations Nullifies Expansionary Fiscal Policy

Automatic Stabilizers

Automatic, or built-in, stabilizers are government policies already in place that promote deficit spending during recessions and surplus budgets during expansions. These policies prevent recessions from becoming depressions. They also help keep inflations from turning into hyperinflations.

Income taxes and antipoverty programs such as Temporary Aid to Needy Families (TANF) are examples of automatic stabilizers. Consider how income taxes are affected as the economy falls into a recession. More and more people become unemployed or make less income as the recession progresses. But when a household makes less income, it owes less in taxes. In other words, government tax revenues will automatically fall during a recession and this is exactly the type of fiscal policy called for to fight a recession.

Automatic stabilizers cannot prevent a recession because the drop in income is necessary for them to begin working. However, built-in stabilizers can prevent a recession from becoming a depression.

Let's consider how a program like TANF would work as an automatic stabilizer. Again, imagine an economy slipping into a recession. More and more households will qualify for TANF funds. Government spending on antipoverty programs automatically increases during a recession and a boost in government spending is just the sort of fiscal policy that is required to fight a recession.

Also notice that income taxes and TANF would work to prevent an expansion from becoming too exuberant. As the expansion continues, inflationary pressures build as households make more and more income. But more income means higher tax payments for households. Higher taxes are the appropriate fiscal policy to fight inflation. Also, fewer households will qualify for TANF funds as the economy expands. This means government spending on this program will be falling. Cuts in government spending are the appropriate fiscal policy to fight inflation.

Automatic stabilizers work to prevent business cycles from becoming too extreme in either direction. Many economists credit automatic stabilizers, not fiscal policy, for the decreased amplitude of business cycles since World War II.

SUMMARY

- Fiscal policy is just one of several options policymakers can use to address economic concerns such as unemployment or inflation. The appropriate fiscal policy to combat unemployment and recessions is to have the government run a deficit by spending more and/or lower tax collections. To fight inflation, the government should run a surplus by cutting government spending and raising tax rates. These policies shift the aggregate demand curve to a more suitable position.

- Students may wonder why we have recessions and inflations if fiscal policy can be used against them. The answer is that fiscal policy has drawbacks and is not completely effective. One drawback of fiscal policy is that the same policies that fight recessions promote inflation. And if the economy is suffering from stagflation, recession, and inflation simultaneously, fiscal policy can address only one of these problems while making the other worse.

- Crowding out and rational expectations can make fiscal policy completely or partially ineffective. Crowding out refers to the rise in borrowing costs to firms and households after the government borrows to deficit spend. Higher borrowing costs can result in lower spending by households and firms that would offset the expansionary fiscal policy. Rational expectations assumes that people and firms will know that an expansionary fiscal policy will result in higher prices. Because prices are expected to be higher in the future, people work less and firms supply less right now. They would prefer to work and supply more later when wages and prices are higher. The reduction in supply offsets the expansionary fiscal policy.

- Yet another problem with fiscal policy is the fact that Congress and the President have to first realize the economy is in trouble, then design a fiscal policy to combat the recessionary or inflationary gap. All of this takes time. Fortunately, there are laws and programs already on the books that will work to fight recessions or inflations. These laws and programs are called automatic stabilizers. Tax laws and antipoverty programs are examples of built-in stabilizers. Automatic stabilizers cannot prevent recessions or inflations, but they can prevent recessions from becoming depressions and inflations from becoming hyperinflations.

TERMS

Automatic Stabilizers government policies already in place that promote deficit spending during recessions and surplus budgets during expansions

Crowding Out the increase in interest rates and subsequent decline in spending that occurs when the government borrows money to finance a deficit

Deficit situation that exists when government spending exceeds tax revenues

Fiscal Policy changes in government spending and taxes to fight recessions or inflations

Inflationary Gap what occurs when the equilibrium quantity of output is above potential output

Marginal Propensity to Consume (MPC) the amount of an extra dollar of income that is spent

Multiplier the degree of magnification that an initial change in spending will have on the economy

Phillips Tradeoff the inverse relationship between inflation and unemployment

Rational Expectations the idea that households and businesses will use all the information available to them when making economic decisions

Recessionary Gap what occurs when the equilibrium quantity of output is below potential output

Stagflation term used to describe the situation when the economy experiences inflation and a recession simultaneously

Surplus spending by the government that is less than tax revenues

FORMULAS

$$\text{Multiplier} = 1/(1 - \text{MPC})$$

$$\text{Change in Real GDP} = \text{Initial Change in Spending} \times \text{Multiplier}$$

MULTIPLE-CHOICE REVIEW QUESTIONS

1. Fiscal policy refers to

   (A) increases in taxes to fight recessions.
   (B) decreases in taxes to fight inflations.
   (C) changes in government spending and taxes to fight recessions or inflations.
   (D) federal deficits.
   (E) federal surpluses.

2. A federal deficit occurs when

   (A) exports exceed imports.
   (B) imports exceed exports.
   (C) federal tax collections exceed spending.
   (D) federal spending exceeds federal tax revenues.
   (E) the federal government spends less than last year.

3. The appropriate fiscal policy to remedy a recession

   (A) calls for the federal government to run a deficit.
   (B) calls for the federal government to run a surplus.
   (C) is increased taxes and government spending.
   (D) is decreased government spending and taxes.
   (E) is increased taxes and reduced government spending.

4. The appropriate fiscal policy to remedy inflation calls for

   (A) the federal government to run a deficit.
   (B) the federal government to run a surplus.
   (C) increased taxes and government spending.
   (D) decreased government spending and taxes.
   (E) decreased taxes and increased government spending.

5. To close a recessionary gap

   (A) the aggregate demand curve should be shifted to the right.
   (B) the aggregate demand curve should be shifted to the left.
   (C) the aggregate supply curve should be shifted to the right.
   (D) the aggregate supply curve should be shifted to the left.
   (E) prices should be raised.

6. To close an expansionary gap

   (A) the aggregate demand curve should be shifted to the right.
   (B) the aggregate demand curve should be shifted to the left.
   (C) the aggregate supply curve should be shifted to the right.
   (D) the aggregate supply curve should be shifted to the left.
   (E) prices should be lowered.

7. One drawback of using fiscal policy to close a recessionary gap is that

   (A) unemployment will rise.
   (B) taxes will have to be raised.
   (C) the equilibrium price level will rise.
   (D) government spending on important programs will have to be cut.
   (E) equilibrium output will fall.

8. Use the following three responses to answer the question: Fiscal policy is not always effective because of

   I. crowding out.
   II. rational expectations.
   III. the balanced budget amendment.

   (A) I only
   (B) II only
   (C) II and III
   (D) I and II
   (E) I, II, and III

9. Stagflation occurs when

(A) inflation falls and unemployment rises.
(B) inflation rises and unemployment falls.
(C) inflation and unemployment both rise.
(D) Inflation and output both rise.
(E) Inflation and output both fall.

10. Study the diagram below.

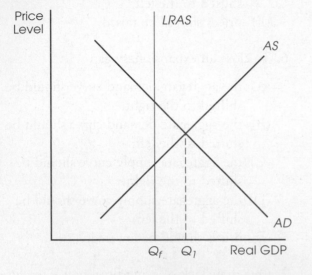

(A) It is incorrect since Qf can never be to the left of Q1.
(B) It is incorrect because AD should slope upward and AS should slope down.
(C) It portrays a recessionary gap.
(D) It portrays an inflationary gap.
(E) It portrays Phillips curves.

11. Crowding out

(A) is one reason fiscal policy is so effective.
(B) occurs when interest rates fall due to government borrowing.
(C) occurs when consumers and firms spend less offsetting expansionary fiscal policy.
(D) causes the aggregate demand curve to shift to the right.
(E) occurs when rising interest rates cause cuts in government spending.

12. The theory of rational expectations

(A) assumes that consumers and businesses anticipate rising prices when the government pursues an expansionary fiscal policy.
(B) implies that fiscal policy will be effective even during stagflation.
(C) supports the notion of a Phillips tradeoff.
(D) assumes that consumers and businesses do not use all the information available to them.
(E) was developed by Keynes as a remedy for the Great Depression.

13. Study the diagram below.

(A) It shows how fiscal policy can work to cure inflation.
(B) It shows how fiscal policy can work to close a recessionary gap.
(C) It portrays the Phillips tradeoff.
(D) It is incorrect because AD should slope upward and AS should slope down.
(E) It portrays stagflation.

14. Automatic, or built-in, stabilizers

    (A) prevent inflation.

    (B) prevent recessions from occurring.

    (C) prevent inflation and recessions from occurring.

    (D) are government policies already in place that promote deficit spending during expansions and surplus budgets during recessions.

    (E) are government policies already in place that promote deficit spending during recessions and surplus budgets during expansions.

15. The Phillips curve

    (A) shows how government spending and tax collections are related.

    (B) is upward sloping from left to right.

    (C) indicates that inflation will be high when unemployment is low.

    (D) shows how the equilibrium price level is related to fiscal policy.

    (E) shows how output and prices are related.

Multiple-Choice Review Answers

1. **(C)**	4. **(B)**	7. **(C)**	10. **(D)**	13. **(E)**
2. **(D)**	5. **(A)**	8. **(D)**	11. **(C)**	14. **(E)**
3. **(A)**	6. **(B)**	9. **(C)**	12. **(A)**	15. **(C)**

FREE-RESPONSE REVIEW QUESTIONS

I. Draw a diagram that portrays a recessionary gap. Be sure to label the axes of your diagram and the aggregate demand curve, the upward sloping aggregate supply curve, and the long run aggregate supply curve.

II. Describe the fiscal policy that would be appropriate to close the recessionary gap. On the diagram show how the fiscal policy works to close the recessionary gap.

III. Draw a Phillips curve. Be sure to label the axes of your diagram. An economy that is in recession would have a low inflation rate but a high unemployment rate. Mark such a point on your Phillips curve and label it "R." Suppose a fiscal policy is implemented and this policy closes the recessionary gap. Mark and label another point on the Phillips curve to demarcate the new inflation/unemployment combination and label it "AFP" for "after the fiscal policy." Explain how you concluded where AFP would be.

Free-Response Review Answers

I.

A Recessionary Gap

II. The appropriate fiscal policy to close a recessionary gap is for the federal government to run a deficit. This can be accomplished by the federal government increasing spending or by reducing taxes or both. Any of these policies will serve to increase aggregate demand. This is shown on the AS/AD model by a shift to the right of the aggregate demand curve.

Fiscal Policy to Close a Recessionary Gap

III.

The Phillips Curve

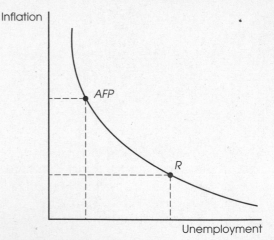

Beginning at point R, an expansionary fiscal policy would lower the unemployment rate but raise prices. After the fiscal policy the economy would have lower unemployment but higher inflation. This is the case at point AFP. Thus, an expansionary fiscal policy serves to slide the economy up the Phillips curve.

Money and Banking

- M1
- M2
- Fiat money
- Functions of money
- Fractional reserve banking
- Money multiplier
- Policy tools of the Federal Reserve

THE SUPPLY OF MONEY

It is best to avoid the word "money" when talking about fiscal policy. It is incorrect to say that an increase in government spending increases the amount of money in the economy and, therefore, aggregate demand. Replace the word "money" with "income" in the previous sentence and it becomes accurate.

The money supply in the United States is controlled by the Federal Reserve. When the government deficit-spends, this does not change the money supply. The money in circulation may be used more intensely, but the number of dollars does not change with fiscal policy.

Money is anything that society generally accepts in payment for a good or service. This is a very broad definition and allows for many things to be counted as money. There have been societies that accepted beads and clamshells in exchange for goods and services.

Experts in the field of money and banking disagree on what should be included in the money supply because they disagree on what our society generally accepts in exchange for goods and services. Certainly, currency—coins and paper money—is the most widely accepted form of money in our society. And checks written on bank deposits are accepted almost as readily as currency. Bankers refer to checking accounts, and accounts that function like checking accounts, as *transaction accounts*. In the opinion of many experts, currency, transaction accounts, and travelers' checks are the only items generally accepted in payment in the United States. This definition of money is referred to as M1 and totaled $1.37 trillion in 2007.

Credit Cards

Credit cards are perhaps more widely accepted than checks, but credit cards are not part of the money supply—they are merely a convenient way of taking out a loan from a bank. When you pay for something with your credit card, the bank that sponsors your credit card is actually paying the merchant for the item purchased. The bank records this transaction like a loan on its books. Then the bank hounds you for repayment of the loan and interest is charged if you do not pay the entire amount in a short period of time. Credit cards are one way banks use their depositors' money to make loans. Since we count the amount of money deposited into checking accounts as part of M1, it would be redundant to count credit cards also.

Savings Accounts and CDs

Many experts think that more than just the three items included in M1 should counted in the money supply. For instance, money in savings accounts might be part of the money supply. True, hardly any merchants will accept your passbook savings account and deduct from it when you make a purchase, but it is very easy to withdraw money from your savings account and make the purchase. Similarly, certificates of deposit are easily cashed (although there are stiff penalties for early withdrawal on these accounts), although no merchant will accept one for payment.

The issue here is liquidity—the ability to turn an asset into cash rapidly and without loss. Savings accounts and certificates of deposit are not generally accepted to pay for things, but they are very liquid and should, therefore, be counted as money. The definition of money known as M2 includes everything in M1 plus money deposited in savings accounts, certificates of deposit, and retail money funds.

M1 and M2 are the most common definitions of money. However, there are several alternative definitions such as "M3" and "MZM". These alternative definitions of money include items that are less liquid such as eurodollars.

TIP

Most people think of money as currency, but transaction accounts (checking accounts) are 50 percent of M1 and savings accounts are the biggest part of M2.

TABLE 18.1

The Money Supply in the United States (as of December 2010) Billions of Dollars			
M1		**M2**	
Currency	915.7	M1	1,830.9
Transaction accounts	910.5	Savings accounts	5,357.4
Travelers' checks	4.7	Certificates of deposit	922.6
Total	1,830.9	Retail money funds	706.1
		Total	8,817.0

Source: Federal Reserve Bank of the United States

FIAT MONEY

There is a lot of gold in Fort Knox and an even bigger stash in the vault of the Federal Reserve Bank of New York, but none of this gold is used to back the money supply. The United States, and most nations of the world, use *fiat money*. This means that the coins and paper money have nothing standing behind them except the fact that they are *legal tender*.

Legal tender means that the coin or paper money must be accepted in exchange for goods or services by the decree of the government. Still, Confederate currency was legal tender during the Civil War and even die-hard Southerners wouldn't accept it. That is because far too much of it was supplied by the Confederate authorities. This reveals the key to understanding how fiat currency works—its supply must be kept relatively limited.

From 1873 until 1933 the United States was on some form of the gold standard. The money supply was backed by gold or a combination of gold and silver. The primary advantage of the gold standard is that the supply of money must be kept limited since the supply of gold is limited. However, this system can be too confining when an increase in the supply of money is warranted and there is not an increase in the amount of gold held by the government.

A fiat monetary system is more flexible in that the gold holdings of the government need not increase in order to expand the nation's supply of money. By the same token, nations that do not keep the supply of their fiat currency limited will see it diminish in value, sometimes to the point of becoming worthless.

What Is Money Good For?

Most people think that money is good for only one thing—spending. True, textbooks refer to money as a "medium of exchange." Money is a much more efficient way to exchange goods and services than barter. Barter requires a double coincidence of wants; you have to find someone who has what you want and wants what you have in exchange. Money obviates the need for this and allows us to spend our time more productively.

However, people use money in another way all the time: to make comparisons. Which corporation is bigger, Procter and Gamble or Pfizer? The assets of Pfizer are worth about $120 billion, while the assets of Procter and Gamble are worth $200 billion; Pfizer is much smaller than Procter and Gamble by this measure. Notice that dollars figures were used to make this comparison. This is using money as a unit of account. Consider another example. Suppose you win a drawing and you can have the grand prize, a Ford Mustang, or $10,000. Most people would take the car based on the comparison that a new Ford Mustang is worth well over $15,000. Again, money is being used to compare things.

Finally, money also serves as a store of value. You can work hard for 40 years and stuff 20 percent of each paycheck under your mattress. After you retire you can live like a king. This is using money to store the value of your hard labor during your working years. Of course, money is a poor store of value during inflationary times. The $600,000 under the mattress can buy less and less as prices rise. On the other hand, money is an excellent store of value during deflations. The $600,000 can buy more and more goods and services as prices fall.

TABLE 18.2

The Functions of Money

- Medium of exchange—money is used to buy goods and services
- Unit of Account—money is used to measure and compare
- Store of value—money is used to accumulate wealth

THE FEDERAL RESERVE SYSTEM

To understand how the money supply can be changed, it is necessary to understand the Federal Reserve System, or FED, for short. The FED is the central bank of the United States. This means that it controls the money supply and supervises all the depository institutions within the country. All of the banks, savings and loans, credit unions, and mutual savings banks report to the FED each week. The FED can audit any of these institutions at any time and would have to approve any mergers and acquisitions.

The FED operates as the bank of banks. If you need a loan, you might go to a bank. If a bank needs a loan, it may borrow from the FED. If you feel uncomfortable carrying around a lot of cash, you might deposit some of that cash in your account at a bank. If a bank feels uncomfortable having a lot of cash in its vault, it may deposit some of that vault cash in its account at the FED.

FACTS ABOUT THE FED

1. There are 12 branches of the FED located in major cities throughout the nation. This makes it convenient for banks and other depository institutions to do their banking.
2. The main headquarters of the FED is in Washington, D.C.
3. The President of the United States appoints the seven members of the Board of Governors of the Federal Reserve System.
4. The President also appoints one of the members to be the chairman of the Board of Governors and another member to be the vice chairman.
5. All the members of the Board of Governors serve 14-year terms.
6. The Board of Governors makes the important decisions concerning the money supply. Should M1 and M2 be increased? Decreased? Held steady?

The FED is a quasi-governmental institution. The people working at the FED are paid by the federal government, but the FED is not part of the executive, legislative, or judicial branches of government. The Board of Governors makes decisions concerning the money supply in complete autonomy. The FED is not responsible to the President or Congress, although it regularly reports to both on its operations and intentions for the money supply.

Fractional Reserve Banking

Banks and other depository institutions keep only a fraction of the money deposited with them on hand. Most of any given deposit is used to make loans or other investments. Nevertheless, banks have plenty of cash on hand to meet their withdrawal needs. A bank manager's worst nightmare is to run short of cash.

The FED's regulation D requires all depository institutions to keep 10 percent of the funds deposited in transactions accounts as reserves. Transaction accounts are checking accounts and other accounts that function as checking accounts, such as NOW accounts and share draft accounts. Reserves must be held against transaction deposits only. Savings accounts and certificates of deposit have no reserve requirement. Banks can hold their required reserves in their vault or in their account at the FED. By the way, currency held in a bank's vault is not counted as part of the money supply.

Many people think that the FED requires banks to keep aside 10 percent of the money deposited in transaction accounts to insure that there will be cash on hand to meet withdrawal needs. This is not true. As stated, bankers will make sure to have enough money on hand to meet withdrawal needs without any requirements from the FED. Reserve requirements, as we shall see below, help the FED control the money supply.

The Money Expansion Process

Imagine that a counterfeiter prints up $1,000 in phony bills and spends the fake money at a jewelry store. At the end of the day the jeweler deposits the counterfeit money into his bank. The bank, not detecting the phony bills, credits the jeweler's transaction account by $1,000. The bank must hold $100 of the $1,000 aside as required reserves. The remaining $900 can be used as the bank sees fit. Typically, excess reserves such as these $900 are used to make loans or buy investments since that is how the bank makes profits.

Now suppose the bank loans the $900 to someone applying for a home improvement loan. The $900 ends up being spent on paint. The owner of the paint store deposits the $900 into a transaction account. Notice that this deposit is boosting transaction accounts by $900 and transaction accounts are part of the money supply as measured by M1 or M2. In other words, the money supply is increased when banks make loans with their excess reserves.

And this is not the end of the story. The bank that received the $900 deposit from the paint store must hold 10 percent of the deposit, or $90, as required reserves. The rest of the deposit is excess reserves and the bank can use these in any way they wish. Suppose the bank buys some real estate as an investment with the $810 in excess reserves. Whoever sold the real estate to the bank now has a check for $810. If this check is deposited into a transaction account, the money supply will be going up again, this time $810.

Again, this is not the end of the story. The bank that receives the deposit of $810 will hold 10 percent, or $81, aside as required reserves. The remaining $729 is excess reserves that the bank may use to make a loan or buy an investment.

When all is said and done, the original $1,000 in counterfeit money will have led to a $10,000 increase in the money supply. This is because of the money expansion process where banks create transaction account money by using their reserves to make loans or buy investments. Table 18.3 outlines the money expansion process for this example.

Remember that money deposited into transaction accounts is part of the money supply. When counterfeiters deposit $1,000 into their transaction account, the money supply ends up increasing by $10,000. This is because of all the subsidiary deposits that occur because of the original $1,000 deposit. The column labeled "deposits into transaction accounts" sums to $10,000.

TABLE 18.3

The Money Expansion Process

	Deposits into transaction accounts	Required reserves	Excess reserves
Bank 1 (Counterfeiter's bank)	$1,000	$100	$900 (used to make a loan)
Bank 2 (Paint store's bank)	900	90	810 (used to buy real estate)
Bank 3 (Real estate seller's bank)	810	81	729
Bank 4	729	72.90	656.10
	$10,000		

Two formulas help us determine how much the money supply will increase because of a deposit from outside the system. The first formula is for the money multiplier:

Money Multiplier = 1 / reserve requirement

In our case the reserve requirement is 10 percent:

Money Multiplier = 1 / .10 = 10

This tells us that any deposit from outside the banking system, such as counterfeit money, will change the money supply by 10 times the amount of the deposit.

The second formula gives the change in the money supply because of the initial change in bank reserves:

Change in the Money Supply = Money Multiplier × Change in Bank Reserves

In our example the money multiplier is 10 and the initial change in bank reserves is the $1,000 in counterfeit money:

Change in the Money Supply = 10 × $1,000 = $10,000

If the reserve requirement was five percent and the counterfeiters deposited $4,000 in fake money, the change in the money supply would be:

Money Multiplier = 1 / .05 = 20

Change in the Money Supply = 20 × $4,000 = $80,000

Policy Tools of the Federal Reserve

The previous examples illustrate why counterfeiting is considered to be such a serious crime. A small amount of counterfeit money can lead to a significant change in the money supply because of the monetary expansion process, but the examples also indicate how the FED could change the money supply.

The FED could print money and deposit it into a bank and the monetary expansion process would take over. The money supply would increase by a multiple of the FED's deposit. And what's more, the initial deposit isn't counterfeit.

As it turns out, there are several ways the FED could change the reserves of the banking system and, therefore, the money supply. These methods are the policy tools of the FED.

1. The FED could *raise or lower the reserve requirements* for depository institutions. If the reserve requirement was lowered, banks would have more excess reserves and could make more loans and investments. This would increase the money supply. To decrease the money supply the FED would raise reserve requirements.

2. Another policy tool involves the *discount rate*. The discount rate is the rate of interest the FED charges when it makes loans to depository institutions. Remember that if you want a loan you might go to a bank, whereas a bank that needs a loan may go to the FED. The FED charges banks a rather low rate of interest on the loans it makes, thus the name discount rate.

   If the FED lowers the discount rate, more banks are encouraged to borrow. These borrowings by banks from the FED increase bank reserves. The money supply will increase by a multiple of the borrowings from the FED.

   As an illustration, suppose the FED lowers the discount rate by half of a percentage point. Say that the lower discount rate encourages banks to borrow $12 million more than usual from the FED. Assuming a 10 percent reserve requirement, the money supply would then increase by $120 million:

   Money Multiplier = 1 / Reserve Requirement

   Money Multiplier = 1 / .10 = 10

   Change in the Money Supply = Money Multiplier × Change in Bank Reserves

   Change in the Money Supply = 10 × $12 million = $120 million

   If the Fed wanted to decrease the money supply, then the discount rate should be raised. Raising the discount rate discourages banks from borrowing from the FED, and banks, therefore, have less reserves. A decrease in reserves translates into a multiple decrease in the money supply.

   During the recent financial crisis the FED made loans to non-depository institutions. For the first time, so-called term auction facilities allowed the FED to make loans to troubled financial institutions.

3. The third policy tool available to the FED to initiate changes in the money supply is *open market operations*. Open market operations is when the FED buys and sells government securities in the secondary market. Government securities are IOUs that the government issues when it borrows money. They

sometimes go by the names Treasury bills, bonds, or notes. The federal government of the United States has borrowed trillions of dollars from individuals and corporations, both foreign and domestic.

The FED expanded its open-market operations as it dealt with the financial crisis of 2008–2009 and set precedent by buying assets other than government securities from a variety of entities holding those assets. For instance, the FED bought mortgage-backed securities from Fannie Mae, Freddie Mac, and the Federal Home Loan Bank.

Secondary Market

When the government borrows money it issues a government security to the lender that states the amount of the loan, the rate of interest, and the length of the loan. However, the lender need not hold the government securities until it matures. At any time the lender may sell the government security to another investor. This is done in the *secondary market.*

Lenders wishing to sell government securities that have a relatively high rate of interest attached to them will experience a profit in the secondary market, while those with relatively low rates will experience a loss. But the FED does not buy and sell government securities in the secondary market with an eye toward making financial gains. The FED participates in the secondary market for government securities in order to change the money supply.

Imagine what happens when the FED buys government securities in the secondary market. The FED pays for the securities with a check that the seller deposits in a bank account. This deposit is an increase in bank reserves from outside the system. The money supply will increase by a multiple of this increase in bank reserves.

To take a specific example, if the reserve requirement is 10 percent and the FED wants to increase the money supply by $50 million, then the FED would buy $5 million worth of government securities in the secondary market.

$$\text{Money Multiplier} = 1 \ / \ \text{Reserve Requirement}$$

$$\text{Money Multiplier} = 1 \ / \ .10 = 10$$

$$\text{Change in the Money Supply} = \text{Money Multiplier} \times \text{Change in Bank Reserves}$$

$$\text{Change in the Money Supply} = 10 \times \$5 \text{ million} = \$50 \text{ million}$$

If the FED wanted to decrease the money supply, it would sell government securities in the secondary market. Persons or corporations that buy the securities will pay with a check. The FED cashes the check to draw the reserves out of the banking system and does not deposit proceeds of the sale back into the banking system. In this way bank reserves are depleted. The money supply falls by a multiple of the decline in bank reserves.

Specifically, if the FED sells $6 million worth of government securities in the secondary market, and the reserve requirement is five percent, then the money supply will fall by $120 million.

TABLE 18.4

Policy Tools of the Federal Reserve

Tool	Description	To Increase Money Supply	To Decrease Money Supply
Change reserve requirements	Change the percentage of each deposit that banks must hold aside.	Lower the reserve requirement	Raise the reserve requirement
Change the discount rate	Change the rate of interest the FED charges on bank borrowings.	Lower the discount rate	Raise the discount rate
Open market operations	Buy or sell government securities in the secondary market	Buy government securities	Sell government securities

$$\text{Money Multiplier} = 1 \,/\, \text{Reserve Requirement}$$

$$\text{Money Multiplier} = 1 \,/\, .05 = 20$$

$$\text{Change in the Money Supply} = \text{Money Multiplier} \times \text{Change in Bank Reserves}$$

$$\text{Change in the Money Supply} = 20 \times -\$6 \text{ million} = -\$120 \text{ million}$$

Table 18.4 summarizes the policy tools of the FED.

SUMMARY

- Money is anything generally accepted to pay for goods and services. Certainly, currency, transaction accounts, and travelers' checks are generally accepted. This definition of money is known as M1. Many experts think that other highly liquid assets should be considered money. These include savings accounts, certificates of deposit, and other liquid assets. Adding these three items to M1 gives M2, another prevalent definition of money.
- The money supply in the United States, like most nations, is not backed by gold or silver or any precious commodity. Fiat money is money because the government says it is money. Experience has shown that it is extremely important to keep the supply of a fiat money relatively limited if it is to function correctly.
- Money is good for spending (a medium of exchange), comparing things (a unit of account), and as an investment vehicle (a store of value). The United States is on a fractional reserve system where depository institutions keep only a fraction of each deposit on hand. Most of the money deposited in a bank is used to make loans and buy investments.
- The Federal Reserve is the central bank of the United States and controls the money supply. It does this mostly with open market operations, but can also alter the discount rate or change reserve requirements. Any of these three techniques changes the reserves of the banking system. The money supply changes by a multiple of the change in bank reserves.

TERMS

Certificate of Deposit debt instrument that is similar to a savings account except the interest rate is slightly greater and the deposit cannot be drawn on without penalty

Currency coins and paper money

Discount Rate the rate of interest the FED charges when it makes loans to depository institutions

Excess Reserves the amount of any deposit that does not have to be held aside and may be used to make loans and buy investments

Federal Reserve the central bank of the United States

Fiat Money money that is not backed by any precious commodity

Government Securities IOUs that the government issues when it borrows money

Liquidity the ability to turn an asset into cash rapidly and without loss

M1 currency, transaction accounts, and travelers' checks

M2 M1 plus savings accounts, certificates of deposit, and other liquid assets

Money anything that society generally accepts in payment for a good or service

Money Multiplier = 1 / reserve requirement, the multiple by which the money supply will change because of a change in bank reserves

Open Market Operations activities in which the FED buys and sells government securities in the secondary market

Required Reserves the amount of any deposit that must be held aside and not used to make loans or buy investments

Reserve Requirement the percentage of any deposit that must be held aside and not used to make loans or buy investments

Savings Account an account at a depository institution that earns interest while the funds are readily available but cannot be withdrawn with checks

Secondary Market place where government securities that have already been issued may be bought or sold

Transaction Account a checking account at a bank or a similar account at some other depository institution

FORMULAS

Money Multiplier = 1 / reserve requirement

Change in the Money Supply = Money Multiplier × Change in Bank Reserves

MULTIPLE-CHOICE REVIEW QUESTIONS

1. Which of the following is not included in M1?

(A) Coins.
(B) Paper money.
(C) Travelers' checks.
(D) Credit cards.
(E) Transaction accounts.

2. Which of the following is not included in M2?

(A) Currency.
(B) Travelers' checks.
(C) Certificates of deposit.
(D) Savings accounts.
(E) Credit cards.

3. Which of the following statements is true?

(A) Some of the things included in M2 are not as liquid as the things in M1.
(B) M2 is smaller than M1.
(C) M1 is backed by gold and M2 is backed by silver.
(D) The biggest component of M1 is currency.
(E) The biggest component of M2 is currency.

4. Fiat money

(A) is not backed by any precious commodity.
(B) can be exchanged for gold.
(C) is backed by gold, but cannot be exchanged for it.
(D) is not legal tender.
(E) can be backed by gold or silver.

5. The Federal Reserve is

(A) part of the legislative branch of government.
(B) the monetary authority for banks, but not other depository institutions.
(C) part of the judicial branch of government.
(D) in control of the money supply.
(E) in control of government spending.

6. Required reserves

(A) can be used by banks to make loans or buy investments.
(B) can be held in a bank's vault or its account at the FED.
(C) must be kept in a bank's vault.
(D) must be used to make loans.
(E) ensure that banks will have enough cash on hand to meet their withdrawals.

7. The secondary market for government securities is

(A) where used items are traded.
(B) located in smaller cities.
(C) where the government borrows money.
(D) where government securities that have already been issued may be bought or sold.
(E) where government securities are issued.

8. If the reserve requirement is 2 percent, then the money multiplier is

(A) 5
(B) 5 percent
(C) 50
(D) 50 percent
(E) one half

9. If the FED buys bonds in the secondary market

    (A) the money supply will increase.
    (B) the money supply will decrease.
    (C) the money supply will not be affected.
    (D) the discount rate would be affected.
    (E) reserve requirements would have to be increased in tandem.

10. Which of the following would lead to an expansion of the money supply?

    (A) The FED raises the discount rate.
    (B) The FED buys government securities in the secondary market.
    (C) The federal government deficit-spends.
    (D) The FED raises reserve requirements.
    (E) Taxes are reduced.

11. Assume the reserve requirement is 10 percent. If the FED sells $29 million worth of government securities in an open market operation, then the money supply can

    (A) increase by $2.9 million.
    (B) decrease by $2.9 million.
    (C) increase by $290 million.
    (D) decrease by $290 million.
    (E) increase by $26.1 million.

12. Assume the reserve requirement is 5 percent. If the FED buys $4 million worth of government securities in an open market operation, then the money supply can

    (A) increase by $1.25 million.
    (B) decrease by $1.25 million.
    (C) increase by $20 million.
    (D) decrease by $20 million.
    (E) increase by $80 million.

13. When the FED lowers the discount rate its intention is to

    (A) give depository institutions a break on their borrowings.
    (B) signal participants in financial markets that a recession is coming.
    (C) signal participants in financial markets that an inflationary period is coming.
    (D) lower prices in the economy.
    (E) encourage borrowing by depository institutions so that the money supply may expand.

14. Lowering reserve requirements would

    (A) force banks to hold more reserves and make more loans.
    (B) allow banks to make more loans and buy more investments thus decreasing the money supply.
    (C) allow banks to make more loans and buy more investments thus increasing the money supply.
    (D) allow banks more freedom to merge and acquire other businesses.
    (E) force banks to sell investments so that fewer funds are held in reserve.

15. The FED's Board of Governors has _____ members, each serving _____ -year terms.

    (A) 14, 7
    (B) 7, 14
    (C) 8, 8
    (D) 50, 2
    (E) 8, 10

Multiple-Choice Review Answers

1. **(D)**	4. **(A)**	7. **(D)**	10. **(B)**	13. **(E)**
2. **(E)**	5. **(D)**	8. **(C)**	11. **(D)**	14. **(C)**
3. **(A)**	6. **(B)**	9. **(A)**	12. **(E)**	15. **(B)**

FREE-RESPONSE REVIEW QUESTIONS

I. Assume the reserve requirement is 10 percent. If the FED buys $10,000 worth of government securities in the secondary market, will the money supply expand or shrink? By exactly how much?

II. Explain why the money supply changes when the FED buys $10,000 worth of government securities in the secondary market. Why is the change in the money supply not $10,000?

III. Suppose that depository institutions did not use all of their excess reserves to make loans and buy investments. For example, if the reserve requirement was 10 percent, depository institutions would hold 20 percent of their deposits idle. How would this affect your answer to I. above?

Free-Response Review Answers

I. If the FED buys $10,000 worth of government securities in the secondary market, the money supply expands. When the Fed pays for the securities the sellers will deposit their checks into the banking system. The reserves of the banking system will increase by $10,000. The money supply will increase by ten times that amount, or $100,000 because the money multiplier is 10 in this case. (Money multiplier = 1 / .10 = 10.)

II. The money supply increases because when the FED buys securities in the secondary market, this increases the reserves of banks where the checks are deposited. The reserves of these banks go up by $10,000. Now these banks are holding more reserves than they are required to by the FED's reserve requirements. The banks make loans and buy investments with these excess reserves and this serves to increase transaction accounts. Transaction accounts are part of the money supply.

III. If banks do not use all of their excess reserves to make loans and buy investments, then money expansion process is not as effective. When a bank makes a loan, this money ends up as a deposit elsewhere, usually at another bank. If banks prefer to hold extra reserves, then the loans will not be as large and the increase in the money supply because of the $10,000 increase in reserves also will not be as large. If banks have a 10 percent reserve requirement and hold 10 percent more in extra reserves, this means that the money multiplier is 5 (= 1 / .2) and the money supply will expand to only $50,000, not $100,000.

Monetary Policy

CHAPTER 19

- Equation of exchange
- Quantity theory of money
- Monetarists vs. Keynesians
- Federal funds rate

DEFINITION

Test your economic intuition by answering this question: If the economy is mired in a recession, should the money supply be increased or decreased? The correct answer is *increased*. Congratulate yourself for having good economic intuition if you answered correctly.

Here is a much more difficult, and less intuitive question: Why does an increase in the money supply stimulate a sluggish economy? After a moment of thought, most people respond that an increase in the money supply would motivate spending. Not bad. But if households and corporations wanted to spend more, why don't they simply use the existing money supply more intensely? They could spend more without increasing the money supply if each dollar was turned over more often. If households and corporations don't want to increase spending, would an increase in the money supply force them to spend more?

You will be able to answer the more difficult questions posed above shortly. First, let's define monetary policy—changes in the money supply to fight recessions or inflations. The Board of Governors of the FED designs and executes monetary policy in the United States. Suppose the Board of Governors decides to increase the money supply. In Chapter 18 we saw that this could be accomplished with a decrease in reserve requirements, a decrease in the discount rate, or an open market purchase of government securities.

The Federal Open Market Committee (FOMC) helps the Board of Governors decide which tool to use. If the open market purchases are selected, then the FOMC plots out exactly how many government securities will be purchased at what time. The FOMC is comprised of twelve members. All seven of the members of the Board of Governors sit on the FOMC, as well as five of the presidents of the twelve FED regional banks.

CHANGES IN THE MONEY SUPPLY

Classical View

Classical economic analysis concludes that changes in the money supply have no effect on the equilibrium quantity of output; only prices and wages are affected. According to Classical theory, an increase in the money supply would increase aggregate demand, but the increase in aggregate demand would result in higher prices.

Workers would immediately realize that their wages could not buy as many goods and services at the higher prices and they would demand wage increases. When the dust settled, if the money supply was raised 10 percent, prices and wages would rise 10 percent and nothing else would be changed.

If the economy was in a recession and the unemployment rate was high, an increase in the money supply would not help. After the money supply was increased, prices and wages would be higher, but the unemployment rate would be unchanged.

The Classical view on how an increase in the money supply affects the economy is reflected in the aggregate supply/aggregate demand (AS/AD) model in Figure 19.1. The increase in the money supply shifts the aggregate demand curve to the right. But suppliers respond to this increase in the demand for their products by raising prices from P1 to P2, but not output. Remember, the Classical aggregate supply curve is vertical. So the increase in aggregate demand has no effect on the quantity of output. Since output is unaffected, so is unemployment.

Fig. 19.1 An Increase in the Money Supply: Classical View

The Classical economists based their conclusions about how money affects the economy on the equation of exchange:

$$M \times V = P \times Q$$

Where M is the money supply
V is the velocity of money
P is the price level and
Q is the quantity of output or real GDP.

The money supply can be defined as M1 or M2. The velocity of money is the number of times the typical dollar of M1 or M2 is used to make purchases during a year. The price level is the average price of a good or service in the economy, the same as the vertical axis in the AS/AD model. The quantity of output can be measured with real GDP and is the same as the horizontal axis in the AS/AD model.

The equation of exchange is a *tautology*, meaning it is true by definition. No economist, Classical or not, disputes the fact that $M \times V = P \times Q$. But the Classical economists take this a step further and assume that V and Q are constant. If this is true, then the arithmetic of the situation tells us that if M increases 10 percent, P must also increase 10 percent.

The Classical economists referred to this result as *monetary neutrality*. A change in the money supply would result in a proportional change in prices. The quantity of output, real GDP, the rate of unemployment, and other real variables are unaffected. This analysis is in line with the Classical notion that the only things that can affect the quantity of output are resource availability and technology.

Monetarist View

It is easy to shoot down the Classical theory of monetary neutrality. The theory is based on the assumption that V and Q are constant. In the United States, the velocity of M1 was 3.6 in 1960 and 8.6 in 2004. Clearly, V is not constant. Similarly, Q, or real GDP, has increased 272 percent in the same time span. With a nonconstant V and Q, we can no longer conclude that a change in the money supply causes a proportional change in prices.

The Monetarist view on how a change in the money supply affects the economy is more realistic. The Monetarist view starts with the assumption that V and Q are stable, but not constant, in the short run. Now if the money supply is increased 10 percent, it is by no means definite that P will increase by 10 percent. Monetarists claim that both P and Q will increase and not necessarily by 10 percent.

According to the Monetarist view, a change in the money supply affects the economy in many ways. For one, interest rates will be affected and this will affect spending levels and, therefore, aggregate demand. For another, more money directly translates into more spending as households and firms try to spend and invest the increment in the money supply. And there are other channels through which a change in the money supply will affect the economy. They are "too numerous to enumerate," according to Milton Friedman, a Nobel Prize-winning economist who is often called the father of monetarism.

TIP 🖉

The FED can affect interest rates in the economy by raising or lowering the money supply. Raising the money supply lowers interest rates.

On the AS/AD model, an increase in the money supply results in an increase in aggregate demand. This translates into an increase in the price level and the quantity of output. We get a different result than the Classical analysis because the aggregate supply curve is drawn upward sloping from left to right instead of vertical.

The Monetarist view on how a change in the money supply affects the economy, like the Classical view, is based on the equation of exchange. However, the Monetarist view is not as rigid. The Classical view maintains that V and Q are constant, so that an increase in M will have a proportional effect on P. Q is not affected. The Monetarist view is that V and Q are stable in the short run, but not constant. This means that both P and Q will be affected when M is increased. Indeed, the Monetarists assert that most of the fluctuations in Q over the years are the result of the FED changing M.

Fig. 19.2 An Increase in the Money Supply: Monetarist View

The Monetarists are highly critical of the FED. If changes in output are caused primarily by changes in the money supply, then all the FED need do is allow the money supply to increase at a reasonable constant rate, say three percent a year. When the FED undertakes monetary policies that reverse the direction of money growth, this results in the recessions and inflations we observe in the economy.

Keynesian View

A third perspective on how a change in the money supply affects the economy is that of the Keynesians. This view, like the monetarist view, is concerned with short run effects and uses an upward sloping aggregate supply curve. The difference is that the Keynesians believe that a change in the money supply affects the economy through one channel, not many—and that channel is the interest rate.

An increase in the money supply would lower interest rates, since more money is available to be borrowed. Lower interest rates encourage households and firms to take out loans in order to increase spending and investment in plant and equipment. This means more aggregate demand.

Money supply ⇑ ⇒ Interest rates ⇓ ⇒ Borrowing & spending ⇑ ⇒ Aggregate demand ⇑

Fig. 19.3 How an Increase in the Money Supply Affects the Economy: Keynesian View

However, Keynesians argue that the increase in aggregate demand will be small. The increase in the money supply will only lower interest rates a bit according to Keynesian analysis. To see this consider Figure 19.4 which shows the supply and demand for money.

The supply of money is vertical because it is not related to the nominal rate of interest. The Federal Reserve determines the money supply. The demand for money is downward sloping to reflect the fact that it is negatively related to interest rates. When interest rates rise, households and firms decrease their money holdings. They would rather put their money where it can earn the higher rates of interest, usually in bonds.

Fig. 19.4 An Increase in the Money Supply Lowers the Interest Rate

The demand for money is also affected by prices and income. If either of these increase, the demand for money will shift to the right. If prices increase, then households and firms will need more money to pay for the things they buy. If income increases, then households will want to buy more things and this means larger money holdings in their wallets or in their checking accounts.

Keynesians believe that the money demand curve is rather flat. That way, if the money supply is increased as in Figure 19.4, then interest rates do not fall very much. Moreover, Keynesians claim that even if the interest rate did fall appreciably, borrowing and spending would not increase all that much.

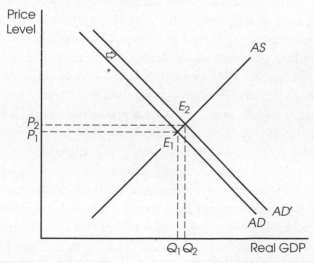

Fig. 19.5 An Increase in the Money Supply: Keynesian View

An increase in the money supply will shift the aggregate demand curve to the right, but only a small amount according to the Keynesian view. This is because a change in the money supply affects spending through only one channel—interest rates—not many channels as the Monetarists believe. Moreover, the interest rate channel does not result in major changes in spending when the money supply is changed. Keynesians argue that fiscal policy should be used to close recessionary and inflationary gaps. Monetary policy is not that effective in their eyes.

Targeting the Federal Funds Rate

When the FED increases bank reserves, interest rates in the economy should fall since more money is available to loan out. One critical interest rate is the federal funds rate. This is the interest rate on loans from one bank to another. Several key interest rates in the economy tend to move in tandem with the federal funds rate.

The current practice of the FED is to raise or lower bank reserves in order to peg the federal funds rate at some desired level. The FED targets the federal funds rate in order to know if more or less money is required in the economy.

For example, if the federal funds rate began to rise, it would indicate that loanable funds are becoming more scarce. If the FED wants to head off a recession, it would add reserves to the banking system, perhaps through open-market operations, in order to keep the federal funds rate from rising.

SUMMARY

- The term "demand management policy" refers to both monetary and fiscal policy because, like fiscal policy, monetary policy shifts the aggregate demand curve. If the government decides to increase total spending in the economy, shifting the aggregate demand curve to the right, this could be accomplished by increasing the money supply, or increasing government spending, or reducing taxes.
- Most economists believe that a change in the money supply will affect both prices and output in the short run. Classical economic theory tells us that in the long run a change in the money supply will only affect prices. Only resources and technology can affect output in the long run, a change in the money supply cannot.
- Monetarists believe that changes in the money supply have a profound effect on the economy in the short run; for instance, a decrease in the money supply would result in lower prices and less output. Therefore, lowering the money supply would be a good way to fight inflation, but it could result in a recession since output decreases. The best thing the FED could do is forget about trying to close recessionary and inflationary gaps with monetary policy and, instead, allow the money supply to grow at a steady, constant rate. This would result in an economy that grows at a steady, constant rate.
- The Keynesian economists disagree with the Monetarists on many points. A change in the money supply would affect the economy through just one channel, interest rates. And the effect would be mild since changes in interest rates do not have a profound effect on aggregate demand. Fiscal policy should be used to close recessionary and inflationary gaps. Monetary policy is ineffective.
- The FED targets the federal funds rate. That is to say, the FED increases or decreases bank reserves in order to put the interbank loan rate at the desired level. For instance, increasing bank reserves lowers the federal funds rate. This should stimulate borrowing and spending.

At the outset of this chapter we asked if households and corporations don't want to increase spending, would an increase in the money supply force them to spend more? Hopefully at this point you can see that the answer is Yes, although "induce" may be a better word than "force." Monetarists think that a significant amount of spending would be induced by an increase in the money supply. Keynesians disagree.

TABLE 19.1

Perspectives on the Money Supply

	Classical	Monetarist	Keynesian
A change in the money supply affects	the price level	the price level and output	the price level and output
through	many variables	many variables	the interest rate
The effect is	strong but limited to prices and wages	strong	weak
V and Q are	constant	stable	variable

TERMS

Board of Governors executive board of the FED that makes major monetary policy decisions

Demand Management Policy monetary and fiscal policy

Equation of Exchange $M \times V = P \times Q$; the money supply times its velocity equals the price level times output

Federal Funds Rate the interest rate charged when a bank makes a loan to another bank.

Federal Open Market Committee (FOMC) a committee within the FED that designs and executes the particulars of monetary policy

Monetarist one who believes that changes in the money supply have a profound effect on the economy

Monetary Neutrality policy in which a change in the money supply would result in a proportional change in prices while real variables, such as the unemployment rate, would be unaffected

Monetary Policy changes in the money supply to fight recessions or inflations

Money Demand the amount that households and firms want to hold in currency and deposits

Velocity of Money describing the number of times the typical dollar of M1 or M2 is used to make purchases during a year

FORMULAS

Equation of Exchange: $M \times V = P \times Q$

MULTIPLE-CHOICE REVIEW QUESTIONS

1. The Federal Open Market Committee

   (A) advises the President of the United States.
   (B) is part of the Federal Reserve System.
   (C) has seven members.
   (D) promotes free trade.
   (E) is part of the legislative branch of government.

2. According to Classical economic theory, a decrease in the money supply would

   (A) raise the price level and output in the economy.
   (B) lower the price level and output in the economy.
   (C) raise the price level in the economy.
   (D) lower the price level in the economy.
   (E) raise the price level and lower output in the economy.

3. According to monetarist analysis, a decrease in the money supply would

   (A) raise the price level and output in the economy.
   (B) lower the price level and output in the economy.
   (C) raise the price level in the economy.
   (D) lower the price level in the economy.
   (E) raise the price level and lower output in the economy.

4. According to Keynesian analysis, a decrease in the money supply would

   (A) raise the price level and output in the economy.
   (B) lower the price level and output in the economy.
   (C) raise the price level in the economy.
   (D) lower the price level in the economy.
   (E) raise the price level and lower output in the economy.

5. In the equation of exchange

   (A) M stands for the money supply and Q stands for quality.
   (B) V stands for the velocity of GDP and Q stands for quality.
   (C) P stands for the price level and Q stands for quarter.
   (D) P stands for the price level and V stands for the velocity of money.
   (E) P stands for population and V stands for the velocity of money.

6. The velocity of money

   (A) cannot be calculated for an actual economy.
   (B) is how fast money can be transferred.
   (C) is required to calculate the money multiplier.
   (D) is the number of times a typical dollar changes hands.
   (E) is the number of times a typical dollar is used to make a purchase in a year.

7. In the equation of exchange, if V and Q are constant, then

   (A) changes in the price level must be proportional to changes in the money supply.
   (B) changes in the money supply have no effect on the price level.
   (C) changes in the price level have no effect on the money supply.
   (D) the equation is invalid.
   (E) the money supply must be zero.

8. In the United States over the years, V and Q

   (A) have not changed significantly.
   (B) are perfectly constant.
   (C) have decreased significantly.
   (D) have increased significantly.
   (E) changed once since World War II.

9. According to Monetarist theory, when the money supply is changed, the economy is affected

   (A) only because a change in the money supply affects interest rates.
   (B) in several ways.
   (C) because interest rates change and so do many other factors that affect spending.
   (D) because many factors that affect spending change, but not interest rates.
   (E) but only insignificantly.

10. According to Keynesian theory, a decrease in the money supply would

    (A) lower interest rates, which would encourage borrowing and, therefore increase spending.
    (B) raise interest rates, which would discourage borrowing and, therefore, increase spending.
    (C) raise interest rates, which would discourage borrowing and, therefore, reduce spending.
    (D) lower interest rates, which would discourage borrowing and, therefore, reduce spending.
    (E) raise interest rates, which would encourage borrowing and, therefore, reduce spending.

11. Which of the following could cause the aggregate demand curve to shift to the left?

    (A) An increase in the money supply.
    (B) Contractionary demand management policies.
    (C) Expansionary demand management policies.
    (D) An increase in government spending.
    (E) There is more than one correct answer here.

12. According to Monetarist theory,

    (A) the FED should actively conduct monetary policy.
    (B) changes in the money supply do not have significant effects.
    (C) fiscal policy is the preferred way of shifting the aggregate demand curve.
    (D) the FED should allow the money supply to grow at a constant rate.
    (E) the FED should randomly change the money supply.

13. According to Keynesian theory,

(A) the FED should not conduct monetary policy.

(B) changes in the money supply have significant effects.

(C) fiscal policy is the preferred way of shifting the aggregate demand curve.

(D) the FED should allow the money supply to grow at a constant rate.

(E) the FED should randomly change the money supply.

14. Milton Friedman

(A) never won a Nobel Prize despite his contributions to economic analysis.

(B) is a Monetarist.

(C) is a Keynesian.

(D) won a Nobel Prize for his contributions to Classical economic analysis.

(E) never won a Nobel Prize despite his contributions to Monetarist analysis.

15. Monetarists believe that V and Q are

(A) constant.

(B) stable.

(C) variable.

(D) not critical for understanding how money affects the economy.

(E) unstable.

Multiple-Choice Review Answers

1. **(B)**	4. **(B)**	7. **(A)**	10. **(C)**	13. **(C)**
2. **(D)**	5. **(D)**	8. **(D)**	11. **(B)**	14. **(B)**
3. **(B)**	6. **(E)**	9. **(C)**	12. **(D)**	15. **(B)**

FREE-RESPONSE REVIEW QUESTIONS

I. Suppose the money supply is increased. What would happen to the equilibrium price level, the equilibrium quantity of output, and the unemployment rate according to

A. Classical economic theory?
B. Monetarist theory?
C. Keynesian theory?

II. Explain why the three schools of economic thought in Part I. reach different or similar conclusions concerning how an increase in the money supply will affect the economy.

Free-Response Review Answers

I. If the money supply were increased then

A. according to Classical economic theory the equilibrium price level would increase and the equilibrium quantity of output would remain unchanged. Since the quantity of output is unchanged, the unemployment rate is unchanged.

B. according to Monetarist theory the equilibrium price level would increase and the equilibrium quantity of output would increase as well. Since the quantity of output increased, the unemployment rate would fall.

C. according to Keynesian theory the equilibrium price level would increase slightly and the equilibrium quantity of output would increase slightly as well. Since the quantity of output increased slightly, the unemployment rate would decrease slightly.

II. All three schools of thought agree that an increase in the money supply will raise the equilibrium price level. However, the Keynesians believe that the price level will only rise slightly. This is because they believe that an increase in the money supply will stimulate only a small amount of extra spending. Another way of saying this is that the Keynesians feel that an increase in the money supply will shift the aggregate demand curve to the right, but only by a small amount.

Similarly, the Keynesians feel that the equilibrium level of output will increase only slightly because total spending is not that sensitive to changes in the money supply. Therefore, unemployment falls modestly. The Monetarists, on the other hand, believe that an increase in the money supply has a significant impact on the economy. The equilibrium quantity of output rises substantially because spending is boosted by the increase in the money supply. Therefore, unemployment falls significantly.

Only the Classical thinkers believe that the equilibrium level of output and the unemployment rate will be completely unaffected by the increase in the money supply. This is because of the Classical emphasis on the long run effects of any change in the economy. The amount of output that an economy can generate depends on the amount of resources available and the state of technology. An increase in the money supply affects neither of these and so the Classical conclusion is that output is not affected by an increase in the supply of money. It only serves to raise prices.

Economic Growth

- Productivity
- Human capital
- Potential GDP

LIVING STANDARDS

In 1948 real GDP per capita (in 2005 dollars) in the United States was $12,646. By 2010 it had risen to $42,722. These figures indicate that the standard of living more than tripled in those 62 years. Real GDP per capita represents how much was produced, per person in the nation. When more goods and services are produced, this implies more material wealth. This is the essence of economic growth—increments in material wealth. The percentage change in real GDP, or real GDP per capita, is the customary measure of economic growth.

Of course, not all growth is good. Some bemoan the congestion, pollution, and loss of simplicity that sometimes accompany economic growth. Nevertheless, generally speaking, more output per person implies higher living standards. Life is more harsh in Tanzania, where GDP per capita is less than $1,000, than in Australia where GDP per capita is over $20,000.

In the United States since World War II, real GDP typically grows about three percent a year. Real GDP per capita has an average growth rate of just under two percent for the same period. This means that American citizens enjoy a standard of life that improves just under two percent a year.

Even small differences in the rate of growth can add up over the years. Imagine two economies, both with a real GDP per capita of $30,000. If real GDP per capita grows by one percent a year in the first economy and two percent a year in the second, then in 25 years the first economy will have a real GDP per capita of $38,500, while in the second it will rise to $49,200.

This brings us to the "rule of 70." It will take 10 years for GDP, or any variable, to double if it grows by seven percent a year. More generally, a variable will double in 70/x years, where x is the annual growth rate of the variable. So if the standard of living grows at five percent a year, we can expect the standard of living to double in 14 (= $^{70}/_5$) years.

It is well known that the fruits of economic growth are not shared equally among the population in America. Since income is unequally distributed, so is the economic bounty. In fact, America has one of the more skewed distributions of income in the industrialized world. Roughly half of all the income goes to 20 percent of the families. The poorest 20 percent of the population earns only five percent of all the income. Growth theorists argue about what can be done about disparities in living standards within a nation. Some see the disparity as a natural consequence of growth, while others insist that economic growth need not result in economic inequality.

DETERMINANTS OF ECONOMIC GROWTH

The production possibilities frontier can be used to summarize the factors that cause an economy to grow. Our previous analysis indicated that two factors could cause the production possibilities frontier to shift outward: (1) an increase in the amount of resources, and, (2) a technological advance that increases productivity. When the production possibilities frontier shifts outward, it implies that the economy's potential for production has increased. Potential GDP is the amount that can be produced using resources fully and efficiently.

Figure 20.1 illustrates how an increase in a particular resource, labor, would affect the production possibilities frontier. If the economy was producing at point A before the increase in the amount of labor in the economy, it could now produce at a point such as B, where more guns and butter are consumed.

Fig. 20.1 An Increase in Labor Force

Figure 20.2 shows a how a technological advance in butter production would affect the production possibilities frontier. Apparently the technological advance has no application in gun production because the intersection of the frontier on the vertical axis has not changed. Nevertheless, the economy can consume more guns and butter after the technological advance. This can be seen by comparing points A and B in Figure 20.2.

The aggregate demand/aggregate supply (AS/AD) model can also illustrate economic growth. If the long run aggregate supply curve is used, then shifts in aggregate demand have no effect on the equilibrium quantity of output. Only a shift to the right of the long run aggregate supply curve can increase equilibrium output. This is shown in Figure 20.3.

Fig. 20.2 A Technological Advance in Butter Production

Fig. 20.3 An Increase in Long-Run Aggregate Supply

The only question that remains is, what can cause the long-run aggregate supply curve to shift to the right? Readers with good retention will remember that there are two factors that could cause the long-run aggregate supply curve to shift to the right: (1) an increase in the amount of resources, and (2) a technological advance that increases productivity. These are the same two factors that can cause the production possibilities frontier to shift outward.

> Economic growth can be portrayed with an outward shift of the production possibilities frontier or a rightward shift in the long-run aggregate supply curve.

Our investigation of the production possibilities frontier and the AS/AD model indicates that there are two general factors affecting economic growth: (1) resource availability, and (2) the productivity of those resources. To dig deeper, we now ask what can affect resource availability and productivity.

The Determinants of Resource Availability

Recall that resources are classified into three categories—land, labor, and capital. One way to promote economic growth is to promote the availability of each of these classes of resources. For instance, you might think that the amount of natural resources, what economists call land, is strictly limited, but that is not true. New deposits of oil, natural gas, and minerals are continually being discovered. Also, advances in agriculture and irrigation can make more land available for farming. Discoveries of mineral deposits and the creation of arable fields are examples of natural resources becoming more readily available. This results in more production and, therefore, economic growth.

The availability of labor is primarily based on demographic factors. These demographics are a major concern in Russia. It is expected that the labor force in Russia will shrink due to a decline in the birth rate. A smaller labor force means an important resource is less available. This will have a negative impact on economic growth in Russia.

But the supply of labor is not only affected by demographic factors. Government-subsidized child care could increase the supply of labor as could education and training programs. Both these policies have been suggested as ways to encourage the supply of labor and economic growth.

Capital is the term economists use to indicate plant and equipment. An expansion of the amount of plant and equipment in the economy would shift the production possibilities frontier outward or the long run aggregate supply curve to the right. In either case, the result is economic growth. Economists have advocated a variety of policies that would promote spending on plant and equipment. Tax breaks for businesses that expand their capital stock have been tried as a means to spur investment spending. Lower interest rates may also help. What would lower interest rates? Expansionary monetary policy, for one thing. Another idea for lowering interest rates and promoting capital accumulation are policies that stimulate savings. Growth theorists have long realized that increased savings could lower borrowing costs for firms and thereby encourage spending on plant and equipment.

The Determinants of Productivity

- Productivity is output per unit of input.
- Labor productivity is the amount of output per unit of labor.
- Capital productivity is the amount of output per unit of plant and equipment.
- Total productivity is the amount of output per unit of all inputs.
- Labor productivity is the standard type of productivity. If a particular sort of productivity is not mentioned, it is safe to assume the discussion is about labor productivity.

Table 20.1 highlights the fact that labor productivity is important for economic growth. From 1948 until 1973 the United States enjoyed robust growth in labor productivity and living standards, as measured by real GDP per capita, increased accordingly. From 1973 until 1999, the growth rate of labor productivity has slowed and so has economic growth.

TABLE 20.1

Labor Productivity and the Standard of Living in the United States		
Period	Average Growth Rate of Labor Productivity (%)	Average Growth Rate of Real GDP Per Capita (%)
1948–1973	2.9	2.1
1973–1999	1.6	1.4

Source: U.S. Bureau of Labor Statistics; Bureau of Economic Analysis; U.S. Bureau of the Census

What determines the productivity of labor? One of the most important factors is the amount of capital relative to the amount of labor. An increase in the amount of plant and equipment per worker will increase labor productivity.

Also, technology can affect the productivity of labor. The innovations that brought a personal computer to almost every office worker's desk undoubtedly raised productivity.

Another factor affecting productivity is the skill level of work force. Education and training can raise labor productivity. Economists call attempts to improve the quality of the labor force investments in "human capital." Human capital is the skill and knowledge embodied in the labor force. A labor force with high levels of human capital is more productive.

TIP

When the word *growth* appears in a question, you should think about the long run and the factors that affect economic long-run growth—resources and technology.

SUMMARY

- Economic growth is defined as the growth of output usually as measured by real GDP or real GDP per capita. In the United States, real GDP per capita has grown about two percent a year since World War II. However, the fruits of economic growth are not shared equally by all Americans. The top 20 percent of families garner 50 percent of all the income earned.

- Economic growth is the result of increased resource availability or increased productivity. Long run output can increase only if more resources are on hand or those resources are more productive; however, there are a variety of factors that can impact resource availability and productivity. Table 20.2 delineates these factors.

- Finally, economists recognize that economic growth has its price. Economic growth can degrade the environment, cause congestion, and lead to more hectic lifestyles. Still, most people would prefer to live where real GDP per capita is high than where it is low.

TABLE 20.2

Determinants of Economic Growth

Increased Resource Availability

- Discovery of new natural resources
- Growth of the labor force
- Growth of the capital stock

Increased Productivity

- More capital per unit of labor
- Technological progress
- Better educated and trained work force

TERMS

Capital plant and equipment

Capital Productivity the amount of output per unit of plant and equipment

Economic Growth growth of output usually measured by the percentage change in real GDP or real GDP per capita

Human Capital the skill and knowledge embodied in the labor force

Labor Productivity the amount of output per unit of labor

Potential GDP the amount that can be produced using resources fully and efficiently

Productivity output per unit of input

Total Productivity the amount of output per unit of all inputs

FORMULAS

Rule of 70 Years it takes a variable to double = 70/the annual growth rate of the variable

MULTIPLE-CHOICE REVIEW QUESTIONS

1. Economic growth is

   (A) measured by the number of businesses in the economy.
   (B) shared equally among the population.
   (C) critical in determining the standard of living in a nation.
   (D) measured by the amount of government spending.
   (E) measured by the unemployment rate.

2. The standard of living is measured by

   (A) GDP.
   (B) GDP per capita.
   (C) Real GDP per capita.
   (D) Actual GDP per capita.
   (E) the unemployment rate.

3. Which of the following will result in economic growth?

   (A) A decrease in the unemployment rate.
   (B) An increase in the unemployment rate.
   (C) An increase in the size of the labor force.
   (D) A decrease in the population.
   (E) A change in political leadership.

4. Which of the following will promote economic growth?

   (A) Government regulation.
   (B) A new production technique that lowers costs.
   (C) Increased taxes.
   (D) More strict pollution standards for corporations.
   (E) Reduced taxes.

5. Which of the following will promote economic growth?

   (A) An increase in the amount of capital.
   (B) Lower wages.
   (C) Price controls that keep prices low.
   (D) Increased government spending.
   (E) A decrease in the money supply.

6. If real GDP per capita was $10,000 in 1990 and $15,000 in 2000, then the amount of economic growth is

   (A) 0.5 percent.
   (B) 5.0 percent.
   (C) 50 percent.
   (D) 3.3 percent.
   (E) More information is required to determine the amount of economic growth.

7. If real GDP per capita was $20,000 in 1980 and $21,000 in 1990, then we conclude that the standard of living has increased

   (A) 0.5 percent.
   (B) 5.0 percent.
   (C) 50 percent.
   (D) 3.3 percent.
   (E) More information is required to determine the amount of economic growth.

8. The standard of living will increase if

   (A) everyone works harder.
   (B) the population grows.
   (C) GDP increases.
   (D) real GDP increases.
   (E) real GDP increases at a greater rate than the population.

9. Output in country A is 1,200 units and its population is 100 persons. Output in country B is 2,400 units and its population is 400 persons.

    (A) Country A has a higher standard of living than country B.
    (B) Country A has a lower standard of living than country B.
    (C) Country A and B have identical living standards.
    (D) Country A is less productive than country B.
    (E) More information is needed to determine which country has the higher standard of living.

10. Output in country X is 30,000 units and there are 3,000 persons working, while country Z has an output of 40,000 units and 8,000 workers.

    (A) The productivity of labor in country Z is 33 percent higher than in country X.
    (B) The productivity of labor in country Z is 25 percent higher than in country X.
    (C) The productivity of labor in country X is 33 percent higher than in country Z.
    (D) The productivity of labor in country X is 25 percent higher than in country Z.
    (E) The productivity of labor in country X is twice as much as country Z.

11. The government can promote economic growth by

    (A) setting a minimum wage.
    (B) regulating industry.
    (C) taxing firms that waste resources.
    (D) job training programs.
    (E) restricting imports.

12. Private industry can promote economic growth by

    (A) implementing innovative production techniques.
    (B) offering products at artificially low prices.
    (C) giving a significant amount of profits to charity.
    (D) hiring workers who are not really needed.
    (E) adhering to environmental standards.

13. The size of the labor force in Japan is expected to shrink beginning in 2010 as a large segment of its population retires. This will

    (A) affect labor productivity more than economic growth.
    (B) affect economic growth more than labor productivity.
    (C) not have a major effect on economic growth or labor productivity.
    (D) affect labor productivity and economic growth equally.
    (E) shift Japan's aggregate supply curve to the right.

14. If the standard of living increases, we can conclude that

    (A) output must have increased.
    (B) population must have increased.
    (C) output and population must have increased.
    (D) population must have decreased.
    (E) output must have increased proportionally more than population.

15. If real GDP per capita grows at a rate of 10 percent a year, then we can expect the standard of living to double in

    (A) 10 years.
    (B) 9 years.
    (C) 8 years.
    (D) 7 years.
    (E) 5 years.

Multiple-Choice Review Answers

1. **(C)** 4. **(B)** 7. **(B)** 10. **(E)** 13. **(B)**
2. **(C)** 5. **(A)** 8. **(E)** 11. **(D)** 14. **(E)**
3. **(C)** 6. **(C)** 9. **(A)** 12. **(A)** 15. **(D)**

FREE-RESPONSE REVIEW QUESTIONS

I. Use the production possibilities frontier to illustrate the effects of a very successful government policy to train the labor force so that workers became more productive. Be sure to label the axes of your diagram.

II.

A. Use the AS/AD model to show the effects of a decrease in the availability of timber due to a depletion of the supply of trees. Be sure to use a long run aggregate supply curve and label the axes of your diagram.

B. Now suppose the government reduced taxes while the supply of timber was depleted. What effect would this have?

Free-Response Review Answers

I. The effects of a more productive labor force due to training.

II. A. A decrease in the supply of timber shifts the aggregate supply curve to the left. This will raise the equilibrium price level and lower the equilibrium quantity of output.

B. If the government reduced taxes while the supply of timber was depleted, this would shift the aggregate demand curve to the right. The equilibrium quantity of output would still fall to Q2, but the equilibrium price level would be higher than if the government did not reduce taxes.

International Trade and Exchange

- Tariffs and quotas
- Balance of payments
- Gold standard
- Exchange rates
- Monetary and fiscal policy in an open economy

THE BALANCE OF TRADE

In 2010 the United States was the world's third largest exporting nation, shipping $1.8 trillion worth of goods and services abroad. However, in that same year, the United States imported $2.4 trillion worth of goods and services. The fact that our imports exceeded our exports by almost $600 billion is troubling to some people. Don't foreigners want our products? We buy their products, but they don't buy as many of ours. Won't this have adverse economic effects? Will we owe foreign nations money? Doesn't this cost American jobs?

A nation's balance of trade is equal to its exports minus its imports. Earlier we called this figure net exports. For the United States in 2010, the balance of trade was negative $600 billion (= $1.8 trillion − $2.4 trillion). When the balance of trade is negative, it can be referred to as a *trade deficit*. The last time America had a trade surplus was 1975. Are these chronic trade deficits a problem, and what, if anything, can be done about them?

Trade deficits can indeed be symptomatic of underlying economic problems. For instance, if a nation's exports are of inferior quality or cost too much relative to the competition, then it may experience a trade deficit. Or a country might rely heavily on imports just to meet its subsistence needs while it has nothing to export. This dire situation would result in a trade deficit as well. Finally, a nation's currency may be overpriced for one reason or another. This would make it expensive for foreigners to buy their products. A trade deficit could be the result.

But there is a more likely explanation for the chronic trade deficits in the United States: We have higher incomes than our trading partners. We are doing so well that we can afford the best of everything no matter where in the world it might be produced. This makes America's imports swell. Unfortunately, many other countries are not doing as well. They cannot afford to buy our exports and our trade balance suffers. If this idea about the origin of our trade deficits is correct, then we should see smaller deficits, or even surpluses, when our economy is experiencing a recession. During the 1991–92 recession the trade deficit shrank to $30 billion. The last trade surplus in the United States was in 1975 on the tail end of a severe 16-month recession.

TRADE RESTRICTIONS

Arguments for Trade Restrictions

Even if our trade deficits spring from the high standard of living we enjoy, they may still be problematic. When we buy foreign textiles, that means there is less demand for domestic textile workers. Imported textiles could mean unemployment for domestic textile workers.

Barriers to free trade across nations have been erected for a variety of reasons. One argument is to protect jobs from foreign competition. However, there is a steep price to pay for this protection. Everyone who buys textiles will be paying more for them because competition was thwarted. We know from our earlier analysis of comparative advantage that free trade enables the countries involved to consume more than under restricted trade.

Other reasons for trade restrictions include the infant industry argument, the diversity argument, and dumping. Infant industries are those that are just getting started. At this point they are in no condition to compete with foreign industries that have all the advantages of being well established. The argument is that these infant industries will be able to compete after they have developed. At that point, the trade restrictions could be dropped.

Another reason to protect an industry from foreign competition is for the sake of diversity. A nation should not rely too heavily on others. What if a war broke out? Do you think our enemies would continue to export to us? We need to encourage some industries despite their inefficiencies because diversity is healthy. Trade barriers can promote diversity.

Dumping is a technical term in international trade. It describes a situation where foreign producers are selling a product in the domestic market for less than it cost to produce it. The foreign firms would like to establish a foothold in our markets, so they are willing to absorb the loss. Domestic producers argue that prices will soon rise once the foreign firms have put them out of business. Trade barriers can be used to prevent dumping.

TABLE 21.1

Arguments for Trade Restrictions

- Promote domestic employment
- Infant industry argument
- Diversity of production
- Prevent dumping

Instituting Trade Restrictions

There are a variety of ways to discourage or prevent imports from coming into a country. Quotas, tariffs, and licensing requirements are the most common.

1. An import quota is a limit on the amount of a product that can be imported. When the import quota is set at zero, domestic producers are completely protected from foreign competition. Figure 21.1 shows the effects of an import quota on the domestic market for rice.

Fig. 21.1 A Quota on Rice Imports

The quota on rice restricts the supply shifting of the supply curve to the left. The more restrictive the quota, the further to the left the supply curve shifts. After the quota is imposed the price of rice will rise and the amount of rice bought and sold will fall.

2. An import tariff is a tax on the specified imported product. The tariff serves to raise the price of the imported product in the eyes of domestic consumers. This gives the edge to domestic producers. Figure 21.2 shows the effects of an import tariff.

   The price of rice would be P1 except that the tariff raises it to P2. The higher price causes a decrease in the quantity of rice demanded and the amount actually bought and sold is now lower (Q2). The tariff, like the quota, raises the domestic price of rice and lowers the amount bought and sold. These higher prices and reduced amounts of consumption are the costs of trade restrictions.

3. Clever administrators can stifle trade in many ways aside from quotas and tariffs. Arcane rules and regulations are often developed with no other purpose in mind than to discourage competition. Governments may require businesspersons to obtain a license granting them the right to import a specific product. The government need only limit the number of licenses it grants and the amount to be imported by each license holder in order to restrict trade. The effects of licensing agreements and rules and regulations

that stifle trade are shown in exactly the same manner as the import quota diagram in Figure 21.1.

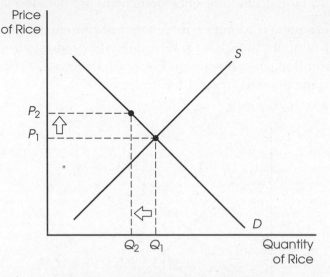

Fig. 21.2 A Tariff on Imported Rice

Economists are generally against any trade restrictions. Comparative advantage suggests that free trade allows nations to consume more goods and services than if trade was restricted. Moreover, the arguments for trade restrictions are dubious while the costs in terms of higher prices and less consumption are more definite.

TABLE 21.2

Trade Restrictions

- Quotas
- Tariffs
- Licensing requirements

THE BALANCE OF PAYMENTS

The balance of payments is composed of the current account, the financial account, and the capital account. The current account is primarily net exports with some additional items. The financial account measures investment dollars flowing into the United States minus investments by U.S. entities abroad. For 2010 the financial account balance is positive, meaning more investment dollars flowed into the United States than flowed out in foreign-asset investments. The capital account is mainly debt forgiveness. Table 21.3 delineates the balance of payments for the United States in 2010.

TABLE 21.3

The Balance of Payments for the United States in 2010 (Billions of $)

Current Account Balance		−470.2
Balance of trade	−495.7	
Net investment income	163.0	
Net transfers	−137.5	
Financial Account Balance		235.3
Foreign purchases of U.S. assets	1244.8	
Minus U.S. purchases of foreign assets	1024.7	
Net financial derivatives	15.2	
Capital Account Balance		−0.2
Net Errors and Omissions		235.1

Source: Bureau of Economic Analysis

The current account, the financial acount, and the capital account should sum to zero. This is an accounting necessity. When the current account is negative, as it was in 2010, this means that we have been spending more abroad than foreigners have been spending here, whether it is on goods and services, or investment payments or gifts and aid. This excess spending abroad puts dollars in foreign hands.

The financial account accounts for those dollars that were put in foreign hands. The financial account for 2010 indicates that most of the dollars that wound up in foreign hands were used to buy assets in the United States. Had foreigners not wanted to use their dollars to buy investments in the United States, they could have just held on to them. Even so, that is an investment—an investment in U.S. currency.

The financial account plus the capital account must be positive by the same magnitude that the current account is negative. This is because all the dollars that wind up overseas must be accounted for. Measuring all these dollar flows is fraught with error. In 2010 these errors and omissions amounted to a significant sum: $235.1 billion.

EXCHANGE RATES

The exchange rate is the value of one country's currency in terms of another's. Exchange rates are determined, as we shall see, by supply and demand. Table 21.4 shows selected exchange rates.

Let us consider the exchange rate between the U.S. dollar and the Indian rupee. One dollar was worth about 45 rupees in May 2010. This implies that one rupee is worth about $1/45$ of a dollar, or 2 cents. Why isn't the rupee worth more or less? Because the supply and demand for rupees intersected at 2 cents per rupee. This is illustrated in Figure 21.3.

TABLE 21.4

Selected Exchange Rates on May 20, 2010

One U.S. dollar equals:

0.94	Australian dollar
0.62	British pound
0.97	Canadian dollars
5.23	Danish kroner
0.70	Euro
44.98	Indian rupees
81.90	Japanese yen
11.68	Mexican pesos
6.90	South African rand

Source: Federal Reserve Bank of New York

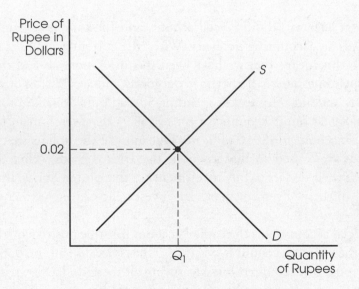

Fig. 21.3 The Supply and Demand for Rupees

The demand for rupees in the international market is downward sloping, which implies that the quantity of rupees demanded will be greater when the dollar price is lower. This makes sense: More people and firms would want to acquire rupees if they could get a lot of them for each dollar. The supply curve for rupees is upward sloping, which implies that the quantity of rupees supplied will be greater when the dollar price is higher. Again, this makes sense: More people would be willing to part with their rupees if they could get more cents for each one.

Changing Rates

The exchange rate between the rupee and the dollar is changing constantly because the supply and the demand for rupees in terms of dollars are shifting constantly. If Americans began to appreciate Indian products more, then the demand for rupees would increase. That's because importers of Indian products would have to place bigger orders and pay for those orders in rupees.

When the demand for rupees increases, the demand curve for rupees shifts to the right as shown in Figure 21.4. The result is a rise in the dollar value of the rupee and an increase in the amount of rupees exchanged.

Fig. 21.4 An Increase in the Demand for Rupees

When the value of the rupee increases against the dollar as in Figure 21.4, this is known as an "appreciation" of the rupee. Or looked at from the other side, the dollar has "depreciated" vis-à-vis the rupee. Previously, a rupee cost 2 cents. Now a rupee costs 3 cents.

Interest Rates

Changing tastes are just one of several factors that influence exchange rates between countries. Interest rates are another. If interest rates in India rise relative to interest rates in America, then it will be more rewarding to lend money in India. However, an American wanting to lend money in India must first turn her dollars into rupees. This increases the demand for rupees. The result will be the same as in Figure 21.4 where the demand for rupees shifts to the right. The rupee will appreciate and more rupees will be exchanged for dollars.

Political Stability

Political stability can also affect exchange rates. If the Indian government finds itself in turmoil with its credibility for maintaining peace and justice in question, fewer foreigners will want to invest in India. The demand for rupees would fall even if interest rates were relatively higher in India. This would shift the demand for rupees to the left. Moreover, Indian citizens will want to store more of their wealth abroad. Who knows what might happen to bank accounts and financial assets in a country where the government is losing control? When Indian citizens want to place some of their wealth in America, they typically start by trading their rupees for dollars. This is reflected in a shift to the right in the supply of rupees.

So political instability in India would decrease the demand for rupees and increase the supply. This is shown in Figure 21.5. The result is a significant depreciation of the rupee.

Fig. 21.5 A Decrease in the Demand and an Increase in the Supply of Rupees

Relative Levels of Income

The relative levels of income in India and America will influence the exchange rate between dollars and rupees. If America is better off than India in terms of income, Americans will be able to afford more of the finer things India has to offer. And India will not be able to enjoy America's exports to the same extent because of her relatively lower standard of living. So if the standard of living in America advanced while India slipped into a recession, the situation would be just the opposite of that portrayed in Figure 21.5—the demand for rupees would increase because Americans could afford Indian exports. The supply of rupees would fall, not increase, since Indians would not be demanding as many American exports as before the recession.

Relative Prices

Relative prices in India and America can also impact exchange rates. If prices rise in India while they hold steady in America, the value of the rupee will depreciate. This is because some Americans will balk at purchasing Indian products because of the higher prices, thus reducing the demand for rupees. And Indian citizens will buy more American products since the prices of these items have held steady. This will increase the supply of rupees. The situation is just as depicted in Figure 21.5.

Astute readers may take the analysis a step further. Once the value of the rupee depreciates, the higher-priced Indian products will appear cheaper to Americans and the lower-priced American products will appear more expensive to Indians. This is because the currencies must be exchanged to obtain each other's products.

If you reasoned this way, congratulate yourself—you have outlined the theory of purchasing power parity. This theory states that the same product, say, a pencil, will cost the same if it is bought domestically or imported because exchange rates change to erase any price differential that may exist. It's an interesting theory, but the real world abounds with counterexamples.

Speculation

Speculators have an important impact on exchange rates. Individuals and institutions buy and sell currencies with an eye toward making a profit. As with all financial transactions, these speculators want to "buy low and sell high." If it is expected that the rupee will depreciate in the near future, speculators will try to sell their rupees now before the price falls. In Figure 21.6, this would increase the supply of rupees, shifting the supply curve to the right. Notice that the result is a depreciation of the rupee from 2 cents to 1 cent. Speculation often results in self-fulfilling prophecies.

Fig. 21.6 An Increase in the Supply of Rupees

Side-by-Side Foreign Exchange Graphs

At least two currencies will be affected by a change in any of the factors affecting foreign exchange rates: the currency under consideration and that of its trading partner or partners. In order to illustrate these effects, side-by-side exchange rate graphs may be used.

Consider a case where Americans suddenly develop a passion for India's exports. If we look at the market for rupees, we will see an increase in demand for rupees. American importers will be required to obtain rupees in order to obtain the goods Americans desire from India.

The increase in the supply of dollars results in a depreciation of the dollar (D_1 to D_2) and an increase in the quantity of dollars traded (Q_1 to Q_2). Thus, we may conclude that when Americans increase their preference for Indians goods, the rupee will appreciate while the dollar depreciates. Figures 21.7 and 21.8 are often placed side-by-side to illustrate these simultaneous effects on the two currencies.

Fig. 21.7 Market for Rupees: An Increase in the Demand for Rupees

The increase in the demand for rupees results in an appreciation of the rupee (R_1 to R_2) and an increase in the quantity of rupees traded (Q_1 to Q_2). However, if we look at the market for dollars, we would see an increase in the supply of dollars. American importers will be supplying more dollars on the foreign exchange market in order to obtain the rupees they want.

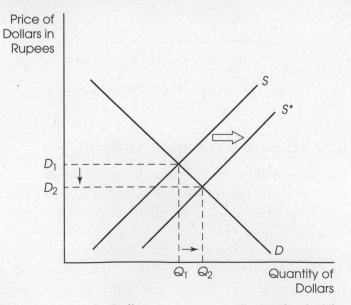

Fig. 21.8 Market for Dollars: An Increase in the Supply of Dollars

TABLE 21.5

Determinants of Exchange Rates

- Demand for a nation's exports (tastes)
- Relative interest rates
- Political stability
- Relative level of income
- Relative prices (theory of purchasing power parity)
- Speculation

Exchange Rate Regimes

Before the Great Depression, most of the large economies of the world were on a gold standard. Essentially, the gold standard kept exchange rates between countries fixed. Since the dollar was worth a certain amount of gold and the franc was worth a given amount of gold, the value of the dollar versus the franc would be established. If the value of the franc appreciated vis-à-vis the dollar, someone could use their dollars to buy gold and then use that gold to buy francs, and then use those francs to buy more dollars than they started with.

Arbitrage of this sort kept exchange rates between nations fixed, but the gold standard was not without flaws. If tastes changed and Americans clamored for French products, the exchange rate did not rise to choke off some of this foreign demand. In such a situation the United States would develop a balance of payments deficit as French citizens and institutions piled up dollar holdings. Many historians and economists point to balance of payment crises caused by the gold standard as one of the central causes of the Great Depression.

Modern international exchange is no longer based on gold. The Bretton Woods regime replaced the fixed exchange rate system based on gold in 1944. In the Bretton Woods system the dollar was as good as gold. Countries pegged the value of their currencies to the dollar and the United States stood ready to trade any dollar holdings of foreign governments to gold at $35 an ounce. This system broke down in 1971 when the United States, running chronic trade deficits, could no longer support the $35 an ounce price of gold.

Managed Float

The current system for determining international exchange rates is referred to as a *managed float.* Supply and demand determine exchange rates between currencies as outlined above. But if exchange rates change in a manner deemed to be detrimental, nations will intervene. Intervention involves coordinated buying and selling of currencies in order to adjust their equilibrium values determined by supply and demand.

For example, because the United States runs chronic trade deficits there is an abundant supply of dollars in international markets. This tends to depress the value of the dollar. A depreciated dollar would lower America's demand for foreign products. This would help with our chronic trade deficits, but it would hurt the countries that export to us. If governments decide to support the dollar, they would intervene by buying dollars. This results in the dollar appreciating in value.

A managed float allows supply and demand to determine exchange rates within a range of values. Once exchange rates exceed that range, governments use their currency holdings to intervene.

MONETARY AND FISCAL POLICY IN AN OPEN ECONOMY

Monetary and fiscal policy can be used to fight inflation or recession. However, our previous discussion of these policies ignored their effects on the exchange rate and the balance of trade. The impacts of monetary and fiscal policy in the context of an open economy are more complicated.

An expansionary monetary policy still stimulates the economy in the short run by increasing the quantity of output and putting upward pressure on prices. This will worsen the balance of trade since the increase in output means an increase in income. Rising incomes tend to drive imports, worsening the balance of trade. And rising prices tend to discourage exports, again, worsening the balance of trade.

TIP

Monetary and fiscal policies are less effective when exchange rates are perfectly flexible.

Policymakers need to keep in mind the effects of monetary policy on imports and exports. In a closed economy, an increase in the money supply stimulates output and income in the short run. In an open economy these effects will be dampened because imports will rise. That is to say, some of the stimulatory effect will be spent overseas, and exports will fall because of the inflation resulting from the increase in the money supply.

The effects of an expansionary fiscal policy are tempered in the same way in the context of an open economy. An increase in government spending and a reduction in taxes will increase output and income in the short run, while putting upward pressure on prices. Higher levels of income tend to raise imports while higher prices tend to discourage exports. This worsens the balance of trade and implies that the effects of the fiscal policy will not be as pronounced.

Also notice that monetary and fiscal polices will affect exchange rates because these policies alter incomes and prices. Remember that exchange rates are impacted by the relative level of income and the relative level of prices in a nation.

SUMMARY

- The United States has been importing more than it has been exporting since the mid-1970s. However, our trade deficits are more a symptom of how well off we are relative to our trading partners than a cause for alarm. Most economists agree that trade restrictions, such as import tariffs, quotas, and licensing agreements, are harmful. Free trade, where countries specialize according to the law of comparative advantage, benefits consumers in the countries involved.
- Nevertheless, most nations restrict trade in one way or another. The arguments for trade restrictions vary from promoting employment to preventing dumping. Infant industries and the benefits of a diverse manufacturing base are two more reasons put forward to justify trade restrictions. However valid

the reason, economic analysis shows that the cost of restricting trade is higher prices to the consumer.

- A nation's balance of payments accounts for the funds that flow into and out of the country. If there is a deficit in the current account, there must be a corresponding surplus in the financial and capital accounts.

- The exchange rate is the price of one nation's currency in terms of another. In today's world, exchange rates are determined by the supply and demand for a nation's currency—up to a point. Occasionally, nations will intervene in the market by supplying more or less of a particular currency or demanding more or less. Nations use their official reserves during these interventions in order to prop up or devalue a given currency. In other words, countries can adjust the position of the supply and demand curves for a currency, but only if they have the cooperation of the major trading nations. Without cooperation no single nation has enough reserves to make much of an adjustment to the supply or demand curves of most currencies. This international monetary system, where supply and demand determine exchange rates with the occasional intervention by a consortium of trading partners is known as a managed float.

- Exchange rates, therefore, are free to float about where supply and demand might take them—just so long as they don't go too far and trigger an intervention. Anything that can affect the supply or the demand for a nation's currency will affect its exchange rate. The demand for a nation's exports affects the demand for its currency, as do relative interest rates. Relative prices and income also affect exchange rates. And speculation can play a role. If market participants expect a particular currency to appreciate in the near future, they will try to buy as much as they can now. As we have seen, this increases the demand for the currency, which, in turn, causes it to appreciate, the fulfillment of a self-fulfilling prophecy.

- Exchange rates are affected when a country pursues monetary and fiscal policy because, in the short run, these policies affect income and prices. Moreover, the balance of trade will be affected by monetary and fiscal policy because imports and exports are impacted by changes in income and prices as well. The short run effects of monetary and fiscal policy are not as pronounced in an open economy.

TERMS

Appreciation the increase of the value of a currency in terms of another currency

Balance of Payments an accounting of the funds that flow into and out of a country comprised of the capital account and the current account

Balance of Trade a nation's exports minus its imports

Capital Account a portion of the balance of payments comprised of foreign purchases of U.S. assets minus U.S. purchases of foreign assets, plus the change in official reserves

Closed Economy a hypothetical economy with no foreign trade

Current Account a portion of the balance of payments comprised of the trade balance, net investment income, and net transfers

Depreciation the decrease of the value of a currency in terms of another currency

Dumping the practice of foreign producers selling a product in the domestic market for less than it cost to produce it

Exchange Rate the value of one country's currency in terms of another's

Gold Standard a unit of currency that is equivalent to a stated amount of gold

Import Quota a limit on the amount of a product that can be imported

Import Tariff a tax on a specified imported product

Infant Industries those industries that are just getting started, perhaps requiring trade restrictions

Intervention situation in which a nation or group of nations use their official reserves to supply or demand a currency in order to alter the exchange rate

Managed Float an exchange rate regime where supply and demand determine exchange rates with occasional intervention when warranted

Net Investment Income amount U.S. citizens earned as interest and dividends from abroad minus how much was paid to foreigners in interest and dividends

Net Transfers money our government and citizens send as gifts or aid to foreigners minus how much foreigners send to us in gifts and aid

Official Reserves government's holdings of foreign currencies

Open Economy an economy with foreign trade

Trade Deficit excess of a nation's imports over its exports

Trade Surplus excess of a nation's exports over its imports

FORMULAS

Balance of Payments = Current Account + Capital Account

MULTIPLE-CHOICE REVIEW QUESTIONS

1. When a country has a balance of trade deficit

   (A) it must make up the difference by shipping gold to its creditors.
   (B) its exports exceed its imports.
   (C) its currency will appreciate.
   (D) corrective actions must be taken.
   (E) its imports exceed its exports.

2. A balance of trade surplus can be the result of

   (A) a loose monetary policy.
   (B) foreigners having no taste for this country's products.
   (C) an appreciation of the country's currency.
   (D) low levels of income relative to other nations.
   (E) high domestic prices.

3. One strategy a corporation may use to gain market share in a foreign market is

   (A) raising the price of its product.
   (B) convincing its government to put an import tariff on the product.
   (C) convincing its government to place a quota on the product.
   (D) cornering.
   (E) dumping.

4. Tariffs and quotas

   (A) result in higher domestic prices.
   (B) promote trade between nations.
   (C) do not necessarily affect domestic prices.
   (D) affect domestic prices: the former raises them while the latter lowers them.
   (E) are ways to fight inflation.

5. Tariffs and quotas

   (A) result in lower domestic prices.
   (B) sometimes raise and sometimes lower the amount of the product sold domestically.
   (C) lower the amount of the product sold domestically.
   (D) raise the amount of the product sold domestically.
   (E) do not affect domestic prices or quantities.

6. Which of the following is NOT an argument for restricting trade?

   (A) to protect infant industry
   (B) to promote employment
   (C) to fight inflation
   (D) to promote a diversity of industries
   (E) to prevent dumping

7. If the value of the U.S. dollar depreciates, *ceteris paribus*, then U.S.

   (A) imports will rise.
   (B) unemployment will rise.
   (C) net exports will fall.
   (D) exports will rise.
   (E) net exports will be unaffected.

8. If a country has a negative value on its current account, then it must

   (A) pay that amount to its trading partners.
   (B) have a positive value of equal magnitude on its capital plus financial account.
   (C) depreciate its currency.
   (D) appreciate its currency.
   (E) send gold abroad.

9. With a managed float

   (A) countries occasionally intervene in foreign exchange markets.
   (B) countries never have to intervene in foreign exchange markets.
   (C) countries must constantly intervene to maintain the value of their currencies.
   (D) exchange rates are fixed.
   (E) each currency is worth a stated amount of gold.

10. Expansionary fiscal policy

    (A) increases unemployment in an open economy.
    (B) lowers the nominal interest rate, which results in currency appreciation.
    (C) is less effective in an open economy with floating exchange rates.
    (D) will not affect the nominal interest rate.
    (E) lowers the nominal interest rate, which results in currency depreciation.

11. In the balance of payments, the trade balance

    (A) is ignored.
    (B) appears in the capital account.
    (C) appears in the current account
    (D) is included in the official reserves.
    (E) is counted as part of "net transfers."

12. If interest rates rise in the United States relative to other nations, then

    (A) the value of the dollar will tend to appreciate.
    (B) the value of the dollar will tend to depreciate.
    (C) exchange rates will be affected but not the value of the dollar.
    (D) the exchange rate will not be affected.
    (E) the balance of trade will tend toward a surplus.

13. If prices rise in the United States relative to other countries, then

    (A) the value of the dollar will tend to appreciate.
    (B) the value of the dollar will tend to depreciate.
    (C) exchange rates will be affected but not the value of the dollar.
    (D) the exchange rate will not be affected.
    (E) the balance of trade will tend toward a surplus.

14. If the demand for dollars rises while the supply of dollars falls, then the

    (A) dollar will appreciate.
    (B) dollar will depreciate.
    (C) exchange rates will be affected but not the value of the dollar.
    (D) exchange rate will not be affected.
    (E) balance of trade will tend toward a surplus.

15. If the demand for our exports rises while our tastes for foreign goods falls off, then

    (A) the value of the dollar will tend to appreciate.
    (B) the value of the dollar will tend to depreciate.
    (C) exchange rates will be affected but not the value of the dollar.
    (D) the exchange rate will not be affected.
    (E) the balance of trade will tend toward a surplus.

Multiple-Choice Review Answers

1. **(E)**	4. **(A)**	7. **(D)**	10. **(C)**	13. **(B)**
2. **(D)**	5. **(C)**	8. **(B)**	11. **(C)**	14. **(A)**
3. **(E)**	6. **(C)**	9. **(A)**	12. **(A)**	15. **(A)**

FREE-RESPONSE REVIEW QUESTIONS

I. Suppose two counties, Alpha and Beta, trade freely and allow investments to flow across their borders as well. Draw two graphs, one of the supply and demand for Alpha's currency and one of the supply and demand for Beta's currency. Be sure to label the axes of your graphs. Show how the value of each currency will be affected if the interest rate on investments in Alpha rises while the return on investments in Beta remains unchanged.

II. Given your response above, how will the imports and exports of each country be affected?

Free-Response Review Answers

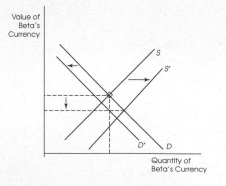

I. With higher returns in Alpha, the demand for Alpha's currency will rise. It also is possible that the supply of Alpha's currency will decline as more domestic investments are undertaken. These two shifts are shown in Figure 21.7. Alpha's currency will appreciate in value.

With higher returns in Alpha, the supply of Beta's currency will rise. It also is possible that the demand for Beta's currency will decline as more of Alpha's investors undertake domestic investments. These two shifts are shown in Figure 21.8. Beta's currency will depreciate in value.

II. Since Alpha's currency is appreciating, Alpha's exports will fall and its imports will rise. Alpha's net exports will fall. Since Beta's currency is depreciating, Beta's exports will rise and its imports will fall. Beta's net exports will rise.

These changes make sense. Alpha's current account is declining, but its financial account is rising. Beta's current account is improving, but its mirror image, the financial account, is worsening.

MODEL AP EXAM IN MACROECONOMICS

Answer Sheet
MACROECONOMICS

Multiple-Choice Questions

1 Ⓐ Ⓑ Ⓒ Ⓓ Ⓔ	21 Ⓐ Ⓑ Ⓒ Ⓓ Ⓔ	41 Ⓐ Ⓑ Ⓒ Ⓓ Ⓔ
2 Ⓐ Ⓑ Ⓒ Ⓓ Ⓔ	22 Ⓐ Ⓑ Ⓒ Ⓓ Ⓔ	42 Ⓐ Ⓑ Ⓒ Ⓓ Ⓔ
3 Ⓐ Ⓑ Ⓒ Ⓓ Ⓔ	23 Ⓐ Ⓑ Ⓒ Ⓓ Ⓔ	43 Ⓐ Ⓑ Ⓒ Ⓓ Ⓔ
4 Ⓐ Ⓑ Ⓒ Ⓓ Ⓔ	24 Ⓐ Ⓑ Ⓒ Ⓓ Ⓔ	44 Ⓐ Ⓑ Ⓒ Ⓓ Ⓔ
5 Ⓐ Ⓑ Ⓒ Ⓓ Ⓔ	25 Ⓐ Ⓑ Ⓒ Ⓓ Ⓔ	45 Ⓐ Ⓑ Ⓒ Ⓓ Ⓔ
6 Ⓐ Ⓑ Ⓒ Ⓓ Ⓔ	26 Ⓐ Ⓑ Ⓒ Ⓓ Ⓔ	46 Ⓐ Ⓑ Ⓒ Ⓓ Ⓔ
7 Ⓐ Ⓑ Ⓒ Ⓓ Ⓔ	27 Ⓐ Ⓑ Ⓒ Ⓓ Ⓔ	47 Ⓐ Ⓑ Ⓒ Ⓓ Ⓔ
8 Ⓐ Ⓑ Ⓒ Ⓓ Ⓔ	28 Ⓐ Ⓑ Ⓒ Ⓓ Ⓔ	48 Ⓐ Ⓑ Ⓒ Ⓓ Ⓔ
9 Ⓐ Ⓑ Ⓒ Ⓓ Ⓔ	29 Ⓐ Ⓑ Ⓒ Ⓓ Ⓔ	49 Ⓐ Ⓑ Ⓒ Ⓓ Ⓔ
10 Ⓐ Ⓑ Ⓒ Ⓓ Ⓔ	30 Ⓐ Ⓑ Ⓒ Ⓓ Ⓔ	50 Ⓐ Ⓑ Ⓒ Ⓓ Ⓔ
11 Ⓐ Ⓑ Ⓒ Ⓓ Ⓔ	31 Ⓐ Ⓑ Ⓒ Ⓓ Ⓔ	51 Ⓐ Ⓑ Ⓒ Ⓓ Ⓔ
12 Ⓐ Ⓑ Ⓒ Ⓓ Ⓔ	32 Ⓐ Ⓑ Ⓒ Ⓓ Ⓔ	52 Ⓐ Ⓑ Ⓒ Ⓓ Ⓔ
13 Ⓐ Ⓑ Ⓒ Ⓓ Ⓔ	33 Ⓐ Ⓑ Ⓒ Ⓓ Ⓔ	53 Ⓐ Ⓑ Ⓒ Ⓓ Ⓔ
14 Ⓐ Ⓑ Ⓒ Ⓓ Ⓔ	34 Ⓐ Ⓑ Ⓒ Ⓓ Ⓔ	54 Ⓐ Ⓑ Ⓒ Ⓓ Ⓔ
15 Ⓐ Ⓑ Ⓒ Ⓓ Ⓔ	35 Ⓐ Ⓑ Ⓒ Ⓓ Ⓔ	55 Ⓐ Ⓑ Ⓒ Ⓓ Ⓔ
16 Ⓐ Ⓑ Ⓒ Ⓓ Ⓔ	36 Ⓐ Ⓑ Ⓒ Ⓓ Ⓔ	56 Ⓐ Ⓑ Ⓒ Ⓓ Ⓔ
17 Ⓐ Ⓑ Ⓒ Ⓓ Ⓔ	37 Ⓐ Ⓑ Ⓒ Ⓓ Ⓔ	57 Ⓐ Ⓑ Ⓒ Ⓓ Ⓔ
18 Ⓐ Ⓑ Ⓒ Ⓓ Ⓔ	38 Ⓐ Ⓑ Ⓒ Ⓓ Ⓔ	58 Ⓐ Ⓑ Ⓒ Ⓓ Ⓔ
19 Ⓐ Ⓑ Ⓒ Ⓓ Ⓔ	39 Ⓐ Ⓑ Ⓒ Ⓓ Ⓔ	59 Ⓐ Ⓑ Ⓒ Ⓓ Ⓔ
20 Ⓐ Ⓑ Ⓒ Ⓓ Ⓔ	40 Ⓐ Ⓑ Ⓒ Ⓓ Ⓔ	60 Ⓐ Ⓑ Ⓒ Ⓓ Ⓔ

Answer Sheet

Model AP Exam in Macroeconomics

Two hours are allotted for this exam: 1 hour and 10 minutes for Section I, which consists of multiple-choice questions; and 50 minutes for Section II, which consists of three mandatory essay questions.

SECTION I—MULTIPLE-CHOICE QUESTIONS

Time—1 hour and 10 minutes
Number of Questions—60
Percent of Total Grade—$66^2/_3$

Directions

Each of the questions or incomplete statements beginning on page 326 is followed by five suggested answers or completions. Select the one that is best in each case and then fill in the corresponding oval on the answer sheet.

1. In the long run an increase in the money supply results in

   (A) a proportional increase in the quantity of output.
   (B) stagflation.
   (C) an increase in the real rate of interest.
   (D) an economic expansion.
   (E) a proportional increase in the price level.

2. You buy 100 shares in XYZ Corporation on the Internet and your broker charges you $29.95.

   (A) This will increase the investment component of GDP and therefore overall GDP.
   (B) This has no effect on GDP.
   (C) This will increase GDP by $29.95.
   (D) This will increase GDP by the cost of the shares minus $29.95.
   (E) This will increase GDP by the cost of the shares plus $29.95.

3. Given the graph above, the opportunity cost of four additional units of butter as the economy moves from A to B is

   (A) seven units of butter.
   (B) 30 units of guns.
   (C) 60 units of guns.
   (D) unobtainable.
   (E) indeterminant.

4. In the short run, contractionary monetary policy causes aggregate demand to _____, output to _____, and the price level to _____.

	Aggregate Demand	Output	Price Level
(A)	Increase	Increase	Increase
(B)	Increase	Increase	Decrease
(C)	Decrease	Decrease	Increase
(D)	Decrease	Decrease	Decrease
(E)	Decrease	Increase	Increase

5. Assume the reserve requirement is five percent. If the FED sells $10 million worth of government securities in an open market operation, then the money supply can potentially

   (A) increase by $200 million.
   (B) decrease by $200 million.
   (C) increase by $50 million.
   (D) decrease by $50 million.
   (E) increase by $150 million.

6. Given the table below, which statement is true?

   Labor hours needed to produce a unit of:

Country	**Wine**	**Cheese**
France	40	80
Belgium	15	60

   (A) France has the absolute advantage in both products.
   (B) France should specialize in and export wine while Belgium should specialize in and export cheese.
   (C) France has the comparative advantage in cheese.
   (D) France has the absolute advantage in cheese.
   (E) Belgium has the comparative advantage in both products.

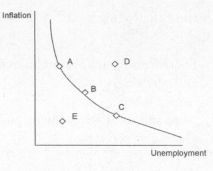

7. At P′ in the diagram above,

(A) inventories will be unintentionally drawn down, and the price level will rise.

(B) inventories will be unintentionally increased, and the price level will rise.

(C) inventories will be unintentionally drawn down, and the price level will fall.

(D) inventories will be unintentionally increased, and the price level will rise.

(E) inventories will be unintentionally drawn down, but prices will not be affected.

8. Suppose taxes are cut in an economy that is in equilibrium at full employment. In the long run the tax cut will

(A) raise real output and raise the price level.

(B) lower real output and raise the price level.

(C) raise real output and lower the price level.

(D) lower real output and lower the price level.

(E) raise the price level.

9. As a result of automatic stabilizers, during economic expansions government expenditures

(A) and taxes fall.

(B) and taxes rise.

(C) rise and taxes fall.

(D) fall and taxes rise.

(E) remain stable.

10. Consider the diagram above. In the short run, stagflation will move the economy from point B to

(A) point A.

(B) point A and then back to point B.

(C) point C.

(D) point D.

(E) point E.

11. Which of the following shifts the production possibilities frontier outward?

(A) A decrease in the price level.

(B) An increase in labor productivity.

(C) An increase in the money supply.

(D) A decrease in the unemployment rate.

(E) A decrease in the minimum wage.

12. In the circular-flow diagram households send _____ to firms in return for _____.

(A) resources; spending

(B) spending; resources

(C) resources; wages and profits

(D) goods and services; wages

(E) goods and services; spending

13. An Italian company opens a shoe factory in the U.S. The production from this shoe company is included in

(A) the Italian GDP.

(B) the U.S. GDP.

(C) both the Italian and U.S. GDP.

(D) both the Italian and U.S. GDP split 50/50.

(E) neither the Italian nor U.S. GDP.

14. Which of the following is NOT included in GDP?

    (A) Federal government purchases of goods and services.
    (B) Imports.
    (C) State and local government purchases of goods and services.
    (D) Exports.
    (E) The change in business inventories.

15. An increase in the price level reduces total spending in the economy because

    I. consumers' incomes cannot go as far now that prices have risen.
    II. foreigners buy less.
    III. higher prices result in higher interest rates, which lower spending.

    (A) Only I is correct.
    (B) I and II are correct.
    (C) I and III are correct.
    (D) II and III are correct.
    (E) I, II, and III are correct.

16. Suppose real GDP increases. We can conclude without a doubt that

    (A) prices are higher.
    (B) employment is higher.
    (C) production is higher.
    (D) prices and/or output is higher.
    (E) unemployment is lower.

17. The appropriate fiscal policy to remedy a recession is to

    (A) increase government spending and taxes.
    (B) reduce government spending and taxes.
    (C) increase government spending and reduce taxes.
    (D) decrease government spending and increase taxes.
    (E) increase the money supply.

18. Which of the following would lead to a decrease in the money supply?

    (A) The FED lowers the discount rate.
    (B) The FED sells government securities in the secondary market.
    (C) The federal government spends less money.
    (D) The FED lowers reserve requirements.
    (E) Taxes are reduced.

19. If interest rates rise relatively more in country A than in country B, then the value of country A's currency will

    (A) appreciate.
    (B) depreciate.
    (C) remain unchanged.
    (D) change indeterminately.
    (E) depreciate by the difference in interest rates.

20. If the marginal propensity to consume equals .75 and government spending increases by $100 million, then overall real GDP can be expected to

    (A) decrease by $133.33 million.
    (B) increase by $133.33 million.
    (C) decrease by $400 million.
    (D) increase by $400 million.
    (E) increase by $75 million.

21. Inflation

    (A) hurts creditors who do not anticipate it.
    (B) hurts creditors who anticipate it.
    (C) hurts debtors.
    (D) benefits debtors.
    (E) both A and D are correct.

22. Which of the following persons is considered to be unemployed?

  I. Mary, who has quit her job to look for another.
  II. John, who fulfilled his dream by retiring from work at age 45.
  III. Diane, who works part-time but would like to work full-time.

  (A) I only
  (B) II only
  (C) III only
  (D) I and III
  (E) II and III

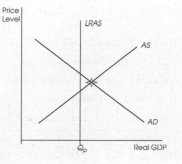

23. The economy depicted in the figure above is experiencing _____. In the absence of monetary or fiscal policy, the economy will eventually move to a point where the price level is _____.

  (A) a recession; higher
  (B) a recession; lower
  (C) extremely high production; higher
  (D) extremely high production; lower
  (E) extremely high production; unchanged

24. The population of country X is exactly the same as country Y, but country X produces twice as much output as country Y. We can conclude that

  (A) the people of country X are smarter than the people of country Y.
  (B) the people of country X enjoy a standard of living twice as much as country Y.
  (C) the people of country Y enjoy a standard of living twice as much as country X.
  (D) the people of country Y work twice as hard as the people of country X.
  (E) country X is bigger than country Y.

25. If the government of country Z increases spending by $12 million dollars and raises tax collections by the same amount, then what will be the overall impact of these moves on real GDP in country Z?

  (A) Real GDP will increase by $6 million.
  (B) Real GDP will decrease by $6 million.
  (C) Real GDP will remain unchanged.
  (D) Real GDP will increase by $12 million.
  (E) Real GDP will decrease by $12 million.

26. Suppose you observe an economy where prices are falling and real GDP is rising. This may have been caused by

  (A) stagflation.
  (B) an advance in technology.
  (C) an increase in government spending.
  (D) a decrease in government spending.
  (E) a decrease in the money supply.

27. Which of the following would reduce economic growth?

(A) A decline in investment.
(B) An increase in immigration from abroad.
(C) A technological advance.
(D) An increase in the labor force.
(E) An increase in the savings rate.

28. Currency held by the public

(A) is not part of the money supply, but currency held by banks is.
(B) is part of M1 but not M2.
(C) is part of the money supply, but currency held by banks is not.
(D) and by banks is part of the money supply.
(E) or banks is not part of the money supply since it is not included in M1.

29. The equation of exchange demonstrates the neutrality of money only if the

(A) velocity of money supply and the quantity of output are constant.
(B) money supply and its velocity are equal.
(C) velocity of money supply equals the speed of transactions.
(D) money supply and its velocity are inversely related.
(E) money supply and the exchange rate are inversely related.

30. Economy X is an open economy with flexible exchange rates. Economy Y is closed. *Ceteris paribus* expansionary monetary policy is

(A) more effective in X because the policy will increase net exports.
(B) more effective in X because the policy will decrease net exports.
(C) equally effective in X and Y.
(D) less effective in X because the policy will increase net exports.
(E) less effective in X because the policy will decrease net exports.

31. An increase in the price of forklifts imported into the United States from Belgium will

(A) increase the consumer price index and the GDP deflator.
(B) increase the consumer price index but not the GDP deflator.
(C) increase the GDP deflator but not the consumer price index.
(D) increase the GDP deflator and the producer price index.
(E) have no effect on the consumer price index or the GDP deflator.

32. An increase in the demand for money in the economy could result from

(A) a recession.
(B) a higher price level.
(C) higher interest rates.
(D) expected future inflation.
(E) a decrease in the supply of money.

33. The international value of the dollar will appreciate if

    (A) American income falls relative to the rest of the world.
    (B) American interest rates fall relative to interest rates in other countries.
    (C) American prices rise.
    (D) foreigners boycott American products.
    (E) speculators expect the value of the dollar to depreciate.

34. The potential amount of money created after the Fed increases bank reserves will be diminished if

    (A) the public prefers to hold less cash.
    (B) the velocity of money falls.
    (C) depository institutions decide to hold more excess reserves.
    (D) the marginal propensity to consume falls.
    (E) the international value of the dollar falls.

35. An increase in the federal deficit may affect the demand for loan funds and therefore the real interest rate and investment spending. Which of the following gives the correct direction of these effects?

	Demand for loanable funds	Real interest rate	Investment spending
(A)	Increase	Increase	Increase
(B)	Decrease	Decrease	Decrease
(C)	Decrease	Decrease	Increase
(D)	Increase	Increase	Decrease
(E)	Increase	Decrease	Increase

36. If the inflation rate is expected to increase in the immediate future, then

    (A) consumers will begin saving more now.
    (B) the velocity of money will fall.
    (C) this will put upward pressure on the nominal interest rate.
    (D) this will put downward pressure on the real interest rate.
    (E) the international value of the dollar will rise.

37. If the economy is in disequilibrium where the price level is such that the aggregate quantity of products demanded exceeds the aggregate quantity of products supplied, then

    (A) prices will be driven upward to restore equilibrium.
    (B) supply will increase.
    (C) demand will decrease.
    (D) supply will decrease.
    (E) a recession is inevitable.

38. If 200 computers with a retail value of $100,000 are domestically produced in 2005, but not sold until 2006, then GDP in 2005 is

    (A) $100,000 higher because of the computers.
    (B) 200 higher because of the computers.
    (C) unaffected until 2006 when the computers are sold and the figure for GDP in 2005 is revised.
    (D) higher by the wholesale value of the computers.
    (E) unaffected and the computers are counted in GDP for 2006.

39. Appropriate fiscal and monetary polices during the contractionary phase of the business cycle include

   (A) budget surpluses and higher discount rates.
   (B) tax reductions and open market purchases.
   (C) budget surpluses and lower discount rates.
   (D) increases in government spending and higher discount rates.
   (E) decreases in government spending and lower discount rates.

40. A change in government spending will have a greater short run impact on real output when

   (A) the marginal propensity to consume is lower.
   (B) the velocity of money is lower.
   (C) the velocity of money is higher.
   (D) the marginal propensity to consume is larger.
   (E) interest rates rise.

41. Suppose a country produces only two goods, pizza and soda. Given the information in the table below, nominal GDP, real GDP, and the GDP deflator in 2005 are (assume 2004 is the base year):

Year	Pizza Production	Soda Production	Price of a Pizza	Price of a Soda
2004	8	20	$10	$1
2005	10	30	$17	$3

	Nominal GDP	Real GDP	GDP deflator
(A)	800	400	200
(B)	130	260	50
(C)	260	130	200
(D)	260	196	133
(E)	800	400	400

42. If the economy experienced a decrease in real GDP and price level, this could best be explained by

   (A) a decline in labor productivity.
   (B) a technological advance.
   (C) a decline in investment.
   (D) an uptick in net exports.
   (E) a reduction in interest rates.

43. The shift depicted in the diagram above could have been caused by

   (A) better production methods in the gun industry.
   (B) an increase in the number of cows in the economy.
   (C) an increase in the number of workers in the economy.
   (D) a technological setback in the gun industry.
   (E) a reduction in farmland available due to pollution.

44. Suppose the real interest rate in a country rises. What can be expected to happen to the demand for this nation's currency and, therefore, the value of its currency and net exports?

	Demand for currency	Value of currency	Net exports
(A)	Decrease	Appreciate	Decrease
(B)	Decrease	Depreciate	Decrease
(C)	Decrease	Depreciate	Increase
(D)	Increase	Appreciate	Increase
(E)	Increase	Appreciate	Decrease

45. According to Keynesian analysis, the Great Depression was caused by

(A) a lack of spending.
(B) a sharp rise in the marginal propensity to consume.
(C) too much investment.
(D) too much foreign influence on the economy.
(E) a sharp decline in labor productivity.

46. An economy in a recession can return to full employment in the long run through

(A) falling wages and prices.
(B) rising wages and prices.
(C) expansionary monetary policy.
(D) increased government spending.
(E) decreased government spending.

47. If the cost of the basket of goods and services the Bureau of Labor Statistics uses to calculate the consumer price index rises from $200 in the base period to $400 in the current period, then the consumer price index

(A) equals 0.5 in the current period.
(B) has risen 5 percent from the base to the current period.
(C) equals 50 in the current period.
(D) equals 200 in the current period.
(E) has risen 200 percent.

48. Contractionary monetary policy implies which of the following about the discount rate, the nominal interest rate, and aggregate demand?

	Discount rate	Nominal interest rate	Aggregate demand
(A)	Decrease	Increase	Decrease
(B)	Increase	Increase	Decrease
(C)	Decrease	Decrease	Decrease
(D)	Increase	Increase	Increase
(E)	Increase	Decrease	Decrease

49. A decline in the demand for money could be the result of

(A) higher prices.
(B) more money placed in checking accounts.
(C) higher returns on bonds.
(D) more credit cards.
(E) open market purchases by the Fed.

50. An important assumption underlying monetarism is that

(A) the marginal propensity to consume is constant.
(B) the money supply is continuous.
(C) the exchange rate is fixed.
(D) the velocity of money is stable.
(E) the exchange rate is flexible.

51. Which of the following policies is most likely to bring about economic growth in the long run?

(A) Imposing tariffs to protect domestic industries from foreign competition.
(B) Placing taxes on savings.
(C) Increasing government spending.
(D) Increasing the money supply.
(E) Promoting improvements in the education of the population.

52. An increase in the price level and a decrease in real GDP in the short run could be the result of

(A) a prolonged period of very bad weather.
(B) a decrease in the money supply.
(C) a decrease in consumer confidence.
(D) an increase in consumer confidence.
(E) an increase in the money supply.

53. In 2010, the United States had a trade deficit of $600 billion; therefore,

    (A) net exports were positive.
    (B) Americans consumed more than they produced.
    (C) America's government spent more than it took in.
    (D) $603 billion worth of capital flowed out of America.
    (E) the government had to make payments to foreign countries of $603 billion.

54. GDP measures a country's level of

    I. production.
    II. stability.
    III. income.

    (A) I only.
    (B) II only.
    (C) III only.
    (D) I and II.
    (E) I and III.

55. Which of the following lists contains only Fed actions that will increase the money supply?

    (A) Raise reserve requirements; lower the discount rate; sell bonds.
    (B) Raise reserve requirements; lower the discount rate; buy bonds.
    (C) Raise reserve requirements; raise the discount rate; sell bonds.
    (D) Lower reserve requirements; lower the discount rate; sell bonds.
    (E) Lower reserve requirements; lower the discount rate; buy bonds.

56. Which of the following lists contains only policies that will close an inflationary gap?

    (A) Increase the money supply; run a federal budget deficit.
    (B) Decrease the money supply; run a federal budget deficit.
    (C) Decrease the money supply; increase taxes; reduce government spending.
    (D) Increase the money supply; increase taxes; reduce government spending.
    (E) Decrease the money supply; decrease taxes; reduce government spending.

57. Suppose the exchange rates are 0.5 British Pound per dollar; 10 Mexican Pesos per dollar; and 100 Chinese Yuan per dollar. Further suppose that a Big Mac costs 3 dollars in America; 2 pounds in England; 50 pesos in Mexico; and 200 yuan in China. In which country is a Big Mac most expensive?

    (A) America ($3).
    (B) England ($4).
    (C) Mexico ($5).
    (D) China ($2).
    (E) England and China are equally most expensive.

58. Potential GDP will fall, *ceteris paribus*, if

    (A) the unemployment rate rises.
    (B) the retirement age is lowered.
    (C) tariffs protecting domestic jobs are eliminated.
    (D) more immigration is allowed.
    (E) the minimum wage is raised.

59. Suppose that an expansionary fiscal policy leads to a large increase in real output and a small increase in the price level. From this it can be inferred that

(A) inflation had already impacted the economy before the fiscal stimulus.
(B) the economy initially had some unemployed resources.
(C) aggregate supply decreased.
(D) aggregate demand is steeply sloped.
(E) aggregate supply is steeply sloped.

60. Imagine someone who is not looking for work because they are embarrassed in the interview process when their inability to read is revealed. However, this person would take just about any job that was offered. According to the Bureau of Labor Statistics this person is

(A) in the labor force and unemployed.
(B) in the labor force and employed.
(C) not in the labor force.
(D) not in the labor force, but counted as unemployed.
(E) not in the labor force, but counted as employed.

SECTION II—FREE-RESPONSE QUESTIONS

Planning Time—10 minutes
Writing Time—50 minutes
Percent of Total Grade—$33^1/_3$

DIRECTIONS

You have 50 minutes to answer all three of the following questions. It is suggested that you spend approximately half your time on the first question and divide the remaining time equally between the next two questions. In answering the questions, you should emphasize the line of reasoning that generated your results; it is not enough to list the results of your analysis. Include correctly labeled diagrams, if useful or required, in explaining your answers. A correctly labeled diagram must have all axes and curves clearly labeled and must show directional changes.

Students should consider doing a "sketch" (main points, quick graph, etc.) of the answer before actually answering the free-response questions. Good luck! When you use graphs on the free-response questions, label the axes and make direct references to any symbols, e.g., MR, P, output, on the graphs when you respond to questions.

> **NOTE**
>
> Recent Advanced Placement exams require *three* questions. Some of the questions may be based on material covered in the common chapters, such as production possibilities frontier or curve when applied to international trade. For these questions, please refer to those chapters.

1. Country X is a closed economy experiencing a falling price level and a low level of real GDP.

   (a) Draw a correctly labeled graph of aggregate demand and aggregate supply that depicts the recession in Country X.

   (b) Assume income taxes are reduced in Country X.
      (i) Explain how a cut in income taxes would affect the equilibrium price level and equilibrium real GDP in Country X.
      (ii) Show the effects of the tax cut on your graph from part (a). Be clear about which curve(s) is/are shifting which way.

   (c) Draw a correctly labeled graph of money supply and money demand showing the equilibrium nominal interest rate.
      (i) Explain how the changes in the equilibrium price level and equilibrium real GDP from part (b) above will affect the equilibrium nominal interest rate.
      (ii) Show the effects of the changes in the equilibrium price level and equilibrium real GDP on your graph of money supply and money demand.
      (iii) Explain how the change in the equilibrium nominal interest rate will impact the macroeconomy.

2. Suppose that interest rates in the United States fall relative to the rest of the world. Explain how this will affect

   (a) the value of the dollar.

   (b) net exports.

   (c) Now suppose the monetary authorities in the United States did not want the value of the dollar to change as you explained in part (a) above. Explain how the value of the dollar could be held stable in this situation.

3. Describe how an open market purchase of $7 million by the Federal Reserve Bank will affect the money supply.

   (a) Assuming a required reserve ratio of five percent, what is the maximum amount by which the money supply can change due to the open market operation?

   (b) How will your answer to (a) above change if banks decide to hold reserves over and above the required amount?

   (c) Suppose a large corporation makes the open market purchase of $7 million. Explain how the money supply will be affected in this case.

Answer Key
MACROECONOMICS

Multiple-Choice Questions

1.	E	21.	E	41.	C
2.	C	22.	A	42.	C
3.	B	23.	C	43.	B
4.	D	24.	B	44.	E
5.	B	25.	D	45.	A
6.	C	26.	B	46.	A
7.	B	27.	A	47.	D
8.	E	28.	C	48.	B
9.	D	29.	A	49.	C
10.	D	30.	E	50.	D
11.	B	31.	E	51.	E
12.	C	32.	B	52.	A
13.	B	33.	A	53.	B
14.	B	34.	C	54.	E
15.	D	35.	D	55.	E
16.	C	36.	C	56.	C
17.	C	37.	A	57.	C
18.	B	38.	A	58.	B
19.	A	39.	B	59.	B
20.	D	40.	D	60.	C

ANSWERS EXPLAINED

MACROECONOMICS

MULTIPLE-CHOICE QUESTIONS

1. **(E)** (Chapter 19) The Classical notion of monetary neutrality is based on the idea that the money supply and the price level are proportionally related.

2. **(C)** (Chapter 14) Financial transactions are not counted in GDP, but brokerage services are counted.

3. **(B)** (Chapter 2) At point A the economy is producing 60 guns and 3 units of butter. At Point B production is 30 guns and 7 units of butter. The 4 additional units of butter come at a cost of 30 guns.

4. **(D)** (Chapter 19) Contractionary monetary policy is a decrease in the money supply. This shifts aggregate demand to the left. A leftward shift in aggregate demand results in a higher level of output and a higher price level. This is seen in the aggregate demand–aggregate supply model:

5. **(B)** (Chapter 18) If the reserve requirement is 5 percent, then the money multiplier is 20 (= 1/.05). Bank reserves fall by $10 million because of the open market operation. The money supply falls by $200 million (= $10 million × 20).

6. **(C)** (Chapter 2) Since Belgium can produce both wine and cheese with fewer labor hours than France, Belgium has the absolute advantage in both products. The opportunity cost of cheese in Belgium is 60/15 = 4 wine; the opportunity cost of cheese in France is 80/40 = 2 wine. France has the lower opportunity cost of producing cheese and therefore the comparative advantage in cheese production.

7. **(B)** (Chapter 16) Since AS > AD at P', inventories will unintentionally increase. In order to lower excess inventories, firms will be forced to lower prices, and the price levels falls.

8. **(E)** (Chapter 16) The trick to answering this question correctly is to use a vertical aggregate supply curve. You know to do so because the question asks about the long run. The tax cut shifts AD right to AD'. This results in a higher price level (P2), but the same level of output (Q1).

9. **(D)** (Chapter 17) During an economic expansion output, income, and employment increase. This results in fewer households qualifying for income maintenance programs such as food stamps and housing subsidies. Government expenditures fall, but tax collections rise because more income means more tax revenue for the government.

10. **(D)** (Chapter 17) Stagflation is inflation and recession (unemployment) at the same time. The only point shown with higher inflation and unemployment than B is point D. Indeed, stagflation causes the Phillips curve to shift right through a point such as D.

11. **(B)** (Chapter 2) Only changes in technology/productivity or changes in resource availability can shift the production possibilities frontier. Many students choose D here, but notice that a decrease in unemployment will move the economy onto the frontier from a point inside the frontier.

12. **(C)** (Chapter 2) Households own the resources (land, labor, capital) in the economy. They sell them to firms in exchange for wages and profits.

13. **(B)** (Chapter 14) It does not matter where the company has its headquarters. GDP counts production within a nation's borders.

14. **(B)** (Chapter 14) Consider the equation GDP = C + I + G + X. X is exports minus imports. So exports are included in GDP, but imports are subtracted out. G is federal, state, and local government purchases; I is business spending on plant and equipment plus the change in business inventories.

15. **(D)** (Chapter 16) When the price level rises, so does total income in the economy. Therefore I is not correct. However, foreign incomes do not rise, so foreigners buy less of our products. II is correct. III is a statement of Fisher's Hypothesis and is also correct.

16. **(C)** (Chapter 14) When real GDP rises it can only be due to more production. Price changes do not affect real GDP. Employment (and therefore unemployment) may or may not change with changes in real GDP.

17. **(C)** (Chapter 17) Increasing government spending and reducing taxes stimulate aggregate demand and fight recessions. Increasing the money supply does this as well, but that is monetary policy.

18. **(B)** (Chapter 18) When the Fed sell securities in the secondary market they get paid with checks drawn on bank accounts. Bank reserves fall and the money supply falls by a multiple of the decline in bank reserves.

19. **(A)** (Chapter 21) When interest rates rise in country A, people from country B will want to place loans there. People from country B will need to obtain the currency of country A in order to do this. The demand for country A's currency rises. This causes it to appreciate.

20. **(D)** (Chapter 16) If the marginal propensity to consume is .75, then the multiplier is 4 (= 1/(1 − .75)). The increase in government spending gets multiplied by 4 to determine the overall increase in spending and therefore real GDP. 4 × $100 million = $400 million.

21. **(E)** (Chapter 15) Inflation hurts lenders because they are repaid in dollars that are not worth as much. Some lenders, however, anticipate this and demand higher rates of interest when the loan is made. Borrowers, or debtors, do not mind inflation because they get to repay loans with dollars that are worth less.

22. **(A)** (Chapter 15) Mary is frictionally unemployed. Retired persons presumably are not looking for work, so they are not part of the labor force. People who work part-time are counted as employed even if they would like to work full-time.

23. **(C)** (Chapter 16) The economy is experiencing an extremely high production level since it is in short-run equilibrium to the right of potential, or long-run, real GDP. In the absence of government policies to correct the situation, the AS curve will shift to the left. Prices are expected to be higher in the future, and so aggregate supply decreases right now. The aggregate supply curve shifts left until a new equilibrium is reached at potential, or long-run, aggregate supply.

24. **(B)** (Chapter 20) The standard of living depends on real GDP per capita. Country X has twice the output per person as country Y.

25. **(D)** (Chapter 17) This is a balanced-budget move—government spending is increasing and tax collections are increasing by the same amount. It is not necessary to know the MPC. In this situation the net impact on real GDP is a change equivalent to the change in government spending.

26. **(B)** (Chapter 16) A technological advance shifts the aggregate supply curve to the right.

27. **(A)** (Chapter 20) Less investment implies less plant and equipment in the future. That reduces economic growth, whereas choices B through D all enhance growth.

28. **(C)** (Chapter 18) Currency in the vaults of depository institutions is not counted as part of the money supply. However, if you withdraw $100 from your checking account, M1 is unaffected. When the money comes out of the bank's vault and goes into your pocket, that in itself raises the money supply by $100—but your checking account went down by $100 because of the withdrawal. It's a wash.

29. **(A)** (Chapter 18) The velocity of money supply and the quantity of output must be constant in the equation of exchange or else, by algebra, a change in the money supply will not have a proportional effect on output in the equation of exchange.

30. **(E)** (Chapter 21) The more open an economy, the less effective monetary policy will be. Consider an increase in the money supply. This will raise real GDP and prices in the short run. However, if the economy is open, then the increase in real GDP will boost incomes and therefore importation (which reduces real GDP somewhat), and the increase in prices will reduce exports (which also reduces real GDP somewhat).

31. **(E)** (Chapter 14) The consumer price index will not be affected by the increase in the price of the forklifts because forklifts are an industrial product, not a consumer product. The GDP deflator is not affected because import prices are ignored by the deflator.

32. **(B)** (Chapter 19) When prices rise people and firms have more money in their wallets and checking accounts in order to conduct their transactions.

33. **(A)** (Chapter 21) If income in America falls relative to the rest of the world, then Americans' demand for imports will decrease. Therefore, the supply of dollars will decrease relative to the demand for dollars. In turn, the value of the dollar increases.

34. **(C)** (Chapter 18) If the Fed increases bank reserves, but banks decide to simply hold onto the new reserves, then the money expansion process will be curtailed. The process depends on banks using their new reserves to make loans out or buy investments.

35. **(D)** (Chapter 17) The government must borrow to finance the federal deficit and this raises the demand for loanable funds. The result will be an increase in the real interest rate and decrease in investment spending. This chain of events is known as crowding out.

Model Macroeconomics Exam

36. **(C)** (Chapter 15) Fisher's Hypothesis states that the nominal interest rate equals the real interest rate plus expected inflation.

37. **(A)** (Chapter 16) If the price level in the economy is below the equilibrium price level, then the quantity of products demanded will exceed the quantity supplied. There will be a shortage, and shortages drive prices up.

38. **(A)** (Chapter 14) Products get counted in GDP in the period they are produced. If they produced but not sold, then they are in inventory. The change in inventories is part of GDP. Inventory changes are included in investment.

39. **(B)** (Chapter 19) Reducing taxes is a stimulatory fiscal policy, and open market purchases are expansionary monetary policy.

40. **(D)** (Chapter 17) The multiplier is $1/(1 - \text{MPC})$. Therefore, the higher the MPC, the higher the multiplier. With a higher multiplier, changes in government spending will have more impact on real GDP.

41. **(C)** (Chapters 14 and 15)

Calculating GDP for 2005

Production	Price	Value
10 Pizzas	$17	$170
30 Sodas	$3	$90
		GDP = $260

Calculating real GDP for 2005

Production	Price	Value
10 Pizzas	$10	$100
30 Sodas	$1	$30
		Real GDP = $130

Calculating the GDP deflator for 2005

$$260/130 \times 100 = 200$$

42. **(C)** (Chapter 16) Aggregate demand must decrease for real GDP and the price level to fall. A decline in investment causes aggregate demand to decrease.

43. **(B)** (Chapter 20) Shifts such as these are the result of a technological advance or increase in resources that benefit only one of the two industries. If the economy produced only guns, then an increase in the number of cows would not help increase production.

44. **(E)** (Chapter 21) Higher real interest rates attract foreign investors. These investors demand the nation's currency which in turn appreciates its value. This makes domestic products more expensive to foreigners and foreign products less expensive to domestic citizens. Thus, net exports decrease.

45. **(A)** (Chapter 17) Real output declined and the price level fell during the Great Depression. This can only be the result of aggregate demand shifting left—a lack of demand or spending.

46. **(A)** (Chapter 16) In Classical theory, a recession causes wages and prices to fall. The falling prices stimulate demand for products, while the falling wages stimulate demand for labor. This pickup in demand ends the recession and brings about full employment.

47. **(D)** (Chapter 15)

$$\text{CPI} = \frac{\text{Total Cost This Period}}{\text{Total Cost Base Period}} \times 100 = \frac{400}{200} \times 100 = 200$$

48. **(B)** (Chapter 19) Contractionary monetary policy means lowering the money supply. The Fed would increase the discount rate, which results in a higher nominal interest rate. Higher interest rates discourage spending which decreases aggregate demand.

49. **(C)** (Chapter 19) When the return on bonds and other assets rises, people and firms want to hold less money in their wallets and checking accounts and, instead, put the money into these assets with high returns.

50. **(D)** (Chapter 19) Monetarists feel that changes in the money supply have a profound impact on nominal GDP. According to the equation of exchange, this would not be true if the velocity of money fluctuated in the opposite direction of the change in the money supply.

51. **(E)** (Chapter 20) Economic growth is stimulated by investment in resources. Education enhances one of the most important resources in the economy—labor.

52. **(A)** (Chapter 16) Only a decrease in short run aggregate demand could cause an increase in the price level and a decrease in real GDP. It sounds odd, but a prolonged period of bad weather (droughts, monsoons, etc.) destroys resources such as farmland and other plant and equipment. Aggregate supply shifts left when fewer resources are available.

53. **(B)** (Chapter 21) A trade deficit means a country's imports exceed its exports. In this case a country is consuming more than it is producing.

54. **(E)** (Chapter 14) The income and expenditure approaches to calculating GDP highlight the fact that GDP measures not only production, but income as well.

55. **(E)** (Chapter 19) The three primary tools at the Fed's disposal for increasing the money supply are lowering reserve requirements, lowering the discount rate, and buying bonds on the open market.

56. **(C)** (Chapters 17 and 19) Aggregate demand needs to be decreased to close an inflationary gap. This can be accomplished with contractionary monetary policy (decreasing the money supply) or contractionary fiscal policy (increasing taxes or reducing government spending).

57. **(C)** (Chapter 21) One way to solve this problem is to put all the different prices in dollar terms:

Country	$ Price of a Big Mac
America	$3
England	2 pounds ÷ 0.5 = $4
Mexico	50 pesos ÷ 10 = $5
China	200 yuan ÷ 100 = $2

The Mexican Big Mac costs 50 pesos, which translates into $5. This is the most expensive Big Mac.

58. **(B)** (Chapter 21) Potential GDP is how much could be produced using all resources fully and efficiently. In order for potential GDP to fall, resources must become less available or inefficiencies must be introduced into the production process. Lowering the retirement age means less labor is available.

59. **(B)** (Chapter 17) Expansionary fiscal policy increases aggregate demand. Increases in aggregate demand raise prices and output. However, if there is a lot of unemployment and capacity to begin with, then the increase in aggregate demand can easily be met by increasing output.

60. **(C)** (Chapter 15) People like this are neither employed nor unemployed according to the Bureau of Labor Statistics because they are not counted as part of the labor force. To be in the labor force, one must be actively seeking employment.

FREE-RESPONSE ANSWERS

1. (a)

(b) (i) An income tax cut leaves households with more disposable income, which results in an increase in spending. Aggregate demand would increase. This would cause the equilibrium price level and the equilibrium level of real GDP to increase.

(ii) Aggregate demand would shift to the right:

The equilibrium point moves from E1 to E2 with the income tax cut. The graph shows that this implies a higher equilibrium price level and a higher level of real GDP.

(c)

(i) The increase in the equilibrium price level serves to increase the demand for money, as does the increase in the level of real GDP. The increased demand for money, in turn, raises the nominal rate of interest.

(ii)

The increase in the demand for money serves to raise the equilibrium nominal interest rate.

(iii) The increased nominal rate of interest will impact the economy in a variety of ways: (1) Higher interest rates will encourage saving and reduce consumption; (2) investment will fall; and (3) higher interest rates will increase the value of the dollar and thereby lower net exports. All in all, higher interest rates tend to reduce aggregate demand and thus reduce the impact of the initial tax cut. The tendency of interest rates to rise with expansionary fiscal policy and consequently reduce the fiscal thrust is called "crowding out."

2. (a) The value of the dollar will decrease because the drop in interest rates will mean that fewer foreigners will want to invest in the United States. This, in turn, implies that the demand for the dollar will fall. A decline in demand for the dollar results in a depreciation.

Model Macroeconomics Exam

(b) Net exports will rise because the value of the dollar has depreciated. A fall in the value of the dollar will raise U.S. exports (our goods are less expensive to foreigners) and lower U.S. imports (foreign goods are more expensive to Americans after the devaluation of the dollar).

(c) The Federal Reserve, in conjunction with the Department of the Treasury, could prevent the depreciation of the dollar outlined above. Basically, the Federal Reserve would use its foreign currency reserves to buy U.S. dollars on the international market. This increase in the demand for dollars would offset decline in demand due to lower interest rates.

3. An open market purchase of $7 million by the Federal Reserve Bank will serve to increase the money supply by more than $7 million. The purchase itself puts $7 million in new reserves into the banking system. Banks then make loans or buy investments with these additional reserves. The loans and investments generate new deposits, which are additions to the money supply.

(a) When the reserve ratio is 5 percent, the money multiplier is 20 (= 1/.05). This implies that any change in bank reserves could possibly be magnified 20 times. Therefore, the open market purchase of $7 million could lead to a $140 million (= $7 million × 20) increase in M1 or M2.

(b) The $140 million figure is based on the assumption that banks use their additional reserves as much as possible to make loans or buy investments. If banks hold reserves over and above the requirements, then the money expansion process will be diminished. The money supply will expand by less than $140 million if banks hold reserves above the required amount.

(c) The money supply is unaffected in this case. The corporation's bank account declines by $7 million while the seller's account rises by the same amount. No new reserves are added to the system, so the money supply does not change.

Model Macroeconomics Exam

Index